SEXUAL LOVING

Other books by the same authors

SEXUAL LOVING

The Experience of Love

Joseph and Lois Bird

DOUBLEDAY & COMPANY, INC., GARDEN CITY, NEW YORK

1976

What the World Needs Now by Hal David and Burt Bacharach. Reprinted by permission of ASCAP.

"Age and Sexual Love" from *Secrets of the Heart* by Kahlil Gibran. Copyright © 1947, 1975 by Citadel Press. Reprinted by permission of Philosophical Library, Inc.

Love Is All, Copyright © 1968 by Joseph and Lois Bird. Reprinted by permission of Doubleday & Company, Inc.

Excerpt from *Please Don't Promise Me Forever.* Copyright © 1972 Hallmark Cards, Inc. Reprinted by permission of Hallmark Cards, Inc.

"The Coital Bond" from *This Is My Beloved,* by Walter Benton. Copyright 1943 by Alfred A. Knopf, Inc., and renewed 1971 by Walter Benton. Reprinted by permission of Alfred A. Knopf, Inc.

Human Sexual Response, Copyright © 1966 by William H. Masters and Virginia E. Johnson. Reprinted by permission of Little, Brown and Company.

LIBRARY OF CONGRESS CATALOGING IN PUBLICATION DATA

BIRD, JOSEPH W

SEXUAL LOVING: THE EXPERIENCE OF LOVE.

1. SEX (PSYCHOLOGY)   2. LOVE.

I. BIRD, LOIS F., JOINT AUTHOR.   II. TITLE.

BF692.B46   301.41'8

ISBN: 0-385-07618-5

LIBRARY OF CONGRESS CATALOG CARD NUMBER: 74–1509

*To young lovers of whatever age
who refuse to believe the honeymoon must end,
this book is dedicated in love.*

Contents

ACKNOWLEDGMENTS

To those pioneers in the investigation of
human sexuality. Many have paid a high price for their
courage in the battle against ignorance and bigotry.
They have opened many doors. And they have placed
us in their debt. They include among others: Mary Calderone,
Robert L. Dickenson, Albert Ellis, Havelock Ellis,
Seymour Fisher, Sigmund Freud, Virginia E. Johnson,
Alfred C. Kinsey, Richard von Krafft-Ebing, William
H. Masters, Margaret Mead, Wardell B. Pomeroy, Abraham
and Hanna Stone, Lewis M. Terman, and Theodore Van de Velde.

And a special acknowledgment to those many men
and women who were willing to share their experiences
and reactions with us. From them we have learned much,
including much about ourselves.

I Thee Wed

My Beloved lifts up his voice,
he says to me,
"Come then, my love,
my lovely one, come.
For see, winter is past,
the rains are over and gone.
The flowers appear on the earth."

Song of Songs 2,
from *The Jerusalem Bible*

We made love
   and everything was re-created.
Our marriage began again;
   it was a wedding night,
      a radiant white wedding night.
Again, last night,
   with our bodies we said "I do,"
      "I take you as my husband."
      "I take you as my wife."

Joseph and Lois Bird
Love Is All

*I*f we were asked to draw conclusions on the nature of breakdown in the loving relationship of a man and woman, we might place the blame on *marriage*. Today, we often hear the institution of marriage indicted as outmoded, unnecessary, imprisoning, stultifying, crippling to women, unnatural, neurotic, and immoral. There are those who feel they "don't need" marriage. They speak glowingly of the LTA's (living together arrangements): "We love each other. What difference would a piece of paper make?" And there are those who are seeking to broaden the legal definition of marriage: "Why should marriage be limited to heterosexuals? Why can't two men who love each other marry? Or two women?" "Why not group marriage? We live in a commune, eight of us, and we consider ourselves all married to each other." Others have suggested one-, three-, or five-year marriage contracts, renewable at the option of both partners. The ideal of monogamy, especially lifelong monogamy, has been attacked as unrealistic. "It may have worked in an age when people had a short lifespan, but how can anyone expect a couple to keep the same interests for forty or fifty years? It just isn't possible." Some extol the "freedom" of an "open" marriage in which both partners pursue a range of interests which may include extramarital affairs.

Yet, despite all the attacks, and in apparent disregard of the divorce statistics, couples continue to marry, and for reasons which have to do with more than social pressures or property rights. Sociologists, who delight in creating vague euphemisms for what often amount to what the average man and woman have known all along, have apparently decided to lump all sexual, cohabitative relationships together. They use the term "pair bonding." Thus, by implication, marriage, legal or common-law, LTA's and homosexual pairings share an indistinguishable equality.

But there are differences, important ones, and they go far beyond the legalities of a piece of paper, a religiously sanctioned union, or the controversial morality of an out-of-wedlock liaison. Marriage is simply *not* the same as an LTA. The differences are legal, psychological, sociological, and philosophical. And for most people, they are deep, profound, and inescapable.

Many of these very differences have led us to conclude that marriage, as our society has defined it, has many things about it which work against the deep love of a man and woman. The problem lies in what we have been told marriage must be, and what we have all too often accepted that it must become. When we think back over our own days before marriage, and that first year or two of our marriage, we have a difficult time recalling anything positive we were told about marriage. Sure, our married friends wished us happiness, but they didn't tell us to expect it. Instead, they gave us veiled (and not so veiled) warnings: The honeymoon can't last; marriage is no bed of roses; love changes; the excitement dies out. To which they added a few discouraging comments about sex. How many couples can sustain their love affair under the weight of such doomsaying?

The effects of such negativism on a couple's sexual relationship can be devastating. The prophecies are self-fulfilling. Sex soon becomes, if not a battleground, a monotonous obligation. Most couples admit to at least occasional boredom in their relations, even where no serious sexual problems are present. And as sex diminishes, it is joined by the other, previously rewarding, dimensions of the relationship. It all starts to go downhill with marriage.

We can, therefore, blame marriage for the breakdown in love without joining the LTA-liberated singles. Our conflict is not with the institution of marriage, but with the negativism associated with it—a social sickness that impels many to expect little and find less. Marriage, we contend, is sorely in need of redefining, restructuring, and revitalizing. But why? Wouldn't it be as well to abandon it altogether?

Our answer: No. Because *marriage* offers unique opportunities for personal growth. Through marriage we can attain our potential as human beings. We can discover our identities as men and women—as persons—through the interactions of marriage. And in ways which cannot be matched by any other relationship. We are not, of course, claiming that such growth *will* inevitably occur, only that marriage holds out the opportunity. Why should the formality of marriage make a difference? The formality, or even the legality, of marriage doesn't. It is what marriage represents to the two persons that makes the difference.

While the word has been overused, and as a result has lost much of its significance, the difference is in *commitment*. The word has two definitions with respect to marriage: a binding or involving of oneself in a course of action, as by a pledge, and a handing over to another for safekeeping. In marriage there is a formal, public pledge to a course of action—the living of one's life in union with another. And in marriage there is a handing over to another of much of what is most valuable to us: the vulnerability of our ego, our dreams, aspirations, and fears; our emotional, and perhaps financial, security; and even, in some cases, our physical well-being. We entrust our hopes for happiness to another person whom we love and trust.

"But we do have a commitment to each other; we don't need to marry to make a commitment," numbers of couples have told us. To which we reply: "There is still a difference, a big difference." The difference is in the nature of the commitment. Certainly the twenty-year-old boy and his girlfriend can decide to share an apartment. They may be very much in love. We would not deny it when they tell us they have made a commitment to each other. But, for that matter, he may have made a commitment to finish college; she may have committed herself to tour Europe with a girlfriend; and both may be committed to promoting conservation of wildlife.

If we are to talk of "commitment," we must speak of the nature of the commitment. Commitment to what? A commitment to a bridge game Thursday evening is hardly the same as a commitment to love and cherish for a lifetime. What commitment is made by our young couple, very much in love, who decide to live together? No one knows. They may not know themselves. It is doubtful they have ever attempted to verbalize it. The words "I love you" do not constitute a commitment. They don't pledge a course of action. Even a promise of "undying" love is no pledge of actions. Generally, it is only a statement of feelings. Let's suppose, however, that our couple have verbalized a course of action, an intent to offer, in deeds as well as words, a lifetime of service to each other. Isn't this *de facto* a marriage? In most respects, yes. It meets many of the tests of commitment we expect of marriage. There is only one thing lacking: a *public* declaration of that commitment. But is this important—really important? Our experience with married and unmarried couples indicates that it is. Not merely because of the legal protection of property rights provided by marriage. Not even because of moral issues or social sanctions. The publicly declared pledge adds something much more, much deeper, more profound. It declares *to the world*, "I choose to pledge all that I am and have to this person. I hold him/her above all others, and I promise, from this time forward, my love, exclusively, to him/her."

This public declaration has two psychological effects. First, it says to one's partner, "I want the world to know you are the one person I choose, and I want the world to know I am yours—now and forever." Second, it says to the world, "I pledge all my responsibility for this man/woman without reservation for the eventualities that life may have in store." The effects are on both the one giving the pledge and the one to whom it is given. When we marry, we put our personal and material future on the line. In many ways, we place ourselves in the hands of our partner; they place the same trust in us. The vows of marriage say, "You can trust in me; come what may, I won't let you down." The promises we make, plus the assurances provided by our performances over time, provide the assurance to another that will permit him or her to surrender that portion of "self" necessary to a close, intimate relationship. These pledges say, "Have no fear, my lover. You can step off this cliff. I shall be here to catch you." "With these words I thee wed. Trust in me. *Trust* in me. Trust in *me*." When we make the pledge, it has an effect on us. We stick our necks out in public, and explicitly we ask the public to judge us on our commitment. It makes an open declaration of our motivation. Consider what effect it might have on you if, at some point in time, you told all your friends you were going to become a millionaire within five years. You would be far out on a limb. If you failed to meet your stated goal, you would have to face your friends with your failure. A public statement of our goals thus acts as a motivator. Not one of us wants to face failure, especially public failure. It may seem that this is a poor motivation for a relationship, but let's be realistic. It takes a great deal of maturity and strong motivation to build a deep and enduring relationship of love. It never just happens. If such a relationship is worthwhile and rewarding—and we contend it is—then any motivation is good. Granted, some motivations are better than others. Anticipation of the rewards of loving and being loved is, everyone would agree, the best of motivations. But the sad truth is that anticipation of reward is seldom, if ever, sufficient in itself to sustain motivation to work toward a long-range goal, and the deep relationship we are talking about is indeed a long-range goal. It isn't reached in a day or a year. We need a combination of positive and negative reinforcement (anticipation of rewards and fear of punishment). The principal negative reinforcement in the relationship, of course, is fear: fear of loss of love, and fear of the loss of the one we love. If that sounds as if one lives with a sword of apprehension hanging overhead, it comes close to what we have found to be an essential element in the total motivation necessary. If fear of publicly admitting to failure or to violation of one's commitment adds to our motivation, and generally it does, it serves a useful purpose—despite the cynics who talk of marriage as a "trap."

We have a further answer to the question, "Why marriage?" It comes down to this: Would we love one another less if we were not married? No. So long as we continue to keep it a love affair, the institution of marriage can neither add anything to our love nor take anything from it. This means, of course, continuing to reject all the negative, anti-loving attitudes and roles of our society's definition of marriage. But would we do it all over again, go through a formal wedding today? Yes, but only because we can think of no more *total* commitment. Our marriage doesn't commit us to each other; it only declares our commitment to the world. If there were some way we could shout it louder, to let everyone know we are committed to each other in a way that goes beyond the marriage vows—a *super-marriage*—we would.

Every married couple with whom we have spoken about the institution of marriage was able to identify with the negative predictions taught by friends and relatives. Marriage is cloaked in cynicism. And in no area of marriage is cynicism preached more than in sex. No one expects sex to retain its excitement, romance, and fulfillment throughout all the years of marriage. And it doesn't. Yet there are couples, although they may presently be few in number, who are "redefining" marriage for themselves. They are dedicated to building and maintaining a marriage which is in all respects a love affair—an affair of love. They would be the first to admit they feel like outsiders in the world in which they live. It is a price they are willing to pay. Some of the couples who opened their lives to us and on whose experiences we drew in the preparation of this book, we would include in this select group. We like to think of them as pioneers in the discovery and development of a brand-new world, of a unique relationship which, in the heights of its love and the depths of its commitment, can be found only in the bond of their "new" marriage.

The material presented in the chapters that follow, and the conclusions we have drawn, is based upon experiences reported by 648 married couples—1296 individuals. We admit we have not resisted the temptation to compile statistical data, percentages, means, etc. We have, however, resisted the temptation to include these statistics for two reasons: first, we do not feel that our sample, the 648 couples, is representative with respect to many relevant variables of a general population of American married men and women. The average age of our sample is older (most are in their thirties). The average number of years of their formal education is high (70 per cent of the men and 55 per cent of the women had completed college). They are in an above-average income bracket. They have been married for from less than one year to thirty-seven years. Close to 85 per cent have been married only once. Many of these couples had initially sought counseling for some problem in their relationship, although in less than 10 per cent of the cases the presenting problem involved self-diagnosed sexual difficulties.

Our second reason for not reporting statistics is our acute awareness of the tendency most of us have to measure our performances against some norm group (the Kinsey response syndrome). Comparing our performance with the "average" can be a two-edged sword. If we are insecure, the comparison may reassure us of our "normality." We may discover we are not strange or deviant or inadequate. On the other hand, we may find we do not "measure up" to the average. This can be not only depressing, but it may lead us to make efforts to "improve" when no "improvement" is called for.

As all who have participated in any type of group psychotherapy can attest, self-understanding can be aided by our attempts to understand, and perhaps find identification in, the experiences and feelings of others. Members of the group serve as a mirror—at times painfully so—in which we are reflected. Not a day has passed when we have not been able to see ourselves in the men and women who have shared their lives with us. We acknowledge our debt to them. They have taught us, repeatedly, how much we are all alike, as well as how important are our differences. And they have shown us the awesome power of human love. For this we are most grateful.

As we have listened to the outpourings of experiences and emotions of spouses joined in the most intimate and profound of human relationships, we have been struck time after time with the dynamic quality of sexual love. It is a kaleidoscope. Ever changing, yet as potentially beautiful today as yesterday, tomorrow as today. The cynics are right when they say that sexual love does not remain the same. But they are wrong when they contend it withers, inevitably, with time. We recall some years ago viewing four paintings. The artist had captured a landscape in each of the four seasons. Viewing the paintings, one would be challenged to judge one superior to another. Spring, with the first greens, the streams running fresh once more, the buds announcing a new germination, the hesitant beginnings. Summer, with the fullness of living things, fields rich in fruits and grains, bursting with fecundity, complete in growth and variation. Autumn, with its warm, deep reds and umbers, the harvest—rewards of the careful nurturance of spring and summer—the lingering twilights and the harvest moons. And winter, an icy blast driving all living things to cover, coating the branches with frost. White and dead. Yet not dead. Merely waiting for a rebirth. "If winter comes, can spring be far behind?" How better can we describe the sexual love shared by husband and wife?

We have seen couples in the early, tentative stages of their union, the spring of their love. We have talked with those who were enjoying the summer of their love, reaching the fullness, the security, and the rewards of their sexual loving. And with those who were luxuriating in the autumn of their love, the languorous, relaxed, total fulfillment of their sexuality, bathed in the deep richness of memories and new dreams born of wisdom in the art of loving. We have also seen couples in the chill of winter—felt their pain in watching the ice form and life (and love) wither. Yet even in the freeze of winter we have seen hope and desire stir. Love was not dead, only sleeping. Calling it to wakefulness is our challenge to live.

CHAPTER 1

Loving Is for Persons

No man loves, but he loves another more than himself. *In mean instances this is apparent. If you come into an orchard with a person you love and there be but one ripe cherry, you prefer it to the other.*

Thomas Traherne (1637–74)
"The Fourth Century" from
Centuries of Meditations

What is love? Ask him who lives, what is life? ask him who adores, what is God? . . .

Percy Bysshe Shelley
On Love

Let us always love! Let us love and love again! Love . . . is the flame that cannot be quenched, The flower that cannot die.

Victor Hugo

What the world needs now is love, sweet love. A cliché, you say? Love. LOVE. LUV. Is any word used more often and in more ways? The word is employed as a noun, verb, and adjective. We learn to accept the ambiguities. Is love a many-splendored thing or a word in the title of an erotic movie? The name of a generation or a biblical injunction? A sacrificial act or a raging emotion? All of these? Or none of these?

Love is indeed the "sweet mystery of life," or so it would seem. We rhapsodize it, anguish over it, compose songs, sonnets, and comic valentines to it. We build monuments to its honor, wage wars in its name. And perhaps, despairing of finding an acceptable, comfortable definition for it, we hang posters, "Love IS."

Man meets woman. Something happens. She embodies something he desires. Something about him turns her on. Emotional reaction. "Chemistry." That confusing combination of thoughts, associations, hormones, and perhaps much more that makes up the awesome, painful, wonderful, tumultuous experience we call *Falling in Love.*

Falling in love, however, is not something that just happened without rhyme, reason, or prior experience. It germinates long before any thoughts of dating, pairing, and marriage. The "chemistry" (and there must be a better word for it) has its genesis in childhood. Male and female, we develop our sexual love potential from childhood on.

No child is born with the ability to love, only the potential. It must be developed and nurtured. In sex, we are endowed with only a biological drive, not a heterosexual orientation. And not with a knowledge of the "opposite" sex, or even of our own. How this knowledge is acquired, and how it is utilized in the growth of sexual love, is as complex as it is essential.

We do not come into the world loving. Quite the opposite. We are born totally egocentric, biting, clawing, scratching, totally self-centered, naked apes. We are born neither good nor bad, only human. And as humans, we are the least instinctual of animals. In the so-called lower animals, inborn behavior patterns, instincts, determine mating habits, food-seeking, natural enemies, and a variety of other behaviors. Whatever instincts our ancestors may have had, they have been all but lost in the mill of evolution. Virtually everything else is learned. We have physiological drives which are powerful, but our drives do not determine specific behaviors or even our goals in their satisfaction. These are learned. How the behaviors and goals relate to the sex drive is even now only vaguely understood. And how they relate to human loving, even less so.

Freud, Krafft-Ebing, Havelock Ellis, and others opened the door to the study of human sexuality during the first three decades of this century. Their observations (and educated guesses) provided more knowledge of human sexuality than all the philosophical and anecdotal writings of physicians and philosophers in the past. Even they left more questions than answers, however, and they were the first to admit it.

Then, during the late 1930s and early 1940s, Alfred Kinsey and his associates at the University of Indiana collected data on the reported sexual behavior of American men and women. Whereas Freud and others had relied on information gathered from psychoanalyses of a small number of individuals and then extrapolated from these cases, Kinsey *et al* interviewed a large number of persons of both sexes, asking specific questions about their sexual history and behavior. No longer were sexologists bound by what writers of various disciplines thought people did (or wished to believe they did—or didn't do). They now had demographic materials. The resulting reports were not, however, greeted with unanimous enthusiasm. Some critics saw the reports as vehicles for undermining the morals of society. The statistics did not console the moralists. The reports made the best-seller lists. The public, it seems, had a thirst for information as to what, how, when, and how often people did things with their genitals. What they learned was that people of both sexes did many things of which society officially disapproved, even condemned as perverted. What disturbed the moralists was the possibility that impressionable readers might use the statistics to rationalize what they wanted to do. It is doubtful they had cause to worry. Certainly no cause-and-effect relationship between the Kinsey data and increased sexual behavior was ever established.

The Kinsey reports, however, did prove immeasurably valuable to physicians, psychologists, sociologists, and others working with men and women troubled by sexual problems. They provided clinicians with something other than their own experiences (and biases) against which to evaluate sexual behavior.

Kinsey's was step one: the behavioral norms. Step two may have been obvious, but it called for even greater courage. In 1966, William H. Masters and Virginia E. Johnson published *Human Sexual Response.** Van de Velde, Dickinson, and others had previously investigated the physiology of sexual response, but nowhere near approaching the scope and rigor of Masters and Johnson. If Kinsey and his associates had succeeded in raising eyebrows, Masters and Johnson rocked the public back on its collective heels. Initially relying on sensational news stories, the public responded. Some were titillated, some outraged, many simply incredulous. Medical researchers had actually studied the physical responses of men and women during sexual activity. To many readers this violated what they believed to be the sacred privacy of sex. For weeks, magazine and newspaper editors were targets of upset readers who objected to stories about the activities of those "immoral people who run that establishment in St. Louis."

All the hysterics in the world, however, could not lessen the import of what proved to be the most significant studies to date in the area of human sexuality. The scientific community now had answers where previously they had had only medical myths.

To Freud, the critics said, "But there is more to sex than oedipal reactions, libido, fixations, and the Id-Ego-Superego." To Kinsey, they objected: "Sex isn't just a collection of statistics." And to Masters and Johnson: "Sex is more than merely physiological reactions." To which Freud, Kinsey, Masters and Johnson, and all others who have studied human sexuality, would answer: "We agree." Each studied one or more dimensions of what all would agree are highly complex emotional and physical interactions. None denied the role of love in sex. Love, per se, was simply not their primary area of scientific interest.

No one has yet been able to study love in anything approaching a scientific manner. Questions on love can provide data on what men and

* Full bibliographical information about all of the books mentioned will be found in Appendix B, p. 256.

women *say* about love (as they understand it), but it can give us no measure of love itself. We might, for example, ask, "Have you ever been in love?" "Do you love your spouse?" "At what age were you first in love?" For our data, we could compute percentages, means, medians, standard deviations, and other statistics. This might, indeed, provide us with some useful information. It might be of value to learn how many husbands and wives claim to love one another. But such information would add nothing to our understanding of the nature of human love. We could not feel confident that the subjects in our sample had similar thoughts and feelings when responding to the word *love*. And our data would add nothing to our understanding of the sex/love relationship.

To qualify as a scientific study, we must have variables which are operationally definable, quantifiable, and objectively measurable. If, for example, we define *loving* as action which gives to another that which meets his/her physical and/or emotional needs and desires, we could get a valid answer to the question, "Is it loving?" only from the recipient. Even then it would be a question of "how much" and "how often." We would know nothing of the motivation or emotions of the lover. If we define love purely as an emotion, we could learn nothing more than what emotional reactions certain individuals *say* they experience. We cannot attach electrodes to the skull or anywhere else to tap emotional response. Physiological response, yes. But feelings, no.

Faced with this dilemma, scientists and most clinicians have left *love* in the hands of philosophers and poets. There have been exceptions. Psychoanalysts have written lengthy dissertations on the subject, but in so doing they have written more as philosophers than as clinicians. While we do not disparage such writings, generally they reflect little beyond the experiences and philosophical bias of the writers. When psychoanalysts speak of love, they speak from the authority of no more empirical evidence than we possessed in the area of sex half a century ago.

Although love can never be subject to *hard* research, we can, hopefully, take a more objective look at the relationships of men and women in our society, their sexual responses, and how they play out their sexual roles within marriage. Beyond that, we can attempt to study how their sexual satisfactions affect other aspects of their lives.

When we first wrote on sexual love (*Freedom of Sexual Love*, 1967), Masters and Johnson had not yet published their monumental work. There were probably almost as many books on sex then, however, as there are now. There were the omnipresent marriage manuals, some still in print from the 1920s, depressing volumes on sexual problems, the "authoritative" writings of social scientists, clergy, and medical practitioners. And always there were the judgmental writings of the puritans competing with the fantasies of under-the-counter sex-book writers. The more we listened to the men and women who were willing to share their sexual experiences with us, the more we questioned the validity of many of the views of these writers. Many of the writers approached marital sex with a singular view. It was reductionism at its worst. This was not because the writer had narrowed his area of research interest (as Kinsey and Masters and Johnson had), but because the writer apparently saw the sum of marital sex as a single dimension, isolated from the other dimensions of the relationship. As we talked with an increasing number of couples, however, we became convinced that all dimensions and problem areas of a marriage are inseparable. And the question of love, with all its definitional problems, runs through all.

Frequently, a husband or wife would tell us, "I'm not sure I love him [or her]." What they meant by the statement reflected the definition of love they employed. If defined as an emotion, regardless of how mixed the emotion might be, then husband and wife might "love" each other, although repeatedly inflicting pain on one another. Remember the words of the song, "You always hurt the one you love"?

For some couples, love is a dependency need. When it is felt mutually, husband and wife may live in a symbiotic and neurotic relationship, each one leaning upon the other. He may feel he cannot survive without her; she may be convinced he is necessary to her very existence. They may tear one another to shreds, but they will stick it out together—and claim to love each other.

A few couples defined love as nothing other than a strong sexual desire for each other. They said they had little in common, little or no liking or even respect for one another, and fought all day and half the night, yet were bound together by a "wonderful sex life," defined as "loving each other."

Others defined love in terms of "respect" and "admiration." No affection, no passion. They may have married for security, social advantage, avoidance of loneliness, or other "practical" reasons. If these goals are achieved, they may (at least for a time) hope for nothing more than a value system in their mate which they can accept and admire. If they find it, they call it love.

Finally, there are those who defined love as a "giving of self," a selflessness in which the needs and desires of the loved one are paramount. This is the love of which the theologians speak. It is a love which demands considerable maturity and rationality if masochism and/or martyrdom are to be avoided. We personally prefer the more realistic definition given by the psychiatrist Harry Stack Sullivan: *"When the satisfaction or the security of another person becomes as significant to one as is one's own satisfaction or security, then the state of love exists."* (*Conceptions of Modern Psychiatry*, pp. 42–43.)

Ask a man or woman to define love and you may hear any of the above, a combination of two or more of them, a denial that love can be defined at all, an assertion that there are many kinds of love, all defined differently, or perhaps none of these. There are even those who say love is a myth, an illusion, even a fraud or a neurosis.

Among the men and women we have interviewed we have seen "love" in all such forms expressed in their sexual relationships. As we prefer to define it, however, we cannot agree that all such couples *love*. We accept the definition of Harry Stack Sullivan. To this definition we would add that intensely pleasurable emotions *accompany* this love. The emotions are not themselves the love, but as the love grows, so does the depth and intensity of the emotion.

CHAPTER 2

The Sexual Roots of Love

*I believe myself that romantic love is the source
of the most intense delights that life has to offer.
In the relation of a man and a woman who love each
other with passion and imagination and tenderness,
there is something of inestimable value, to be
ignorant of which is a great misfortune to any
human being.*

Bertrand Russell (1872–1971)
Marriage and Morals

*Were the bright day no more to visit us,
Oh, then for ever would I hold thee thus,
Naked, enchained, empty of idle fear,
As the first lovers in the garden were.*

John Milton

*One thing I am sure of: While perhaps not everything
in a marriage is sexual, everything which is loving,
and makes life worthwhile between us, is very, very
sexual.*

A wife

*M*an in a unique animal. He may choose not to love, find loving difficult, or fail in his attempts to love, but he is born with the potential of loving. In this respect, he is unique in nature. He may walk erect, express humor, build moon rockets, or compose symphonies, but it is in loving that man is most distinguished from the other members of the animal kingdom.

Every act of sex is not an act of love, and every act of love is not sexual. Only in humans, however, can sexuality be expressed in loving. In romantic novels and motion pictures it is sex appeal which draws man and woman together toward marriage. Sex appeal is the magic chemistry.

It is on a purely physical level. A glandular, visceral level. It is the stuff of which erotic dreams and fantasies are built. We may not be able to identify the genesis of our sexual stimuli, those physical features and mannerisms which trigger our sexual responses: large breasts, narrow hips, broad shoulders, slender build, dark eyes, long legs, curly hair, full lips, blond (or brunet) hair, youth, maturity, rugged individualism, delicate personality, or some combination of these or other features which may be incomprehensible to our friends and family. Our sexual preferences are formed early in life. We may be turned on by a girl "just like the girl who married dear old Dad" if our relationship with Mom was positive. If the relationship was unpleasant, we may look for someone quite her opposite—or someone we initially believe is her opposite. A woman may be turned on by men with slender legs because she admired an uncle who had slim legs, or perhaps because long, thin legs were "in" when she was younger. During the 1940s, female legs and buttocks were the thing. In the 1950s and 1960s, large breasts were displayed as the dominant object of sex appeal. The culture and the times play an important part in determining what we see as sex appeal.

Less than half the wives we interviewed in the sample of 648 and only about two thirds of the husbands said "sex appeal" was a strong element in their choice of mate. Almost a fifth of those of both sexes said they felt little or *no* sexual attraction for the person they married!

We asked a group of sixty unmarried college students to list the attributes and characteristics they would look for in a mate. Most lists were extensive. They had apparently given the question considerable thought. Most included educational achievement, common interests, consideration, humor, and similar values. Some of the men included the "traditional" housewife skills—cooking, housekeeping, entertaining. Some women included being handy with tools, good health, and athletic ability. But not a single man or woman included sexual attraction in their list. The male students may have swapped stories with their male friends about this or that female, her anatomy, sexual attractiveness, and what experiences they claimed to have had with her. The female students might have had late-night, after-the-date conversations with girlfriends, comparing this "sexy" male with that one. Yet when it came to stating what they looked for in one they might marry, not one said, "I want someone who can stir my sexual impulses." As one young man said, "That isn't a thing you look for when you go out to find a wife—at least, not if you have any maturity."

Almost every woman in our college sample, as well as the wives interviewed, recalled the education in mate selection they had been given by parents, relatives, teachers, and friends. Some, of course, was by way of parental model—positive or negative. Much of it was more direct. The girl received hours of unsolicited advice on what to look for in a prospective husband. Earning capacity, stability, education, status, "decency," and kindness (prized highly by mothers) were high on the list. So were family background, religion, occupation, politics, and approval of friends. Perhaps, above all, they were told to marry a man they could trust (translation: a man who will never "look" at another woman).

Men admitted they also had been "educated" in mate selection. They were taught what a "good" wife was, and what to look for in "the mother of your children." One husband in our sample summed it up: "There is the kind of gal who gives you a hard-on when she walks through the room, but she sure as hell isn't the kind you marry." Over half the wives interviewed said they had, at some time prior to marriage, dated a man who stirred their sexual impulses, who had "that animal magnetism." "He would touch me, maybe just only on the cheek or hold my hand," one wife told us, "and I would get so aroused it would scare me. But you don't build a marriage on that; it would be like living on a roller coaster."

The following is the consensus we drew from the views stated by those husbands and wives who said that "sex appeal" was not a significant factor in their choice of a spouse:

1. Sex is not very important to the success of a marriage.

2. If a couple places undue emphasis on sex, their relationship will run into trouble when the sexual attraction starts to fade (as it inevitably will).

3. If the criteria of an acceptable spouse are met (i.e., if he/she is what you want in all other ways), sexual satisfaction will follow "naturally."

4. Sex is a natural function. It doesn't demand analysis, discussion, or development. Stripping sex of its "privacy" cheapens it and lessens its "higher" value.

5. Sexual satisfaction is dependent on satisfaction in a wide variety of other, nonsexual, areas; if the other satisfactions are not found, sex will not be satisfying. (You cannot find sexual satisfaction with someone you do not admire, in whom you do not have confidence, etc.)

6. Sexual satisfaction is dependent on performance (i.e., concern, duration of foreplay, technique) of one's partner, not on sex appeal.

Does "sex appeal" play a significant part in the overall satisfaction husband and wife find in their relationship? Or is there validity in what these husbands and wives say? We asked the men and women we interviewed to rate their marital satisfaction and their sexual satisfaction with their spouse. We then correlated these ratings with their ratings of sex appeal of their spouse. The relationships were highly significant. Those who rated their spouses high in sex appeal reported the greatest satisfaction in their marital sex relationship. They also were among the group who rated their overall happiness in marriage the highest. We must conclude that sexual attraction is a very important variable in predicting fulfillment in marriage.

Two further questions were raised: How is sexual attraction learned? Can it be developed if it did not exist initially in the relationship? The answers to both questions call for an understanding of how we develop our sexual feelings.

"Develop" is perhaps not the right word. Sexually, we are born free. We have no inborn sexual fears or inhibitions, no sexual attitudes pro or con. These are learned. What we learn and how well we learn it establish the limits of our freedom. Few individuals remain even relatively free. Nearly every husband and wife interviewed admitted to at least some fears and inhibitions in the area of sex at the time they married. A majority of those married over five years still had some. The development of freedom in sex begins with acceptance of one's genitals. In early infancy every individual is taught not to expose the genitals. We are taught that our genitals are "offensive," and that we must never touch them except when necessary for elimination or hygiene, never for pleasure. And we are taught to show no curiosity toward the genitals of others. They are referred to as "privates." Most of those we interviewed, of both sexes, recalled being caught by a parent and punished, by scolding or worse, for "playing" with their genitals. Many had played *I'll-show-you-mine-and-you-show-me-yours* games with their friends. When caught, the punishment was often severe. Generally the explanation was no more than "because we don't do that," or "because it's not nice."

Girls were taught to cover parts of their bodies which boys could leave uncovered, even at an age when there was no discernible difference between the sexes. Adults kept more covered than children, and talked about what was covered even less. When they went to the bathroom, they locked the door and didn't announce their intentions. Privacy meant secrecy.

Early in life the child experiences sexual feelings which are pleasurable. But he learns not to speak of them. Since no one else speaks of such feelings, he has no way of knowing that anyone else has such feelings.

Most interviewees of both sexes learned where babies come from before learning about sex. They learned that the mother carries the baby in her "tummy." How the baby got there was a mystery. When the question was pursued, they were given non-answers: "When Mommy and Daddy marry and love each other, God sends them a little baby." Or, "The baby grows from a little seed inside the mother."

Even those who had "liberated" parents who answered the questions without evasion were given only lessons in the anatomy and physiology of pregnancy. Sex remained as the great unknown. Much later, the "facts" were learned. The majority learned it from friends. They usually came away from the conversations still more confused. Many said they could not see how such a thing was even physically possible. How could a man put that "thing" where they said he did? And how could a woman receive it? Wasn't a woman too small down there? And how did the man make his seed come out? They were left with far more questions than answers.

Very few, however, asked the all-important question: "Is there any reason to do *that* except to have babies?" It wasn't until much later in life that we learned something of the pleasure in sex, usually not until adolescence. And even then, moral and social limitations were placed upon the pleasure. Sex was far from free.

During childhood we learned our sexual self-image and the sexual image of the other sex, what those of our sex should feel (and do) and what those of the other sex should feel (and do). This learning became our sexual identity—what it meant to be male, what it meant to be female. With this sexual identity went a sexual role. Confirming what feminist writers have pointed out, most of the men and women said they were aware of having learned specific sex roles. Boys were taught to have interests and activities different from girls. They didn't play with girls. They didn't even like girls, at least not much, and never openly. And girls wanted nothing to do with boys.

The alienation was, of course, not permanent. At least it seemed not to be. With the onset of adolescence, boys developed an interest in girls, girls became turned on to boys. In the future they would marry. Before that happened, they would fall in love, perhaps many times.

During adolescence, sex awakened. The awakening came with little warning. All of a sudden it was there. And we hadn't been forewarned. Powerful glands secreted hormones which rapidly transformed us into new persons—physically, emotionally, and behaviorally. Still, the big secrets of sex were not revealed by the adults who were teaching us by their words and actions. Some recalled lectures on the facts of life in school. Others were given material from a pamphlet supplied by the family doctor. Most of the women interviewed were told something (although very little) about their menstrual cycle—half of them shortly prior to its onset, the other half after the first bleeding appeared. Yet few recall either parent ever talking about the *experience* of sex. The rule seemed to be: "We won't mention it; and you are not to ask questions about it." Whatever the child might be feeling, he or she was not to talk about it. Whatever the adults felt and experienced, they would never admit.

Nearly every man and woman interviewed recalled significant misinformation in sex which they carried into adolescence, if not into adulthood and marriage. The misinformation, negativism, and secrecy which surround sex make it unique as a socialized—and distorted—drive. Those who object to what they consider the "overemphasis" on sex, question why it is necessary to instruct people in something which should be "natural." The answer is that society has not permitted it to be in any way natural.

Not when we consider the following: *Of our several physical drives —e.g., hunger, thirst, sleep—sex is the only one for which society permits no outlet for satisfaction during the first one fourth to one third of our lives. We are taught that sex is to be expressed (and even fantasized) only within a limited social context. And we are taught that the sex drive is to be satisfied only in a relationship with an appropriate member of the other sex in a sexual act which has "meaning."*

Unlike hunger or thirst, the child is not even permitted to discuss, or even mention, the existence of the drive. The fifteen-year-old boy charges through the front door, drops his books on the kitchen table, and announces, "I'm starved! I'm going to make myself a sandwich." His mother reminds him only to clean up afterward. What would be her reaction if he said, "I'm feeling real horny. I'm going to my bedroom to masturbate"? If eating carried similar social injunctions, meals might be eaten only at the family dining table, only during a dinner alone with one's wife, only seated in specified positions, the entree to be eaten only after tempting one's partner with hors d'oeuvres, lavish compliments on the quality of the food, praise for each other's table manners and eating style, and words expressing anticipation of the entree. In addition, no expression of hunger would be permitted to anyone other than one's spouse, and then only in private. Never would one be allowed to eat alone, no matter how hungry. And thoughts of dining with anyone else would be considered evil.

From earliest infancy on, sex is presented as a series of *Thou shalt nots.* We are taught to turn off reactions. For twelve to fifteen years, boys and girls are taught to turn off an incredible variety of potential sexual stimuli: persons, objects, acts, and relationships. We learn to turn off sexual responses to members of our own sex. We learn to turn off parents and siblings. We also learn turn-offs on the basis of age, socioeconomic status, education, ethnic-group membership, and certain physical characteristics.

By the time we begin actively seeking sexual relationships—dating, going steady, having love affairs, engagement and ultimately marriage —we have drastically attenuated our sexual selections, both persons and actions. We have also been taught to turn off to those of the other sex who, though within the "acceptable" group, do not consistently meet the established mores of sexual behavior. Each sex is taught a set of turn-offs. If female, she is taught to turn off if the man does not create a "romantic" environment. She learns to turn off if he doesn't consistently profess his love for her, if he doesn't invest great effort in trying to turn her on, if he uses the wrong words or fails to use the right ones, if he doesn't treat her family, friends, pets and interests with proper respect, if he forgets to shave or remembers to phone his office when he "should" be paying attention to her, if he admits being turned on by another woman or not being turned on enough by his wife, if he acts too aroused by his wife at a time when she has a headache or is otherwise not interested.

The male learns to turn off if his advances are rejected, if the woman doesn't act enough like a lady when he expects her to, or behaves too much like a "lady" when he wants something else, if she acts too "cold" or too sexually aggressive, if she behaves too much like his mother—or not enough.

It is not so much that we had to learn our sexual arousal. We were born with all the physical and emotional potential to be fully sexual beings. We learned the "switches" to throw to turn ourselves off. If we install enough switches, and practice employing them, we may in time come close to extinguishing the functioning of our natural sex drive, and with it the ability to establish and maintain a fulfilling marriage.

It seems evident that the most effective "switch" employed, often unconsciously, to turn off sexual response is the one which says, "Any sexual act motivated solely by the desire for sensual pleasure is *wrong*." Almost every husband and wife interviewed recalled words they had heard in adolescence condemning "lust." Sexual pleasure for its own sake was animalistic, debased, sinful, filthy, beneath the dignity of a human being. And above all, it was devoid of love. The teachers of morality did not say that sex is good and can be even better if there is mutual respect, admiration, and especially love. They said that unless it was intended *primarily* to communicate those values and feelings, it was *bad*.

To illustrate the psychological problem this creates, let us return to our analogy with hunger and eating.

Food and drink are frequently used in rituals heavy with meaning. Unleavened bread and grape wine are employed in Christianity to link man with his Redeemer. The ritual meal has deep significance in Eastern religions as well as in Judaism. Yet no religion teaches that the eating of food is wrong or bad unless endowed with religious significance. An intimate dinner for two may be rich in meaning. The lovers touch their glasses together before tasting the wine. The action communicates something known only to them. It has meaning. If she feeds him fruit while he rests his head in her lap, it says more than, "Have some grapes; they're delicious." If we were taught to view food and drink as we do sex, we would approach our food only when it is served in a setting of "meaning."

Dogs, rabbits, and koala bears copulate, or mate. Humans *make love*. If a man and woman engage in sexual intercourse but do not make love in doing so, they have done something less than "supremely human." Their act has been "meaningless." A majority of husbands and wives interviewed said that they subscribed to this value to a degree. The answers given to the question, "What makes it 'lovemaking'?" were indeed puzzling. While some said, "mutual satisfaction," "concern for the other's satisfaction," and "an absence of exploitation," most said the act was lovemaking if the motive was to "make love." This seems to say nothing, to be at best circular. But it is not. Most of the individuals presumed the motive involved was the desire to "make love" if there was commitment present. And they further presumed there was commitment if the couple were husband and wife!

This position might seem to tie love and marriage tightly together in the thinking of these husbands and wives, at least where sex is concerned. Further questioning, however, led to a different conclusion: Husband and wife do not (properly) engage in sexual relations for the fun of it, primarily for the sensual pleasure they experience. They do it to express their love for one another. Parenthetically, the attitude of many seemed to be: Sex for pleasure and sex as an expression of love do not go hand in hand.

Yet all evidence we have collected points to the conclusion that the most fulfilling relationships are built upon and motivated by the sexual love of the man and woman. In structure it is an inverted pyramid. At the base, the core, is sexual attraction which draws the man and woman together. The attraction motivates them to find ways to be together. As they spend time together, strong sexual desire develops, which in turn motivates them to want to spend even more time together. In time, they decide they don't ever want to part, and they marry. They don't marry for security or status or companionship or escape. They marry because the thought of not living and loving together is intolerable. It is rooted in sex. It grows into love, and blossoms into a fulfilling oneness.

CHAPTER 3

Communication

We talk: your voice, your thoughts, and the words you use to express them are the most familiar in the world to me. Each of us can end a sentence begun by the other. And you are—and we are—a mystery.

Anne Philipe
Le Temps d'un soupir

If the first condition for the achievement of understanding is the will to understand, the second condition is that of expressing oneself.

Paul Tournier
To Understand Each Other

We talked. My God, how we talked! But it was only after she said she wanted a divorce that we began to communicate.

A husband

*W*eather, as Will Rogers was fond of pointing out, is something everybody talks about but nobody does anything about. Sex, on the other hand, is something most of us think about a great deal, and most of us do something about, but talk about very little.

We may not be able to change the weather by talking about it. But we can change our sexual attitudes and actions only if we are willing and able to talk about them. Most of us talk about the weather more than sex for two reasons: Weather is a "proper" topic; sex is not. And weather, even when hurricane warnings have been hoisted, is usually a less anxiety-arousing topic than sex.

It is tempting when asked, "Why talk about sex?" to ask in reply, "Why not?" No one asks a gourmet why he talks about food, or a philatelist why he talks about rare stamps. The gourmet is turned on to food; the philatelist is enthusiastic about stamp collecting. We expect them to talk about their interests to the point of boredom. Then, what of the individual who finds sex exciting and fulfilling? Wouldn't we expect him or her to talk about it? Yet men and women who claim to experience joy in sexual love tell us they find discussion of sex, even with their spouse, either in poor taste or painfully difficult.

Only a small percentage of the couples interviewed said they "frequently" talked about sex. And of those, nearly half said the talk usually centered on a sexual problem or complaint. The vast majority, however, admitted to at least some lack of freedom in discussing sexual love. This, in an age when popular writers would have us believe we are all "liberated."

For those who freely accept and enjoy sex, and who trust the acceptance of their spouse, talking about sex is as natural as singing in the shower. And this is as it should be. Learning to communicate in the area of sex, and to feel comfortable in doing so, is essential to marital closeness. "I can't know you unless you permit me to know you; you can't know me unless I reveal myself to you," are statements of humane communication which bear particular relevance to our sexuality. Living together, even loving together, does not give men or women the ability to read each other's minds. Telepathy is not a fringe benefit of marriage. There are those, however, who apparently believe it is. One of the most frequent complaints is, "If he/she loved me, he/she would know what I want." And, on the other side of the coin, "I know him/her better than he/she knows him/her self. He/she doesn't have to say a word."

There are three reasons why communication in sex is so important as well as so difficult. First, we have all been raised to view sex as a strictly private matter, not to be discussed. Second, men differ from women in their sexual anatomy, in the sexual orientation they have been taught, and, perhaps, in their sexual psychology. Not being a woman, a man cannot possibly *know* what a woman thinks and feels, what turns her on and turns her off. He can know only what she tells him. *If* she tells him. It is something that cannot be learned in a few suggestions or even by reading a score of sex manuals. The same, of course, is true of a woman's attempt to understand a man. Third, there are substantial differences between members of the same sex and even within the same individual. These differences seem, in fact, greater in sex than in any of our other primary drives.

In sexual communication, it is imperative that a couple begin with a mutual pledge: "I will unconditionally accept what you tell me about yourself, your fantasies, desires, and experiences. No reservations. No judgments. No rejections." The assurances need not be verbalized each and every time, but they are always implicitly offered and accepted by both spouses. Both must at all times be keenly aware how fragile the lines of communication are in sex. Criticisms, judgments, and rejections can so easily sever the lines.

"But you're not *listening* to me," is a common complaint in most marriages. Authentic listening is a major challenge for most of us. Self-interest tends to close our ears. When it comes to sex, it is especially difficult, carrying as we do residual taboos, fears, and prejudices. Unless husband and wife abide by the assurance of acceptance, listening but not judging, they will react to their fears and prejudices, lash out in condemnation, and force each other to withdraw into silence. Or worse, lies. Then neither will discover the secrets of what gives pleasure in their sexual loving.

If there is to be a meeting of mutual needs and desires, sexual communication must be marked by mutual concern and candor. Honest expression of one's feelings and desires is most important—so long as it is tempered with a concern for the feelings of one's spouse and the possible effect such candor may have on the relationship. As ambiguity is eliminated, frustration is reduced. There is a virtue in the straightforwardness of the following:

"I like it when you . . ."
"It turns me on when you let me . . ."
"I like it when you . . . while we are . . ."
"I would like you to . . . more."
"I like it when you . . . my penis."
"Caressing your . . . is very arousing to me."
"When we make love this evening, I would like you to . . ."

And the self-revealing statements of our sexual feelings which, uncomfortable though they may be, are declarations of our humanity, the real person within us:

"At times I have had thoughts of . . ."
"Sometimes when we make love, I have feelings . . ."

Expression of thoughts and desires should not be a one-time experience. Our sexual thoughts are too numerous and complex to be expressed or even recognized in an hour or two. And they are changing constantly as we gain experience and freedom.

Sex may not be everything in the relationship, but what we feel about sex, our attitudes toward men, women, and ourselves sexually, reveals much about *what we are*. And what we are, as well as what we want to become, is dynamic. It is not constant.

Communicating thoughts and desires as a prelude to sexual relations offers benefits which make it worthwhile as a regular part of lovemaking. It gives the spouses the opportunity to express their moods *as of that moment*. Such expressions can also be highly arousing to the lovers. Can we fail to respond to the words of a lover speaking of erotic desires to please us? From our interviews we learned that one reason many couples find conversations about sex so unrewarding is that they keep such conversations on a level which is proper, clinical, and (we would say) sterile. Some couples discussed their sexual activities and feelings as if they were lecturing on anatomy. And understandably so. It is less emotionally threatening that way. It is virtually devoid of feeling. But how ironic. Sexual love without feeling is not love. And discussion of their sexual love by lovers without feeling can only separate the lovers, not bring them closer together.

There is no such thing as an objective discussion of sex between lovers. Nor should there be. There are some experiences which are, by their nature, always subjective. Religious experiences and sexual experiences are two such classes. At best, we can only hope to express a fraction of what we feel. The expressions are only the tip of the iceberg. And always we are left with the question: "Could anyone else feel what I feel?" And the question which follows this one: "If I reveal my feelings and desires, will I shock him/her; will he/she think I'm a pervert or sex maniac?" Avoiding discussion of sex altogether, or at best keeping it clinically "objective," may make us less vulnerable, but at the price of intimacy. A sizable majority of couples interviewed had not developed even superficial lines of communication in sex. In a recent television interview, a psychologist who directs a sex-information telephone service said that the majority of calls revealed a "total lack" of husband-wife communication. In our society, as one authority pointed out, "the goal should be to reach a point where we can talk about sex as freely as we talk about what we would like to eat for lunch." To this we would add: "We don't talk about lunch in terms of the digestive system, using correct anatomical and physiological words." To be able to do so, however, it is necessary to "desensitize" (reduce a fear by exposure to the fear-eliciting stimuli) sexual material by frequent "practice" sessions. Despite the discomfort husband and wife may initially experience in such conversations, the discomfort will pass as they discover that "such things" can be talked about without fear of rejection.

We have encouraged couples to develop their own vocabulary of sex. The so-called correct, proper words can have the effect of maintaining uneasiness and emotional distance. It is indeed unfortunate that common sexual words, four-letter words and others, are condemned as "dirty" or "smutty" or "filthy" or "vulgar." Words are words. They are neither moral nor immoral, proper nor improper, clean nor dirty, virtuous nor obscene. They are *words*. Yet we were taught that they were *bad*. Their use is banned on radio and television, censored in the press, and, until recently, they were considered shocking in novels and motion pictures.

Since a majority of wives and a substantial minority of husbands said they found vernacular sex words offensive, we were interested in their reasons. This is the consensus in order of frequency:

1. Such words show a lack of respect for one's spouse. They show a desire to exploit, and an attitude which views women as sex objects.

2. If one knows the "correct" words, they will not use "obscenities." Vernacular sex words mark the user as a person of low character or intelligence.

3. Vernacular sex words degrade marital sex. Relations between husband and wife should be treated with respect. It is lost when such words are used.

4. The words are themselves obscene. Everyone knows and accepts this. No further explanation is needed. They are just dirty.

These words are capable of eliciting an emotional response. Novelists are very aware that these words are emotionally loaded. They use them:

"They expressed their mutual affection in a physical embrace."

"They engaged in marital relations."

"They made love."

"They fucked."

All may be descriptive of the same act, but they do not touch off the same reactions. Novelists know this. The more explicit the words, the stronger the reaction. The words "sexual intercourse" are cool, detached. They are descriptive only. The word "fucked" is emotionally loaded. It is a word of minimal interpersonal distance. And it is this loss of distance which makes the word disturbing to so many. It is difficult to understand how these words could be destructive to a good relationship. Or degrading. Or exploitive. Shakespeare said it well when he pointed out that renaming a rose would not diminish the flower's fragrance. The words we choose, however, do reflect our attitudes. While we seldom observed negative attitudes toward sex, spouse, or the other sex related to the use of vernacular sex words by those interviewed, we did find that husbands and wives who were disturbed by such words were frequently those with a lower sex drive (as measured by behavior and desired sexual encounters) and strong aversive reactions to sexual matters. Typical was a thirty-two-year-old wife and mother of three: "I'm totally turned off when my husband uses words like that. It takes away my romantic feelings." She claimed she had no negative attitudes toward sex or men. When questioned, however, she admitted she viewed the male genitalia as "ugly," and oral sex "repulsive." She had never experienced orgasm.

Conversely, a majority of wives who were consistently orgasmic admitted they found such words decidedly arousing when employed by their husbands during lovemaking. More women than men were aroused by use of these words during sexual relations.

Only a small minority of women found the words degrading or representative of an exploitive attitude on the part of men. "They show a rape mentality," said one wife. "To the average man, sex isn't something you do *with* a woman; it's something you do *to* her." She told us she was staying with her husband only for the financial benefits. Along with a minority of other women interviewed, she saw men as the enemy.

The argument that vernacular sex words indicate a lack of education or moral character is unsupported by any of our interviews. Well-educated, articulate individuals with excellent working vocabularies were as apt to use such words as were those with less education. The college professor may speak of a "three bagger" in baseball, a "knock down and drag out" with his department chairman, and of "flunking out that undergrad who bombed the final." The words enrich his vocabulary. They don't prove its limitations. As far as the morality of such words is concerned, we can only say: "The actions a word describes can be immoral; the words cannot be."

In developing their sexual vocabulary, some couples who previously felt inhibited in discussing sex found it helpful to list vernacular synonyms for the names of sexual parts and actions, then circling the words they found acceptable. When they have each selected vernacular sex words and have chosen to employ them, recognizing the benefit to be derived from it, and not falling back on the emotionally safe, "acceptable" words, they have found themselves able to be increasingly open in sharing their sexual thoughts, desires, and dreams. This has come as a surprise to many who felt that the use of "improper" words would inhibit them still more. One wife told us, "I thought I would never be able to listen to words like these, let alone use them. I was foolish. Since we started a week or two ago, Jim and I have talked more about sex than in all the years we have been married."

Communication in sex is, of course, going to be correlated to the overall communication the couple have attained. Communication is a learned skill. It is not unlike playing the piano or typewriting. It is in no sense a "natural" skill or the gift of some special "types." It takes practice. And motivation.

A lack of topics for discussion, the tendency to misunderstand what the other one is saying, talking around an issue without ever reaching it, and attempting always to "make points," are the most frequent blocks to communication. Only a small minority of couples found they could sustain a two-hour conversation, except when faced with a crisis. Most said they could not find enough to talk about.

There are several explanations for this. For example, neither one may bring to the conversation sufficient material to share. If the wife limits her intellectual input to housework and children, and the husband limits his to his job, the couple will have little to talk about other than their mundane activities. Then how long will it take for boredom to set in?

Imagine one is seated beside a stranger on a bus. He strikes up a conversation, turning it toward politics. He says, "Well, I don't know much about what's going on in Washington, but do you want my opinion?" Is there any reason why anyone should? The stranger disqualified himself in advance. It may be that we often expect our interests, views, and off-the-top-of-the-head comments to grab the attention of our listener, usually a spouse, regardless of our lack of authority or information. To sustain conversation day after day with someone we know well, and with whom we wish to share all the important as well as trivial thoughts and experiences of our past and present, we must have organized and integrated thoughts to share. This means keeping abreast of what is going on in the world. A shocking majority of husbands and wives said they were "frequently" bored by the conversations of their spouses. In a world of "instant media," we are informed of the events of the day almost as soon as they happen. And so is everyone else. "Have you heard . . . ?" then becomes a question with a certain answer: "Yes, I have heard." Being well-informed is not just an asset to conversation, it is essential. But for the conversation to get off the ground, spouses must have something to say *about* the information they have gathered. Otherwise, in a short time they will find they both have the same information and nothing more to say. Couples who conversed very little were generally those who read very little. Most of us in our daily lives have little that is stimulating to bring to a partner. Although television viewing occupies thirty hours per week of the average family time, little of the programing provides food even for trivial conversation, and a half-hour TV newcast equals the word count of a mere quarter page of newspaper print. Yet a majority of husbands and wives admitted they did not usually do more than scan the daily paper. Furthermore, there was a noticeable split in interests between husbands and wives. Husbands might read the financial and sports sections. Wives might read society and fashion pages. Few couples consistently read the same materials, even in general news.

Even with a wealth of conversational material, communication does not always come easily. It is a skill which cannot be learned effortlessly or quickly. Casual conversation, perhaps. Communication, never. It is a long-range goal, and the trouble with long-range goals is just that: They are long range. The rewards are not immediate. Until a couple is communicating really well, their attempts may approximate exercises in frustration. To hang in there, continuing to try to reach each other over a barrier of words, calls for strong resolve and a clear recognition of the benefits to be derived.

Good conversation is enjoyable. Good communication is even better. So is playing the piano well or shooting par golf. We are not likely to become as emotionally battered playing a piano or swinging a nine iron as in trying to communicate. What motivates us to keep trying even when it hurts is the greater pain felt when there is separateness and the awful feeling of isolation from the one we love. Without communication, husband and wife watch love die and intimacy never develops.

In a previous work, *Marriage Is for Grownups* (pp. 57–69), we offered several suggestions which we feel are worth repeating and expanding:

1. *Examine what you already know.* We learn a great deal about people just by living with them. They reveal their needs, preferences, idiosyncrasies, and desires in food, dress, entertainment, politics, reading, art, etc. And sex. If we are observant, we discover a lot in a short time. When we hear a husband or wife, married a year or more, say, "But I don't know what he/she wants from me," or "what he/she likes," we suspect there has been little attempt to find out. For an obvious reason. If we don't find out what our mate wants, we won't have to give it.

The late Robert Lindner, psychologist/author, in his *Must You Conform?* (pp. 183–210), listed *awareness* as one of the signs of maturity. It is also the first and most important step toward communication—awareness of self and spouse. It means being alive, receptive to persons, objects, events, sights and sounds. Lindner also speaks of the "prophetic sense," the ability to foretell, within limits, the outcome of one's activities and the activities of others. The mature individual is capable of understanding the relationships of separate items of information, and to predict consequences. If we know an individual's reactions to situations A, B, and C, we may be able to predict how he will react when faced with D. The man who enjoys reading about the exploits of Hannibal, Alexander the Great, and Napoleon Bonaparte, will probably enjoy the motion picture *Patton*. Our behavior has a remarkable unity. If we employ the collected pieces of information about the other person to generalize to new, but similar situations, and to discriminate when there are some similarities yet significant differences, we are a long way toward understanding him.

2. *Eliminate the buffers and excuses.* Buffers, and the excuses we offer to justify them, keep us at a comfortable distance in communication. Couples who find their attempts at communication painful may fill their time together with projects, work, friends, and a variety of hobbies and recreation. If nothing else, there is always television. Or children. If they are serious in their attempts to build communication, they will plan their time and eliminate the buffers. A television set can be turned off. Children do eventually go to bed. And most parents have a bedroom of their own.

3. *Schedule a time for talking.* When habits of communication have not been established, the best resolution to try to talk more may go the way of so many good intentions. The answer is obvious: Set aside a period each day during which to share thoughts, observations, desires, and perhaps gripes. *Marriage Encounter,* a program designed to help couples improve the quality of their relationship, advises those who go through the weekend program to practice each day, individually, writing out the thoughts he/she wishes to share, then bringing these so-called "love letters" to each other. The writings are then, of course, discussed. The concept has merit. A program such as this may seem uncomfortably structured and lacking in spontaneity. And so it is. But, then, so is practicing the piano. Only with practice does communication become "free expression."

4. *Analyze your conversations.* Individually and together. We all experience communication breakdowns, especially during the "learning period." The breakdowns are painful, but we can learn from them. If we mentally replay our conversations, we may discover when and how the breakdowns occur. When did one of us become threatened? Were invalid inferences or gratuitous verbal mediations the problem? Husband-wife conversations tend to form patterns of interactions. Formats are es-

tablished which tend to become rigid. And we seldom are aware of the patterns. We act out well-learned roles: parent, child, teacher, autocrat, seductress, therapist. They can so easily lead us into frustration and annoyance. Discovering these roles and how they interact with one's spouse can do a lot to reduce defensive hostility. Destructive role-playing games can continue only if both spouses cling to their half of the hyphenated interaction. One can play "child" only if the other plays "parent." Let the "child" stop playing "child" and the game is over.

5. *Clarify and define.* We like to think we know what our spouse is saying, thinking, and feeling. More often than not, we don't. Not only are our words definitionally muddy, our emotions often get in the way. We leap to conclusions, snatch at inferences, and stretch for interpretations. It may slow down the conversation, but the only way to avoid serious misunderstanding is to ask for clarification and definition. Repeatedly. It is a mistake to assume that our words communicate what we intend them to communicate. The answer: amplify, expand, define, rephrase, and clarify. It may be tedious, but it may save the communication from collapsing.

With groups of married couples we have explored various communication techniques. One that we developed has proven most effective. We call it *Tennis Match* (tape recording). It has clearly defined terms and rules, as does the athletic game of tennis. In the communication game of tennis, however, *both* win or *both* lose. The following is a brief description:

The court: anyplace where two can carry on an *uninterrupted* conversation. No television. No children. No neighbors dropping by. Phone off the hook, if necessary. No buffers. A parked car is ideal.

The net: the defensive reactions of either or both partners. Think of the height of the net as variable, under the control of either husband or wife. With the press of a button, either one can raise the net, i.e., react defensively. The object is to keep the "net" as low as possible.

The ball: the topic or issue. It must be narrow and specific rather than broad and general. A couple cannot play the "ball" of family finances. It is too broad. They might play a ball labeled "weekly grocery budget," but not "family finances." "I would like to play a tennis match over my desire for oral sex" can be played through to conclusion. "Let's talk about our love life" will lead to a conversational smorgasbord with no satisfaction for either player.

The object of the tennis match is to keep the "ball" in play, back and forth, until a resolution is reached. Or at least a mutual understanding.

The first and most important rule of the game is, therefore, to continue until either a conclusion is reached with an agreed course of action, or until both players agree that there is a "meeting of the minds." Many of our conversations have an uncertain start, a sputtering progression, and an inconclusive finish. They literally "go nowhere."

We can talk around an issue indefinitely, returning to "worry" it time and again like a cat with an old stocking, never able to say, "We are now in agreement; we understand each other; we can now act." In some instances, we actually may *not* want the issue resolved. We may want to avoid a compromise in which we have to give up something. "If I can't win all the chips, I don't want the game to end."

We have all sometime started a discussion only to have the phone ring, or to suddenly remember a chore or appointment, or feel the onset of fatigue. "Let's turn in, we can always finish talking about this in the morning," is a plea we have all employed. It virtually insures that the matter will *not* be brought up the following day. Conversations cannot be placed on the shelf, to be retrieved later. A new day is a new day. We rethink what we said the night before. We modify positions and marshal new arguments. Or simply decide to drop the whole thing to avoid the discomfort. If it is brought up again, it starts from the beginning, from ground zero. By agreeing to continue the tennis match until it is concluded, the couple may lose some sleep, but certainly this is a small price to pay for communication. If an important match cannot be concluded (e.g., a spouse has an important appointment in fifteen minutes), it would be better not to start it. It can wait until later. But not too much later.

Another, equally important, rule: Play only *one* ball at a time. Listening to tape recordings of a typical husband-wife conversation, we may hear a dozen or more topics touched upon within less than a half hour. The husband begins with the checking account she overdrew. She parries with the amount he spent on golf clubs and, incidentally, how fed up she is with him going off to play golf Saturday mornings while she is stuck with housework and kids. He returns with a dig about how she might get her housework done if she didn't spend so much time with her mother. To which she replies, "Well, I need someone to talk to; I don't get any conversation from you." And so on. A score of tennis balls are served, but not one of them is played. We cannot play more than one ball at a time, yet frequently we start a conversation by serving two or more in the opening sentence. "Darling, I'd like your opinion of this dress I picked up today for $69.95. I know that's more than we can afford, especially since you spent all that money on your hunting trip, but Mother called today to say she'll be here next week." Four balls served at once. But only one can be returned at a time.

The next rule is one many couples view as unrealistic: *Turn off display of emotion during the match.* Since most of us think of our emotional reactions as something over which we have little control, we may tend to turn them on whenever the conversation gets at all upsetting. (Or when we feel an emotional display will act to our advantage.) Actually, we can learn to turn off our temper and tears. And we do when we need to. The husband who manages to stay under control when chewed out by the boss, may have a short fuse when talking with his wife. Husband and wife can agree to turn off these emotional reactions during the tennis match (and for that matter, at other times as well). A match cannot be played well under extreme heat. Not can it be played on a wet court. So temper and tears are out.

We have also found that when couples use the words of tennis (court, net, ball, serve, etc.) it helps to keep the goal in mind. It also assists them in keeping those emotional responses cooled. A husband may find it easier to hear his wife say, "You slammed that one over the net; would you mind serving it again?" than to listen to her say, "That was a hostile remark you just made." "You just played a second ball," is easier to hear than, "You're trying to change the subject."

When husband and wife come together each day with several "balls" ready to be played, communication rapidly develops into more than a skill; it becomes an art. We are frequently asked, "What should we talk about?" Our answer: There should be nothing a husband and wife cannot talk about. Whether playing a tennis match over preferences in music, political opinions, where to spend a vacation, or likes and dislikes in sex, conversation which is developed to the level of communication helps us open the doors on our private worlds. Through it, we learn the myriad ways to love. And loving, after all, is what it's all about.

CHAPTER 4

Fantasies

*It is in the nature of sex fantasies that
they are, to a large extent, so unrealizable that
they are seldom acted upon. And that is exactly
their therapeutic function. They serve as mental
aphrodisiacs and psychological stimulants, underlying
"normal" sexual behavior.*

Drs. Phyllis and Eberhard Kronhausen
Sexual Fantasies

*. . . and please
don't ever think about someone else
when I kiss you.*

Dean Walley
Please Don't Promise Me Forever

*I*f we were robbed of our dreams, what would life be? If we were to find ourselves incapable of imagery and imagination, what voids we would have to endure in living. Sexual fantasies are human. And they are unique to humanity. We can't conceive a cat or orangutan dreaming of erotic nights and sensual days. Only humans can mentally recreate past pleasures, and shape dreams of a future. What a wonderful gift!

If our minds were suddenly wiped clean of all sexual memory traces, and, in addition, we were to become incapable of imagining desired sexual events we have never experienced, sex drive might still be present, but the number and kind of stimuli capable of eliciting arousal would be substantially reduced. In "lower" animals, sexual response is instinctual, triggered by specific stimuli. It is not a learned response; it is innate. The animal reaches biological maturity, and the response is present, fully developed, elicited whenever the instinctual stimulus is presented. The stimulus may be a color, odor, sound, or pattern of behavior. The animal doesn't "remember" the stimuli or anticipate its recurrence. The response is automatic; the animal doesn't know or care why. The salmon returns from the sea to begin a tortuous route upstream to complete the reproductive cycle. The fish doesn't decide it is homesick. Nor does it conclude that jumping all those rocks and dams may be more work than it is worth. When the instinct is triggered, the journey starts. The salmon doesn't analyze, or dream, or exercise any choices. If we humans, however, at some time in our evolutionary past, responded to sexual stimuli instinctively, no traces remain. We must *learn* what to respond to, and what response is most rewarding. Human sexual response is not a light bulb, bursting into full brilliance when the switch is thrown. Our responses are not purely psychogenic, with no accompanying sensory input. There are also our fantasies, memories, and associations.

We all fantasize. Our fantasies provide color, perhaps even meaning, in our lives. They allow us to expand our reality, to make it "larger than life," at times to escape. Apparently, some fantasize more than others. A small minority claim never to fantasize in sex. We have found three possible explanations for this apparent deficiency: (1) a disinterest in sex (whether due to physical, e.g. hormonal, problems or severe inhibitory attitudes), (2) suppression of sexual thoughts and fantasies, (3) a general lack of imagination, tendency to daydream, and/or artistic-creative thinking. Difficulty in accepting our sexual fantasies is common. Many attempt to deny, avoid, or suppress them. And still more experience guilt when their fantasies break through into consciousness. They agree with the well-indoctrinated value that "the thought is tantamount to the act." Strict moralists have traditionally taught that taking pleasure in thoughts of sexual acts is as heinous a sin as commission of the act itself. A noted theologian of the Middle Ages, Francis de Sales, cautioned the faithful that a "decent" man thinks of his meal only when he sits down to it, and afterwards washes his hands and mouth to remove the smell and the taste of what he has eaten. He then went on to ask couples to draw from this comparison a lesson pertaining to their sex life!

This reasoning is puzzling. Nowhere do we read that an adolescent who daydreams of being Billy the Kid is committing a sin. Are fantasies of robbery and murder moral, while fantasies of sexual acts are punishable by hellfire? It strains rationality to the breaking point. A fantasy may be severely neurotic or psychotic. If we become convinced that our fantasies are real, they are delusions. Fortunately, most of us have no trouble distinguishing fantasy from reality, and we can enjoy our fantasies without ever trying to turn them into reality. That is the wonderful thing about fantasy. It eliminates all the distasteful things that might crop up should the dream become real. On a clear day with blue skies and a mild breeze, we might dream of sailing through the Western Antilles. In our dream there are no blistered hands from furling sails, no tropic squalls to leave us bone-weary and soaked, no boredom with long days and nights at sea. Fantasies are all champagne nights with no hangovers and no picking up the tab. But if we dream of sailing the Caribbean, we don't feel guilty for having deserted our children and running out on our creditors. If we act out some of the fantasies, we may feel guilty. And perhaps we should. But fantasies are fantasies, nothing more.

Puritans will argue that fantasy is father to the act. What terror-filled lives they must lead. Haven't many of us fantasized what it might be like to maneuver a sports car at high speed over a freeway from one city to another? Or to swing from a trapeze high above the upturned faces of the circus spectators? Or perhaps to shoot it out with a desperate criminal? What if we lacked any rational impulse control (which is what these poor uptight souls fear) so that we tried to act out these daydreams with no thought of possible consequences? Don't daydream; you might be killed! What utter nonsense. Unless we are talking about psychopaths or three-year-olds, human beings are capable of weighing the rewards and punishments resulting from their actions. How *do* the anti-sex moralists view human beings?

There is more than a rational argument for not suppressing sexual fantasies. Indeed, there are valid reasons for developing them. They build and maintain sexual arousal. The individual, male or female, able to respond with arousal frequently and to a variety of stimuli, including fantasies, is more apt to find sexual satisfaction with his or her partner. Fantasies help maintain a level of erotic responsiveness, an almost chronically turned-on feeling. Also, fantasies can enrich sexual relations. Monotony and boredom are always lurking in the physical relationship. Fantasizing during sex can prevent sex from going stale. Dreams can provide a new "reality," a change in the daily pattern of life; living, in fact, is often described in terms of change. And just as dreams of wealth can lead to plans which may ultimately be set in motion and result in success, sexual fantasies may prompt a couple to explore adventures that will enhance their love life.

There is a further, and important, benefit to be derived from sharing fantasies. Our dreams and fantasies reveal much about us. Psychoanalysis has always emphasized the importance of dream analysis in understanding the unconscious. But waking dreams, aspirations, hopes, and fantasies can also open windows to our inner self. The more you know about your lover's dreams and fantasies, the better you know him or her. As Herbert and Roberta Otto have pointed out in *Total Sex* (p. 276):

> Invariably sexual fantasies present an important creative communication possibility. *The sharing of sexual fantasies can bring*

*greater openness to communication and often has a marked effect
on the sex life of partners. The basic ground rule of all sex fantasy
communication involves an agreement by both partners that all
sexual fantasies that occur when the couple is together will be
shared verbally. Also included are important sexual fantasies that
occur when the couple is not together. This is done with the clear
understanding that* sharing a sexual fantasy does not necessarily
have any implications for action. Roman type is the Ottos'.)

While a number of our couples have experimented with sharing fantasies both during sex and at other times and have reported it has increased their closeness and understanding as well as enhancing their
enjoyment, perhaps an equal number have run into trouble in doing so.
The usual problem is the obvious one: jealousy and rejection. A wife
might describe her fantasy of having sexual relations with her boss, but
how many husbands could take it? In our experience with couples, very
few. The Ottos may speak of the couple having a "clear understanding
that sharing a sexual fantasy does not necessarily have any implications
for action," yet such a "clear understanding," may be far from a realistic
goal for many couples. How can the husband be sure that, given the
opportunity, his wife would not have an affair with her boss? Or that
she isn't saying she finds her husband an unsatisfactory lover? It is true,
as the Ottos state, that "the sharing of sex fantasies introduces a new
freedom and a whole new dimension to the spectrum of communication," but equally true, as they point out, that "very few people at this
point in Western culture have the openness and courage to share their
sexual fantasies with their spouse or partner." We concur. Before exploring the possibilities of sharing fantasies, we strongly suggest that the
couple make sure they have a far-above-average relationship, that both
have a positive self-image, and that they have an understanding of each
other and their respective "vulnerable spots." They should talk it over,
evaluate the possible advantages and disadvantages. There are risks. It
would be foolish to lose sight of them. But then, there are risks involved
in all high adventure. And sexual loving is the greatest adventure of all.

Fantasies reported by men and women differ in several respects.
Some psychotherapists contend that most women never fantasize about
sex. "They don't know how to dream erotically," writes Dr. Allan
Fromme (*Enjoy Being a Woman*, p. 113). "More than ever, they have
become deeply interested in their sexual fulfillment, hope for it, look
forward to it, and yet only rarely do they actually allow this to inflame

their imagination enough to enjoy the delights of a sexual fantasy." He goes on: "The reason for this is simple and obvious: *women haven't been brought up to enjoy sex.*"

These observations have not been supported by our data. This may be due to differences (e.g., socioeconomic, age, educational, emotional adjustment) between the group populations interviewed, or the extent to which individuals are willing to reveal fantasies. Many women, we found, were initially reluctant to admit to fantasizing about sex. They thought of it as something a man, but not a woman, might do (similar to the fallacy that men, but not women, masturbate). To admit fantasizing, therefore, might, in their view, make them appear less feminine. For this reason, we did not ask the women we interviewed *if* they ever fantasized sexual acts. We told them, "Most women daydream about various sexual actions, and this is, of course, perfectly normal. We wonder if you would tell us some of your sexual fantasies." The result, we have found, is that women report fantasies as frequently as men.

There are observed differences in the content of the fantasies. Female fantasies tend to be more elaborated and enriched with detail not specifically sexual in nature. They frequently fantasize a romantic love relationship with the partner in the fantasy. A twenty-seven-year-old woman related the following:

> *I had gone to my dentist. He's young, probably about thirty-five. And thin, but athletic-looking. He must be an outdoors type; he has this great tan. I don't think he is married. He doesn't wear a wedding ring. I've been trying to figure some way to ask his nurse. I'm sure he doesn't have anything going with her. She's just sort of fat and dumpy. Anyway, I was lying in bed late on Sunday morning and I started thinking about him. I imagined I had gone for my regular check-up, and his nurse was on her lunch hour. He wasn't in any hurry. He told me I had a beautiful smile, and I could tell from the way he looked down into my eyes he was interested in me. When he finished checking my teeth, he removed that long drape from me but he didn't put the chair upright. He just stood there talking about nothing much at all, moving those dark eyes of his up and down me. I was wearing a sort of sheer white blouse, and I was braless. I have rather prominent nipples, which is why I usually don't go braless—unless, of course, I'm deliberately trying to get a rise out of a man [laughs]. I knew even*

*without glancing at the fit of his slacks that he was aroused, really
turned on. And I also knew he was going to ask me to spend the
day with him. We drove in his sport car to a yacht club. He had
this long, sleek-looking white boat. It was a powerboat, not one with
sails, and it had this low, purring motor that sent off almost sexual
vibrations. I didn't have a swimsuit along, so I made a bikini out
of a couple of scarves, which was a lot sexier. I sat on the railing,
next to him, while he steered the boat, and I watched the muscles
in his arms move as he turned the wheel. It was a warm day and
the spray felt good. Soon I was as wet as if I had been swimming,
and it made my scarf bikini as revealing as tissue paper. He
couldn't take his eyes off me. About sunset, he headed the boat into
an inlet. There were woods on the shore and we were all alone. I
showered while he started dinner. When I got out, I wrapped in a
towel like a sarong. We sat down to a dinner of thick, rare steaks,
sliced tomatoes, and red wine. He served. The last slivers of purple
and orange of the sunset were fading when we went up on deck
again. We stretched out on the wide deck and he opened a bottle
of champagne. From then on, we didn't talk much. We just
watched the stars come out and the moon rise through the trees. I
was lying on my back, staring straight up, but I could feel his eyes
on me. He brushed his fingers against my shoulder and down my
arm. So very slowly, and with a feather-light touch. Then he
stopped before going on. He brushed my hair back with his fingertips, and he whispered my name over and over. Then he helped me
to my feet, slipped the towel from me, and took me in his arms.
We kissed for a long time while he moved his fingers over me. But
still there was nothing rushed. He seemed content to hold me close,
kiss me, and share something unspoken. When we finally made
love, I felt every part of me crying out to accept his maleness. He
was gentle, but strong; sensitive, but very much in command. We
did it on deck, and I could watch the moon above the silhouette of
his face. As I fantasized him dropping the towel from me, I started
to masturbate, but very slowly, lazily. When I finally climaxed, it
was fantastic, just about as overwhelming as I've ever experienced.
Since then, I've fantasized the same scene several times. Sometimes we're in a mountain cabin or a penthouse, on a balcony,
looking down on the lights of the city. But the rest is basically the
same.*

If her fantasy sounds a bit like something one might read in a women's magazine, it is because women's magazines either reflect the fantasies of women or inspire them. Probably both. These are seldom the type of fantasies reported by men. The following, from a thirty-seven-year-old married father of two is typical:

> *There's this girl who works in my office. She's one of the clerk-typists. Her face isn't much, but she's got this great-looking ass, a pretty fair set of boobs, and she walks around wearing these short miniskirts that fit over her buns tighter than hell. I guess every guy in the office spends time watching her move her fanny. Well, this one day I was getting something from one of the bottom file drawers. The files are behind and over to one side from where her desk is. I was looking her way when she swiveled around to answer the phone on the desk behind her. She had that short skirt hiked up, and her legs were spread like you wouldn't believe. I saw just about everything she had and then some. Oh, she was wearing panties—red ones—but they were pulled up, you know, tight into her snatch. I could see the hair. She's a blond, but she isn't a "true" blond, if you know what I mean. She caught me staring at her. I glanced up and she was looking straight at me. But you know something? She didn't even make a move to pull her legs together. I got the impression she even kind of smiled. Anyway, I've had a lot of fantasies about her since then. Not really fantasies, more just thoughts of how I can get into her pants. She sure acts like she's hot to go. She sometimes works late. Maybe one of these nights. No, I've never masturbated thinking about her. I'm usually looking at pictures in one of the men's magazines when I jack off. The last time was, I think, about a week ago. There was this picture of a redhead lying back on a couch, nude of course, with her legs spread and her hand up between her thighs. It looked like she was doing it to herself. I didn't have any thoughts in particular. The picture just made me hornier than hell.*

One might argue whether these should be classed as fantasies. They were more properly visual, psychogenic stimuli. In any case, they are not the elaborated, highly imaginative fiction of the usual female fantasies. These distinctions between the sexes are by no means sharp. Some of the men related very enriched fantasies. Some of the women reported only the most basic sexual fantasies. The most frequently reported fantasy by the women was virtually impoverished: *"rape" by a nameless, faceless, man.*

Next to infidelity, the thing most worried about in fantasies is "normality." The fantasies of emotionally healthy individuals of both sexes include virtually every conceivable—and socially unacceptable—sexual act. The woman, however, who fantasizes a sexual act with a dog may, however, feel she is "perverted." The man who daydreams of sexual relations with his sister may be convinced he is "sick." Yet fantasies are no more indications of abnormal behavior than dreams. They may say something about us, but they do not necessarily "label" us. Among the fantasies of perfectly well-adjusted, happily married women, we have recorded the following:

> *Two men having sex with her simultaneously, one vaginally, one anally, their penises moving against one another as they move in and out, and copiously ejaculating in mutual orgasm with her.*
>
> *Being orally stimulated to orgasm by a pet dog trained to perform in this way. Or being mounted while in a rear-entry position by a large dog (or by a Shetland pony).*
>
> *Initiating a young (i.e., adolescent) boy into a variety of sexual acts. This has sometimes taken the form of conducting a "school" for teen-age boys in which she "instructs" them how to perform a variety of sexual acts with her (the "Sex Goddess" fantasy?).*
>
> *Being "gang raped" by a group of criminals or quasi-criminals (e.g., a motorcycle gang).*
>
> *Seducing and engaging in sex with one's pastor, or other "sacrilegious" sexual acts (e.g., sex within a monastery or nunnery).*
>
> *Having sex with a woman or women. This has included oral sex with a woman, mutual masturbation, tactual and oral stimulation of the breasts and nipples, and mutual use of vibrators and dildos.*
>
> *Exhibitionistic acts, including stripping for men (or women), being observed in coitus, and sexually arousing a man by masturbating while he watches.*
>
> *Being tied to a chair or bed and being sexually "tortured" (stimulated) by a man or men (or woman).*
>
> *Spanking or other sadistic acts performed on a man as a preliminary to or part of the act of sex. Or having such acts inflicted on oneself.*
>
> *Engaging in sex as a prostitute (This is another common fantasy). Some women may fantasize themselves as streetwalkers;*

others fantasize themselves as expensive call girls; and a few, familiar with the early work of Masters and Johnson, daydream of the role of sex surrogate helping to "treat" men suffering from sex problems.

Engaging in sexual acts with a close relative, including relations with one's father, brother, sister, son, or daughter.

Engaging in sex in unusual places—e.g., in church, parents' bedroom, doctor's examining table, public conveyance.

Fantasies of men have included:

Sex with one or more sexually insatiable women ("nymphomaniacs"). Similar is the fantasy of being taken captive and held in sexual service to an erotic princess and her court.

Sexually satisfying a previously unresponsive woman (e.g., frigid, lesbian).

Defloration of a virgin.

Sex involving sadomasochistic or master-slave acts (i.e., whipping, bondage, humiliation—either as perpetrator or victim).

Participation in mate swapping or group sex.

Observing spouse in sexual acts with another man.

Sacrilegious sex (e.g., sex with a nun, sex in a holy place).

Being seduced by an aggressive woman (usually this involves accepting her desire to perform fellatio).

Observing a woman in masturbation, sex with another woman, an animal, etc.

Engaging in sex with a woman of another racial or ethnic group.

Only two fantasies commonly found among the members of one sex were rarely found among members of the other sex. In our sample population, the rape fantasy and the homosexual fantasy were reported by more than 60 per cent of the women but less than 1 per cent of the men. We suspect, however, that even these apparent differences should be viewed with some suspicion. It may be that men are less willing to admit to a fantasy (rape) in which they are the wrongdoer rather than the victim. (Note that men frequently fantasize being captured and "raped" by Amazonian women.) Since homosexual acts are far less acceptable in men than in women, and since male-male sex is extremely threatening for most men even to think about, it would not be surprising if many men are reluctant to report such fantasies if they have them.

Fantasies are part of the creative life of normal men and women. And the word "normal" should be emphasized. They are *fantasies*. They are *not* first steps toward a life of depravity or mental illness. It is our impression, in fact, that the ability to fantasize is correlated with both intelligence and creativity, recognizing and accepting the fact that fantasies indicative of neuroses and phychoses are not represented in our population sample. Even though some fantasies enjoyed by most of us are condemned by a rigid, puritanical society as "perverted," they still intrude themselves on our consciousness. They may be arousing, but they do not compel us to action, to "acting out." Normal, healthy, creative men and women immerse themselves in the exhilaration of sexual fantasies. They accept them, and they take pleasure in them. While they may choose to live out some of their fantasies, they would never consider acting out others. The fantasies are pleasurable, and that is enough in itself. And since they are arousing, they may lead to lovemaking with one's spouse, and perhaps to its enhancement. This, alone, should be more than sufficient justification for fantasizing—if one needs justification.

For those who have little experience in fantasizing, it may not come easy at first. It is, however, a part of one's total sexuality that is worth developing. The following suggestions have been found helpful:

1. Set aside time each day, even if only ten minutes, for fantasizing. It should be at a time and place with a minimum of distractions, a time when you can be alone. If your daily life is filled with pressures and demands, you may at first find it difficult to clear your mind enough to allow the fantasies in. With practice, it will come easier.

2. Begin by fantasizing times and places. Without fantasizing sexual partners other than your spouse (which at first may be threatening or guilt-producing), try imagining a variety of unusual places you might have sex (e.g., a beach in Tahiti, in the vestibule of a commuter train, beneath a table in a plush restaurant, on horseback, in a canoe, in a swimming pool).

3. Fantasize sex with a variety of partners, all imaginary, or individuals with whom you are not personally acquainted. These could be faceless men or women, or simply "types" (e.g., "a tall, swarthy Latin," "a delicate Oriental girl," "a rough, muscular longshoreman") or they might be movie or television personalities or public figures. The important thing to keep in mind is that these are *sexual* fantasies; they are not fantasies of an emotional/intellectual/social relationship. As soon as the fantasy is "expanded" into a more complex relationship (e.g., "I

wonder what it would be like to be married to him?"), the probability
of guilt feelings is increased, and just as reality can seldom be as rich
and stimulating as fantasy, injection of reality factors by expansion of
the sexual fantasy into a larger relationship fantasy can diminish the
erotic quality of the initial fantasy.

4. Try expanding your repertoire of fantasies. Nothing is more individual than fantasies. They are almost as unique as fingerprints, and
they run the gamut of everything possible and impossible in sex. Some
men and women with no sex hangups and who are perfectly healthy
and well-adjusted either do not fantasize or fantasize very bland, pedes-
trian fantasies. Others, equally well-adjusted and happy, have elaborate
fantasies of highly unconventional sexual acts (e.g., sadomasochism, sex
with animals, homosexual acts). What turns someone else on may do
nothing for you; it may even be a decided turn-off; but you'll never
know unless you explore it. Try out some of the more far-out fantasies.
Don't slam the door on them, rejecting them out of hand because of
fear, guilt, or inhibitions. If you hang onto the knowledge that a fantasy is only a fantasy, you may discover some highly rewarding areas for
daydreams.

5. When possible, physically stimulate yourself as you fantasize.
Whether to orgasm or not, masturbatory stimulation may not only be
motivated by your fantasies, it can serve to increase the vividness and
pleasure found in the fantasies. On the other hand, there is no reason
to limit fantasizing to those "ideal" times when you have an hour or
two of privacy without distractions in a place where you can undress,
enjoy favorite sexual aids, etc. Since your fantasies are yours alone, who
needs to know what thoughts are going through your mind?

6. If you are not in the habit of fantasizing, you may find it helpful
to establish regular "practice" times until fantasizing is established. As
psychogenic stimuli, well-developed fantasies have few rivals. They are
limited only by the limits of your imagination. They can contribute immeasurably to building and sustaining a strong sexuality.

Two works which seriously attempt an examination of sexual fantasies are well worth reading. *Erotic Fantasies* by Drs. Phyllis and
Eberhard Kronhausen is a study of the subject through extensive sur-
veys and interpretations of writings they term "erotic realism" (an attempt to distinguish it from "pornography") and folklore. The fantasies
they gathered fell into several major categories: homosexuality, incest,
sadomasochism, animal contacts, fetishism, pedophilia, bondage, and
trans-sexualism (sex-role reversal). The writer of fiction can only suc-

ceed in holding the reader's interest if the reader is able to identify, if only in fantasy, with the characters in the story. The popular erotic novel must, therefore, tap the fantasy world of the reader. We question, however, whether there is sufficient evidence to conclude that the fantasies of the erotic novelists are anything more than the sexual daydreams of the authors which find acceptance and identification among the aficionados of erotic literature. This is a question, not a conclusion. We suspect, in fact, that the more common fantasies in erotic writing *do* tap the fantasies of most men and women, albeit they are elaborated. Nevertheless, it would be of value if we could know what the average man or woman next door fantasizes. Through interviews and letters solicited in response to advertisements placed in underground newspapers, freelance writer Nancy Friday collected a sample of four hundred sexual fantasies of women. She has published the accounts in a work entitled *My Secret Garden*. This is neither a collection of titillating vignettes written to turn on primarily male readers nor an anthology of "riding across the desert sands astride a proud stallion, held in the arms of a handsome Arab prince" romance tales. They are *sexual* fantasies, covering a broad spectrum of thoughts and desires which make up the secret life of many women. It is written with considerable insight. Miss Friday demonstrates the objectivity of a researcher as well as remarkable understanding and compassion. The book is highly recommended to women seeking to discover more about themselves and their sisters, and by men who want to understand a very important dimension in the life of a woman.

The only difference between a "pornographic" story and a personal sexual fantasy is the author. If the author shares his fantasies in print or in a movie scenario, he may go to jail for publishing obscenity. If he keeps them to himself, he can become the judge who sends others to jail for "peddling smut."

The history of erotic writing is probably as long as the history of the written word. And the first pictorial representation of sexual acts probably appeared on the walls of a cave. Yet we still cannot agree on what it is, what effect it has, what harm (or good) it may do, or who has an interest in it. One noted jurist achieved a high in legalistic obfuscation when he said, "I can't tell you what pornography is, but I know it when I see it" (or words to that effect). He may not be able to define it, but we know how he recognizes it, don't we? It's very simple: whether it turns him on.

Each time a legislator or a judge or a politician seeking re-election attacks the claimed spread of such writings, movies, and such, the claim is made that the materials in question appeal to the readers' "prurient interest." In other words, produced or written with the view of turning on the reader or viewer. What else? If it doesn't, it won't sell. And if it does, it is obscene. Definitely so if it is lacking in "redeeming social importance." Sexual arousal, in *their* thinking, can have no "redeeming social importance" or value. They might agree that perpetuation of the species has some social value. But pleasure? Never.

Remarkable changes in public attitude, however, have occurred over the past two decades, and legislative and judicial thinking has followed (admittedly with dragging feet) these changes. When one of the authors was living in Paris in 1950, a topic of conversation among American students and artists was how to smuggle the works of Henry Miller into the United States. Today these writings can be found in college bookstores and small-town libraries, and few eyebrows are raised. We have topless, bottomless, totally nude dancers appearing in our big-city nightclubs. And we have exposure of the genitalia of both sexes featured in magazines on sale at the neighborhood drugstore. Without taking count, we feel we are safe in saying that more books on sex have been published in the past ten years than in the preceding several decades. Certainly the writings have been more explicit. And, in the main, more factual. Hardly a year has gone by over the past ten years without at least one book devoted to sex hitting the best-seller lists. Some have been serious contributions to the psychology or physiology of sex. Others were "how to" books. And still others were "exposé" books. To all these can be added the fiction best-sellers, most of which would have been banned for their sexual explicitness not many years ago. How do we account for this phenomenon? Who are buying these books, and why are they buying them?

The answer is, of course, most of us—because we like sex, it is important to us, and we are forever curious about it, about ourselves. And the most significant reason, perhaps, of all: we hope in some cases to find it arousing.

It is a less than favorable comment on the attitudes of our society that anyone should find it necessary to develop a rationale to justify the reading of erotic material or the viewing of an erotic film. Yet repeatedly we have found adults of both sexes, married and unmarried, who must be persuaded there is nothing "wrong" in the reading or viewing, and that there may actually be some "right" reasons for doing so—other than pleasure. Are there, in fact, other valid reasons? Not excuses or rationalizations, but legitimate reasons? Definitely!

The first is an irony. One of the principal arguments against the printing or reading of "hard core" erotic literature is that it is not representative of reality; it is detached, amputated from the totality of a human relationship. And the argument is forceful. It *is* detached. Whether we call it "hard-core pornography" or, as the Drs. Kronhausen do, "erotic realism," it is fiction with a sexual theme which is detached from any context of a total human interaction. There is little romance, sparse communication, and only a semblance of a relationship. One human being (male or female) sexually interacts with another human being (male or female). What happens the following day or the day after is irrelevant. Only physical sex is important. But it is this, we contend, which gives erotic writing and films their value as a contribution to the growth of the individual's sexuality. We are not arguing for a depersonalization of sex or against the importance of human physical *love*. Nothing could be of greater importance in sex than the overall relationship of love. But before sex and love can be blended into the most sublime of human experiences, sex—the purely physical, sensual encounter—must be freely accepted and relished. Hard-core erotic writing, with its impoverishment of characterization, plot, and relationships, allows us, in our imagery, to confront our physical passions as they *are*, not as we may have been taught they should be. It is raw, amoral, and generally, far, far from reality. It is this lack of reality which keeps us from identifying with the characters in the story, and carrying what may be an anti-erotic personal reality into the induced fantasy of the fiction. Then, through our responses to the writing, we can learn a lot about our individual sexuality.

Like sharing fantasies, sharing erotic writings, pictures, and motion pictures with one's partner can be a great vehicle of communication. A straightforward "Tell me what turns you on" may not come easy. It may be even harder to answer, both because he or she may not know, and because we may be reluctant to admit some of the answers we might give to that question, and so may our partner. Reading and sharing our reactions to fiction, however, are usually much easier. A couple can go through the pages of a picture book of sexual acts, pointing to those they find appealing, without the awkwardness that shows up when they try to use words to describe the same thing. And swapping observations following an X-rated movie is a delightful preliminary to an evening of closeness and excitement.

Good erotic writing *should* be a turn-on. It is intended to be. And that is the best reason for reading it. Sharing such erotic material, however, is not without its risks. And for the same reasons, sharing fantasies may be risky: jealousy. This is a particularly vexing problem to many women. A majority of women reported at one time or another feeling jealous and even resentful when their husbands evidenced an interest in erotic magazines, especially the photographs accompanying the erotic writings. Even the centerfold models in men's magazines were objects of jealousy as well as envy. Wives discovered their husbands admiring the models, and they reacted: "He would rather be in bed with her than me." Reactions of husbands since women's magazines began publishing photographs of male nudes (especially uncovered frontal nudes) is no less one of jealousy. But there is frequently a difference. A number of husbands simply denied the possibility of erotic response by their wives. "My wife wouldn't be turned on by those muscle-bound faggots." "Why would she get aroused by a photo of some guy when I give her everything she could ask for?" That male ego can show a lot of vulnerability. Often the same man who will react with something close to rage if his wife shows interest in photos of nude males, will be surprised when his wife is annoyed by his interest in a photo of the Playmate of the Month.

Writers in the area of sex, following the unsubstantiated assumptions of many previous writers, have traditionally held that women are not aroused by erotic writing and pictures. Only men are. And why not? Aren't men more sexual? And aren't women more interested (and aroused) in a context of romance and relationship? Hard-core eroticism is not a turn-on to women. But have these assumptions been substantiated? Not at all. When male nudes were first featured in centerfolds of women's magazines, chastely concealing their genitals, many female readers wrote in to protest the concealment. The audiences of X-rated films are no longer "dirty old men." Now, couples are standing in line to view *Deep Throat, Behind the Green Door,* and other nothing-left-to-the-imagination films. Women no longer feel abnormal or masculine by admitting an interest in erotic realism. But they may encounter very threatened husbands when they verbalize their interest. In this, as in so many areas of sex, our advice to husband and wife is: Tread lightly; take each step toward mutual growth with understanding of the sensibilities, inhibitions, and, perhaps, fears of your lover. And make no mistake, not one of us is totally secure. The deepest love is an adventure taken by two—hand in hand.

Most hard-core material—writings, films, photographs, etc.—is vulgar, in bad taste, almost completely devoid of beauty. If it "panders" to any particular group, it is those with the most limited literary and esthetic taste. Ten per cent of it is disgusting; eighty per cent is boring. The fact that hard-core books and magazines are big sellers, and hardcore movies gross millions, seems less an indication of a mushrooming interest in genitalism than a measure of cultural drought. The paperback porno novel is probably no more trashy than the paperback murder novel. And erotic films are certainly no more tasteless than the television commercials for feminine hygiene sprays and stomach antacids. Yet few of us would label all fiction in which crime is a major theme "trash." Who would consider Hamlet in poor taste? Nor do we damn all movies and television. If the porno novel is trash, it is trash, but not because of the subject matter or theme. The same novelist could be writing a religious novel and still produce trash. The same goes for films. Most hard-core films are produced for a budget less than that of the average one-minute television commercial. And with actors whose talent would not qualify them for a high-school play. This is understandable. In the early days of television, we were willing to watch almost anything, fascinated as we were by the flickering figures on the small screen. As the audience grew, television became big business. More money was spent on production, sets, scripts. Actors of stature were attracted to the medium. A fierce competition for ratings ensued. Many predict that something similar will occur with erotic films. They see it happening already, and they make a good point. Today leading actors and actresses are doing nude scenes, and even explicit sexual acts, on the screen. Not too many years ago, Marilyn Monroe's famous calendar nude was "scandalous." In the future, therefore, we may see art replace the "skin flick" in erotic realism.

In the meantime, however, it may take some shopping around to find much of merit. There are few writers of erotic realism of the caliber of D. H. Lawrence. Nevertheless, the shopping may benefit both of you even if the harvest is slim. You may learn something about your own responses as well as those of your mate. And it is on the never-ending search for this knowledge that sexual love is built.

We feel one other problem deserves mention. Theaters which feature exclusively "adult" (porno) films are generally as inviting as the drunk tank of a jail. Forty-second Street near Times Square in New York City and the Tenderloin district of San Francisco are prime examples of what can happen when the "sex shops" take over. Forty-second

Street, once a street which gave title to a delightful motion picture about life on the stage, has become a freak show of muggers, hookers, pimps, and junkies, unattractive during the day, frightening at night. San Francisco's Tenderloin is a jungle of prostitutes and psychopaths whose viciousness and depravity defy description. The North Beach area of San Francisco, long a birthplace of greats in show business, is now a tourist trap for men on the loose crowding into the nightclubs featuring "live sex acts on stage" and "nude coeds," and, of course, hole-in-the-wall 100-seat skin-flick movie houses. In economics, one may question whether good money drives out bad or bad money drives out good. Perhaps *good* erotic films will, in time, drive out the trash. So far, regrettably, they have not driven out the sewer environment of the skin-flick movie houses. During the 1920s, the establishments in which one could drink in public were frequently "upholstered cesspools." The laws prohibiting the consumption of alcoholic beverages in the United States made outlaws of drinkers. And outlaws could expect nothing better than these sleazy holes-in-the-wall. Only when drinking again became "respectable" (and legal) could the environment improve. Perhaps the same applies to erotic films. Until then, we face the choice of patronizing the "sewer" (which is as "anti-erotic" as a cold shower) or seeking out the "soft core" films shown in a theater where esthetics and personal safety are not dominant.

In the bibliography are listed several books on sexual fantasies. Some are better than others, but all of them are worth the reader's attention. Expanding one's sexual imagination is more than worth the time and effort. The reading and sharing can do more than that. It can provide a vehicle to help in the re-evaluation of our sexual attitudes. What might at first seem unnatural, strange, or even disgusting, may, through exposure, come to be regarded as a healthy expression of sexual love. It is a freedom husband and wife can find together. And of all the freedoms in marriage, one most highly to be treasured.

Chapter 5

Sensuality and Sexual Love

you are a hundred times beautiful
I stroke you with my loving hands
pink-nailed long fingers
I caress you
I adore you
my finger-tips . . . my palms . . .

Lenore Kandel
The Love Book

I feel trapped by the boundaries of my skin,
the limits of my senses,
trapped and locked in
by the separateness of my world.

I want to love him completely;
I want to share his skin,
feel with his senses,
lose my identity in his.

Joseph and Lois Bird
Love Is All

*W*e are born with our senses ready to respond. Touch, smell, hearing, taste, and sight form our link with the external world. Internally, our bodies send messages to the brain telling of contracting muscles, visceral tensions, drive states, and our reactions to the secretions of our glands.

What happens from that initial introduction to life until we face the adult world spells out the story of our sensuality. Like so much of what we are as functioning human beings, we do not fully understand our sensuality. Perhaps if we did, we could do more to protect the gift we have been given in our senses. We might better be able to develop and enrich it.

We do not even have a satisfactory definition of *sensuality*. It is more than the enjoyment of one's senses. It is awareness, perception, sexuality, sexual pleasure, and being "one with the world"—being alive.

Strictly defined, sensuality is not itself pleasurable. It is a vehicle which we may employ to increase our pleasure in being alive. Take it away, suppress or deny it, and little that makes life worth living remains. All that is sensual is not sexual, and all that is sexual is not sensual. But all that is pleasurable in sex *is* sensual. Each of our senses contributes to our sexual pleasure, and in striving to enhance our enjoyment in sex, we work to increase the pleasurable input from each of our senses.

The sensual experiences which are the prelude to adult sexuality are introduced (and discovered) in infancy. They are the beginnings of intimacy. We are touched, held, nursed, and caressed by our mothers and fathers. This touching may be second only to nourishment in its importance to our well-being, both physical and emotional. Some years ago, psychologists discovered that infants raised in institutions in which touching and holding of babies was minimal (due to a staff shortage) tended to be physically weaker and more prone to illness. Dr. Harry Harlow, in a series of studies conducted at the University of Wisconsin, discovered a compelling need in young monkeys for a touching physical closeness to the mother. When the natural mother was removed, the infant monkeys would cling to cloth surrogate "mothers" in much the same way they had clung to their real mothers.

Desmond Morris, in *Intimate Behaviour* (pp. 11–12), has said, "In early childhood, before we could speak or write, body contact was a dominant theme. Direct physical interaction with the mother was all-important and it left its mark. Still earlier, inside the womb, before we could see or smell, let alone speak or write, it was an even more powerful element in our lives. If we are to understand the many curious and often strongly inhibited ways in which we make physical contact with one another as adults, then we must start by returning to our earliest beginnings, when we were no more than embryos inside our mothers' bodies."

Far from being an environment of sensory deprivation, our first home, the womb is a highly sensual, intimate environment. Bathed in the warmth of the amniotic fluid, gently rocked by our mother's movements, comforted by the rhythm of the maternal breathing and heartbeat, we wait in a comforting cocoon of sensuality. It is an environment we strive to recapture during the remainder of our lives.

We are pushed, pulled, assaulted into the world. Squeezed through the birth canal, we arrive in a world of glaring lights, loud noises, and a lack of supportive touching. We are, of course, held, diapered, fed, and bathed. But from the moment of our birth, intimacy is a pervasive need never again to be fully met.

To the various definitions of *love* we might add one more: *Love is the desire to touch the loved one, and to be touched in return.* We may feel that the definition is too narrow, and it may be. But is it because we feel we must philosophize love? Or at least desensualize it? We do not, unfortunately, live in a sensual, touching culture. Society imposes so many restrictions on physical contact: The persons we may touch. Where. When. And what areas of the body. Age and sex are restricted. Frequency and duration must be considered. And the sexual implications are essential considerations.

The younger we are, the more touching we receive. When we are infants, even total strangers pat, stroke, and hold us. We are hugged, rocked, and kissed. It is the first step from the total sensuality of the womb. Then quickly it comes to an end. Small boys no more than six or seven have learned to step back from more intimate contact. They extend their arm in a handshake. Fathers feel uncomfortable with their sons. They no longer hug their sons (if they ever did). Now they learn to tousle Junior's hair and give him a playful punch. Mothers, in their efforts to avoid turning their sons into sissies, curtail their maternal embrace. From there it is almost all downhill. Not until we enter into the intimacy of sexual relations will we again fill the need for touching. And probably not even then. We don't turn off a basic need, keep it turned off for years, and expect it to respond the moment we press the "on" button. Inhibitions are not that easily overcome. And touching becomes one of our strongest inhibitions. Just look at the inhibitions of the typical thirteen-year-old boy. He is not to:

1. Embrace other males his own age, older, or younger (except his father or close family member—if older—in situations of high emotion).

2. Embrace females other than his mother, and then only on her initiative and when it is inescapable. (Embracing girls may be something he fantasizes but fears initiating.)

3. Touching of male peers is to be limited to aggressive acts—hitting, wrestling, etc.—out of fear of being suspected of homosexuality.

4. Nonperson pleasurable touching experiences (intimacy substitutes) are to be strictly limited. Soft, highly sensuous fabrics are not for males. A fur muff or a velvet-collared coat may provide intimacy substitutes for girls, never boys. And this applies as well to sensual touching of self. At a time when girls are learning the benefits (pleasuring) of hand and body lotions, boys are being encouraged to take brisk showers, and to exercise to "toughen up the body."

(A majority of husbands said they had no interest in satin sheets, bath oil, sensuous massage, and caressing which was not a prelude to sexual contact.)

The pressure to suppress sensual intimacy is not as great on girls. But it is still formidable. Fathers do not hold and embrace their daughters. Only about a fourth of our sample of women remembered frequent physical affection from their fathers. And the same percentage said they recalled physical intimacy expressed by their mothers only on occasions of sorrow or great joy. Some attempted to explain it in terms of their own choices rather than their mother's. Holding Mother's hand, some felt, was a sign of dependency and immaturity. As the girl gets older, her hair is no longer brushed by Mother. It is no longer "necessary." And by the time she enters school, Mother has stopped washing her back or massaging her neck and shoulders when she is tired and sore.

It is an irony that about the time we are pressured to stamp out the vestiges of the touching intimacy of childhood, we are introduced to adult sexual behavior. Seldom, however, does this satisfy the need we have for touching intimacy. Often, in fact, it works to inhibit its expression still more. The following is a consensus of the observations of individuals of both sexes:

Touching intimacy between adults is generally heavy with sexual messages and implications, and any sexual activity and expression is rigidly proscribed. There are few areas of a woman's body a man can touch without the touch being interpreted as a sexual overture. He may shake hands, but should he hold her hand too long, it may communicate desire. He may place an arm across her shoulder to console or, if they are close friends, to greet, congratulate, or express "platonic" affection. But not an arm around her waist. And not *both* arms around her. That's a no-no. Stroking her hair, cheek, back, or almost any other customarily nonsexual area of her body, may be interpreted as a seductive gesture. In a culture which attempts to prohibit any sexual expression outside of marriage, and equates sexuality (even within marriage) with genitalism, any touching of a female below the neck is fraught with danger.

Most husbands and wives interviewed saw sexual touching as directed toward a genital goal. There is a virtual maxim that says touching is antisexual, a support of the pleasure-as-evil precept handed down by this society of ours. Popular sex manuals call it *foreplay*. The authors of how-to-do-it manuals instruct how to touch, stroke, and manipulate the "erogenous zones" of the female. These maneuvers are designed to arouse the female. Seldom do they talk about what she might do to (or for) him.

In recent years, sexologists have given almost equal attention to the woman's role in arousing the man. The goal is the same: fulfillment of the sexual act—i.e., orgasm. Under this demand, all sexual touching (that which is labeled "sexual") is then a means toward the end, the orgasmic climax. Each embrace, each kiss, each touch becomes part of the total contract. One of the parties—it may be either the man or the woman (but is "traditionally" the man)—makes an "advance." He/she touches his/her partner. This embrace is taken as an offer to contract for sexual intercourse. If the partner responds, it is interpreted as acceptance of the offer. The contract made, the initiator now progresses to the next step in arousing and seducing. The initiator is committed by this unverbalized contract to continue the "foreplay" and to carry it "all the way." His partner, by accepting an arousing overture, makes a commitment. She tacitly agrees to permit and encourage repetition of these actions. It progresses step by step, each set of actions calling for the next more arousing actions. At a certain stage in the progressive actions (commonly understood by both), they are committed to "go all the way." If either of them backs off at that point, it is considered a serious breach.

Between husband and wife the ritual may be well formalized. The initial movement or two may formalize the contract, freezing it in a series of actions and reactions. The wife may be standing at the kitchen sink preparing dinner. Her husband tiptoes up behind her. He kisses her on the nape of the neck. His hands encircle her waist, squeeze lightly, and caress down over her hips and thighs. She stiffens her back. Her hands grasp his to stop his "advances." "Please, not now; the children." The "not now" means, of course, sexual intercourse, since in a contractual view of sex, all "advances" are aimed at that singular goal (or at least at some orgasmic conclusion).

But what if sexual union is not the husband's intent? Is there any way he can satisfy his desire to touch without it being interpreted as the initiation of sex? Perhaps not if over a long period of time such actions have always signaled an intent to go "all the way."

Almost half the wives interviewed said they would interpret the described actions in the kitchen as "meaning he wants sex." Almost all said, however, they would enjoy more affectionate touching. Both husband and wife lose the joy of touching when the touching becomes such a contractual interaction. Since we are all limited in the frequency of coital engagements (as well as by our desire for same), the contractual interaction severely limits opportunities to touch in affection. If intimate touching is limited to preliminaries of orgasmic sex, touching can be enjoyed a very few hours each week (if that much!). The satisfaction of one drive (touching) is thus limited by the strength of the other drive (sex).

Non-demand sex eliminates this problem. It is sexual in the sense that many of our actions, verbal and tactual, are sexual. But non-demand sex does not *necessarily* involve the genitals. Nor is it goal-specific oriented. It is *not* aimed at orgasm. It *may* culminate in orgasm, but there is no "contract" compelling it.

In non-demand sex, touching may go on for hours without culminating in orgasm. That is the beauty of it. And the love. Not that orgasm is not a wonderful experience. It is only that in non-demand sex, orgasm is not a "demand." Relieved of responsibility to "perform," the spouses are free to caress one another virtually anytime they are together. And, reasonable limitations of social propriety considered, without reservations as to body areas. They are each free to enjoy sharing sexual fantasies and desires without fear of rejection. Either one may or may not become aroused and desire to go further without any need to prove anything, without any demand felt to "follow through." Since touching and being touched is a drive conditioned prior to birth and reinforced throughout early childhood, non-demand sex fulfills a drive-need we each have to relate, on the most intimate level, to a human being we value highly.

The key word is *value*. The word *love* is ambiguous; the word *like* doesn't say enough. As these words are commonly employed, *valuing* says much more. In the marriage ceremony we promise to *cherish*. We cherish, protect, and guard the things we value. We don't risk losing those treasures. And we don't leave them in a state of benign neglect. If we own a great work of art, we take extraordinary care to insure it against harm. We take pride in showing it to others, and in letting them know how much we treasure it. At the same time, we are aware of how much others covet our treasures. Hence, we don't take chances. We don't gamble on losing what we value. This is shown in our actions. A lover values his loved one, and one way this valuing is shown is in talking and touching. The lover has a strong desire to *know* his loved one. It is this desire which motivates him to strive for communication, to talk into the small hours of the morning exchanging views, opinions, experiences, and feelings. And if lovers are free of crippling fears and inhibitions, they will express their desire for physical intimacy. They will hold and caress each other. They will seemingly never get enough skin contact.

We find it interesting that objects which are valued highest—great works of art, precious jewels—are treated with *sensual* care. Diamonds are boxed in velvet; antiques are placed on deep carpeting; works of art are cushioned in silk. The diamond does not need the protection of velvet. It cannot be scratched by cotton or cardboard. The softness of velvet says, "We cherish this jewel." Valuing a treasure, we feel almost compelled to touch it. We admire a piece of sculpture in a museum, and we feel a strong urge to run our fingers over its surface, to feel the coarseness of chiseled granite, the cool smoothness of marble, the warm softness of polished wood. And we have clasped our hands behind our backs, inhibited by the *Do Not Touch* rule.

Lovers feel the need to touch each other, as alcoholics feel the need to drink. Touching is not something they do as an obligation. Or as a means toward an end. They do it because they can hardly *not* do it. It is a loving compulsion.

How is it, then, that we find loving human beings who seemingly show little interest in touching or being touched? If valuing and desiring compel touching, must we conclude that the spouse who is "not the touching type" shows a lack of valuing? We do not think so. We are all born "touching types." A combination of upbringing in a nontouching family, a fear of rejection, and sexual inhibitions can turn any one of us into a "nontouching type." It doesn't necessarily indicate a lack of loving, valuing, caring. Nor a lack of desire to touch and be touched. Fortunately, the walls can come down.

Although we knew this to be a problem for many couples (and the complaint of many wives), we were not prepared to find that a large majority of wives said they were not satisfied with the amount of touching they received from their husbands. The sensory deprivation apparently experienced by wives is, we must conclude, a major factor in their frustration. The first step toward developing tactual loving—touching—involves reducing the physical distance between partners. Ethologists, natural scientists who study the behavior of animals in their natural environment, have described what they call "flight distance." When the animal is approached by a potential enemy, it is as if there is a territorial line surrounding him. Should the enemy invade the boundary, the animal fights or flees. If escape is possible, most animals will flee. If no escape is offered, they will defend themselves. They will attack. Invasion of that unseen territory which surrounds the animal is an act of aggression. We also have our flight distance. It varies with the circumstances and the relationship we may have with the "invader." If we board a thirty-passenger bus and find only four passengers, all strangers, we will probably not sit down beside one. We respect his flight distance, and we expect him to honor ours. Should the bus have standing room only, however, all passengers will, by unverbalized consent, reduce their flight distance. A feeling of comradeship may even develop out of this "packed like sardines" experience.

In a one-to-one interaction, flight distance will be determined by the nature of the overall relationship, the nature of the momentary interaction, the security of the participants, the physical environment, and the emotional loadings (positive and/or negative) of the material under discussion. The nervous young salesman, hoping to close his first big deal, meets with the client, president of a large company, in the client's spacious office. He attempts to establish the maximum flight distance (within, of course, the bounds of convention and the dimensions of the office). The two men confront each other at a distance far greater than "arm's length." Yet that evening, the same young salesman, sitting on the sofa with his fiancée, attempts to reduce the flight distance from her to literally zero. When she finds herself annoyed at a remark of his, she increases their flight distance by moving to the far end of the sofa. If he follows, she may further increase it by moving to a chair several feet away. Or she may leave the room.

Ironically, many husbands and wives increase, rather than decrease, their respective flight distances after they marry. During the engagement period, they may be virtually inseparable. Physically, they can't get close enough. As they sit side-by-side in a car, or before a bonfire on a beach, or standing in line at a theater, they touch in every way the law allows. Yet after they are married a year or two, they view television from chairs eight feet apart. They sit against the doors in the front seat of the car. They sleep in a king-sized bed, an arm's-length between them. Or they sleep in twin beds. With the end of the honeymoon, the distance may widen. The touching may decrease. The natural, biological need they have for tactual stimulation is frustrated.

What accounts for this increase in distance after marriage? We might suppose that the insecurity and fear both feel before marriage is greater, hence more conducive to flight distance, than any they might experience after they are living together. Our evidence, however, suggests a different conclusion. During the premarital dating, the partners are careful not to threaten or attack. Neither wants to risk destroying the relationship. Once married, however, things do not stay the same. The marriage contract gives them the security to lay bare their vulnerable spots. And it gives them the security to attack each other's soft spots without fear that doing so will destroy the relationship. Also, the relationship gives rise to demands and obligations; it can easily become judgmental. And finally, a lack of effort may result in boredom. Followed by hostility. Followed by withdrawal.

One or both may be unaware of their need for touching or the deprivation they experience in its absence. Even if acutely, painfully, aware of it, they may not know what to do about it.

Where there is a genuine caring and valuing of each other, most couples have found they can reduce their flight distance through a program of desensitization. Desensitization is the process of gradual and repeated exposure to a fear-producing stimulus in order to reduce, and eventually extinguish, the fear response. Many couples found the following effective:

1. *Agree to work together to develop or recapture physical intimacy.* These needs and desires can seldom be communicated in any subtle or nonverbal way. They should be expressed in "I want . . ." statements.

2. *Agree to explore the freedom of husband/wife nudity.* Clothes provide what one husband called "my armor." Our clothing can serve as a facade, a shield, a psychological defense. It tells much about us—what we want others to believe, and what we don't want them to know. The military speaks of respect for the uniform rather than respect for the wearer of the uniform. If all the troops disrobed, general down to private, what would happen? Would respect be lost? It might. Without the ribbons, gold braid, and his stars of rank, would the general still be able to play the role of commander? Unless he had sufficient innate leadership ability to rise above the loss of status symbols, he might find the challenge too great. Our "uniforms" go a long way toward establishing our status and roles. They separate rich from poor, young from old, liberal from conservative, doctor from farmhand, bishop from bartender, housewife from model. And they protect us from exposure, emotionally more than physically.

When we reveal our innermost thoughts and feelings, we speak of "baring ourselves" or "letting it all hang out." If we reveal these thoughts while in the nude, we have even fewer defenses. In a physical as well as verbal manner, we are saying, "This is me."

Since they are more psychologically vulnerable, most couples find conversing in the nude a difficult undertaking, at least until they get used to it. And especially when the topic is one which is "emotionally loaded." Almost a third of the husbands and wives interviewed said they could not bring themselves to do it, although they were not inhibited in nude sexual activity together. Few felt they could discuss family finances, for example, in the nude. For most couples, nudity was limited to bathing, sleeping (a smaller percentage), and sexual relations. To linger over their breakfast coffee or sit together on the living-room sofa watching the late movie on television *in the nude* had never occurred to them.

There are two main benefits to be derived from social nudity between husband and wife. In discarding our clothes, we discard a wall of defenses, layers which hid us from one another. Husbands and wives, for example, argue from positions behind a wall of defenses. Including their clothing. Stripped of their defenses, it is unlikely they would continue firing shots at each other. It would be hard to find a couple who could argue with hostility in the nude. (This alone might be a point in favor of husband-wife nudity.) What is most important: With lowered defenses an openness is made possible. As husband and wife adjust to nudity in a variety of communication situations, any initial anxiety they might experience is lost. It is one more step toward an open, free acceptance of self and spouse, and, ultimately, toward the "oneness" which marks the living, loving relationship.

Second, nudity is essential to the development of "non-demand" sex. Since mutual nudity is so often associated with sexual relations and its preliminaries, to many couples any disrobing together is a signal for orgasmic sex. Just as with touching which is interpreted as a demand, nudity initiates a sexual "contract." It is as if husband and wife agree to disrobe together only if prepared to go "all the way." The pleasures of touch and sight to be found in mutual nudity are their own reward. And they are obvious. No fabric or texture is so sensually satisfying as the touch of human skin, especially the skin of one's lover. Holding, caressing, moving against one another, skin surface to skin surface, can anyone find reason for lovers to avoid the pleasure whenever they find the opportunity?

Some find reasons. The reason given to us most often had to do with the presence of children. The following statement of a wife was typical: "I certainly don't favor running around the house naked in front of the kids. Even in our bedroom we can never be sure the kids aren't going to pop in." In answer to our obvious question, she said, "I'd feel terrible locking the bedroom door on the children. It's such an obvious rejection." And in reply to another question: "I just feel more comfortable wearing a nightgown. I've always worn a nightgown. It seems right." In other words, inhibitions. In the name of modesty. It is all well-learned. No sooner are we old enough to remove our training pants than we are told not to. What we are taught to call modesty is drummed into our unconscious as shame. Few of us are fortunate enough to reach maturity with a healthy pride in our body. An infant in the nude may be cute, but we are taught to scorn our bodies as we get older. The nude models in men's magazines (and recently the male centerfold models in some women's magazines) may qualify as sexually stimulating (some would say "sex objects"). But the less-than-perfect bodies of the rest of us? Well, they should be kept covered, right? Why? Our faces differ. We don't all have perfect profiles. Some of us have noses which are too large, lips which are too thin, or eyes that are less than perfect. Yet we don't veil our faces. Why do we feel such shame for the rest of our bodies? There can be no rational reason, yet the attitudes are hard to shake. Irony: Many of those who loudly proclaim the body as the "Temple of the Soul" condemn any display of it —even between husband and wife.

In recent years, large-group social nudity, previously confined to nudist camps, has gained widespread acceptance, especially among the young. Nude beaches have increased in number and spread in popularity. Nude encounter groups have been given support by respected psychotherapists. Suburban nude swimming parties and group saunas are no longer the interests of only avant-grade liberals. In some cases, this openness has expanded to include total permissiveness in sexual activities. Most notable was the *Sandstone* experiment in Southern California described by Dr. Alex Comfort (*More Joy*, Crown Publishers, New York, 1974). Whether social nudity becomes generally accepted in the future is difficult to predict. Many feel that the pendulum of permissiveness is due to swing back. If it swings back to the suppression and puritanism of previous years, it would indeed be tragic. Especially if it were to mean a return to the Jansenistic attitudes which did so much to devalue our bodies. The pros and cons of group nudity may be debated, but nudity between husband and wife offers such distinct advantages to the relationship, it is worth whatever effort may be necessary to overcome inhibitions and embarrassment.

3. *Develop a touching relationship.* Marital intimacy depends on touching as it depends on caring. This is not a need of women only, despite the finding that women complained most of the deprivation. Men have as strong a need. Since as boys they are taught to suppress this need—and even though as young men they learn that it is their responsibility to take the romantic initiative—they frequently neglect touching unless sex is desired. It is not that the husband cares less, only that he expresses the caring less in touching.

Among some sensitivity-therapy groups the benefits of massage are stressed. Several books on sensuous massage for couples have been published in recent years, some with beautiful photos. They are welcome contributions to the art of sensuality. Deep massage, a good rubdown to relieve sore muscles, is not the object. Such a massage may be therapeutic, but it is seldom arousing. In the sensual massage, the fingers communicate "I value you" in a unique, deeply meaningful way. Moving the hands and fingertips slowly, lightly, and lovingly over the arms, legs, torso, and genitals of the lover is a powerful bonding experience. The softness and warmth, the aliveness and response, are rewarding, equally, to both the active and passive partners. Can there be a man, woman, or child who would not yield to the pleasure of being stroked? We even use the word "stroking" as a synonym for complimenting or praising. And is there a lover worthy of the name who cannot find pleasure in caressing the body of his or her lover?

The following is a consensus from those of both sexes who have experimented with sensory enhancement and non-demand sex:

At first it was somewhat strained. The sexual "demand" message of nudity, they found, had been strongly reinforced. As they practiced, however—for some couples as much as forty-five minutes each day— the uneasiness left them. The majority said it took only three or four sessions for them to find mutual nudity "very natural." The sessions varied. Sometimes it consisted of nothing more than sitting together in the nude listening to music or talking, only lightly touching. At other times they engaged in stroking, holding each other, bathing or showering together, exchanging massages. The husband discovered a freedom from the demand of performance. He might or might not have an erection. The enjoyment of the experience was not dependent on it. One or both spouses might experience orgasm (or neither might). The goal was not to achieve orgasm. But neither was it to avoid it. The wife discovered a new meaning in physical intimacy. When sex is compartmentalized and physical intimacy is limited only to those times of high sexual urgency, suspicions of self-centeredness may arise. ("He's not interested in me; the only time he gives me any affection is when he wants sex.") She also experienced, both in fact and in feeling, a timelessness in sex. In non-demand sex, lovemaking could go on literally for hours. They learned to express love in the language of their bodies.

4. *Explore ways to expand your total sexual sensuality.* Perception

through a single sensory modality can be likened to a solo. Perception through all senses in concert can be likened to a symphony. The solo can give us the melody line, but it is only when the strings, brass, woodwinds, and percussion are added that the richness of the composition can be heard. A sizable majority of couples interviewed admitted they tended to limit their sexual relations almost entirely to tactual stimuli. Input from the other senses was virtually ignored, and there was seldom any attempt to enhance other sensory stimuli. The stimuli may have been present. The afferent impulses travel to the brain. But our perceptions are selective. We can be attentive to some stimuli while ignoring others. The salesman who is pushing hard to close a contract over a business lunch may be almost unaware of what he is eating, and later may not recall the décor of the restaurant. He is attentive only to the stimuli that pertain to his goal. Sexual stimuli are stimuli which contribute to the response of arousal from whatever sensory modality. The sound of a voice, or a sigh, sensual music, even the roar of the ocean, can be arousing stimuli. The sound of sexual words spoken by one's lover can be highly arousing. And the sounds of sex are, for most couples, some of the most arousing auditory stimuli. Some couples have found that tape recordings of their lovemaking provide a highly erogenous background to non-demand sex.

We are all aware of the strength of visual stimuli in arousal. The slope of a shoulder, the highlights of well-brushed hair, the glow of warm skin by firelight, the curve of a breast, the muscles of an athletic leg, the aliveness in a lover's eyes, the form and mystery of the human body, most perfect of God's creations. These are visual stimuli unsurpassed in the pleasure they give.

Yet only a few couples said they "usually" made love with some sort of illumination present. A sizable minority said they "rarely" made love with the lights on or in daylight. They chose to deprive themselves of the visual enjoyment of sex. There is an irony in this. What first attracted most of us to the one we married was what we *saw*. We may not have married "for looks," but what we *saw* contributed much to the chemistry. Then these couples marry and promptly turn off the lights!

Scent plays perhaps a greater role in sexual arousal than we are aware. Odors play an important role in communicating sexual receptivity and aggression in many mammals. Until recently, it was believed that primates do not secrete pheromones, odoriferous sexual attractants. But Dr. Richard Michael, physiological psychologist, and his associates at Emory University have reported that some primates, including humans, do secrete a sexual scent. Apparently the scent is carried in the fatty acids of the vagina. Other investigators, Drs. George Preti and Richard Doty, have found that a woman's scent varies during the menstrual cycle and that during her fertile period her odor is the most pleasant. They submitted scents from women throughout their menstrual cycles to volunteers who did not know the origin of the samples. Extracts from the fertile period were selected as being the most pleasant. The researchers were not willing to say that a pheromone definitely exists. Whether a woman's odor can subliminally trigger a man's response is something they are not ready to assert. But it is something worth considering.

Recently, musk oil has gained popularity as a perfume. The commercial product is not genuine musk. Musk is the glandular secretion of the male (!) musk deer, long used in expensive perfumes and believed to have aphrodisiac qualities. The real substance would cost a fortune. Its popularity, however, is understandable. Endow any food, drink, or odor with a reputation as a sex stimulant, and the public will storm the market. Whether musk has the desired effect on any but the female musk deer is unimportant to our discussion. For most of us, the fragrance of human skin and the odors which are emitted with sexual arousal are potent stimuli. And powerful motivators to intimacy.

Even taste can be a sense modality contributing to arousal. Among women who were "highly sexual" the taste of seminal fluid was a powerful aphrodisiac, albeit psychological. A wife said, "Those drops of clear fluid that come out of his prick when he's really aroused have a taste that drives me wild!" Actually those drops of clear fluid which are secreted by the male as a preliminary to ejaculation are almost tasteless, but her perception of the "taste" was enough. A number of couples in the high sex group reported they found the "taste" of skin to be highly arousing. Kissing or licking the skin of the loved one were definite turn-ons.

When we are challenged to define a romantic, sexual stimulus, do we point to sight, touch, odor, or sound? What do we find romantic in a rose? The color, texture, odor, or all of these? Isn't it much the same with the body of a lover? The scent and taste, as well as the touch, movement, and sounds of the lover, interact to arouse and gratify. This is poetically expressed in the Old Testament in what is one of the most moving professions of erotic love, the Song of Songs of King Solomon:

Sweet, sweet are your caresses,
my bride, my true love;
Wine cannot ravish the senses like that embrace,
nor any spices match the perfume that breathes from you.
Sweet are your lips, my bride,
as honey dripping from its comb;
Honey-sweet your tongue, and soft as milk;
the perfume of your garments is very incense.
My bride, my true love,
a closed garden, hedged all about,
a spring shut in and sealed!
What wealth of grace is here!

The Song of Songs 4:10–12

The development and expansion of one's sensuality is not directed solely toward sex. Sex is important, to be sure, but it is broader and more important than sexuality alone. Being fully sensual is almost synonymous with being fully *alive*. This is understandable if we pause to consider that *everything* we perceive about the world in which we live, all that brings us pleasure from our environment and from those about us, comes to us through our senses. Even our memories are *sensory* memories. Advocates of sensory-awareness programs have rightfully stressed the importance of our sensory perceptions. They have charged that most of us have "lost touch" with the world of sensory pleasure. We believe they are right, and our data support their position. Touches, fragrances, sounds, and tastes in which we once took pleasure come to be ignored and rejected. It is not so much that we lose our taste for these sensory pleasures; it is simply that we build up the calluses of a busy life in a plastic, sanitized, nonsensual (and antisensual) world.

The calluses, however, need not be permanent. They can be stripped away. And we can reclaim our birthright of sensual sensitivity. Incense, satin sheets, delicate perfumes, bath oils, romantic music, fine wines, rich pastry, ocean breezes, firelight, soft furs, massages, words of love and touches of desire. Sensual stimuli. Sexual turn-ons. When enjoyed with a loved one, they take on a special character. They carry the surprise, the releasing joy, and the eroticism which we stamp as romantic. By introducing, then enhancing mutually pleasurable sensual stimuli, a loving couple can enhance their romantic relationship—their aliveness—their *bonding*.

Could anything be more worth the effort?

CHAPTER 6

Man/Woman: The Sexual Anatomy

*If problems in the complex field of human sexual
behavior are to be attacked successfully, psychologic
theory and sociologic concept must at times find
support in physiologic fact. Without adequate support
from basic sexual physiology, much of psychologic
theory will remain theory and much of sociologic
concept will remain concept.*

William H. Masters
Virginia E. Johnson
Human Sexual Response

*It has never been difficult for me to believe in
God; I have spent my life studying His work.*

A retired physician

*T*here is a saying among sexologists: "The most important sexual organ is the brain." It recognizes the importance of thoughts, images, and attitudes. And the emphasis is well-
founded. But the saying bothers us. It establishes a hierarchy of factors
which play a role in human sexuality. To imply that intellect and
emotions play a more important role in our sexual response than the
roles played by the endocrine glands or the neuromuscular system is
absurd. A bit like saying water is more essential to life than air. This
is not, of course, what the sexologists are suggesting. They are merely
attempting to counter the thinking which treats human sexuality as no
different from sexuality in other primates. We can, however, err in
the other direction. In doing so, we attempt to split mind from body,
spirit from flesh.

Man functions holistically. He is more than a collection of parts, a
brain added to a skeleton added to muscles added to organs, etc., etc. A
dog has four legs, a tail, a sex drive, and a brain. We don't have four
legs, only two. We don't have a tail, but we do have a brain and a sex
drive. Dogs are incapable of reasoning and forming attitudes. They respond to instincts. They are almost totally nondiscriminatory in matters
of sex. The female dog is not selected on attributes. Old, young, fat,
skinny, light, dark, mangy, well-groomed, purebred or mongrel. The
male dog's sexual instincts are triggered by *his* drive and *her* stimuli. It
is a direct stimulus/response mechanism.

The human response is not so simple. Human beings are almost in-
stinct-free. Our brain and the discriminations (and generalizations) of

which we are capable take sex out of the realm of the simple instinct-triggered stimulus/response. How does this sexual drive work? If love of husband and wife is rooted in sex, what are the roots of sex? This is a question which may have many, many answers. We presently have but a few. We do not know, for example, the part played by certain centers in the brain. We know only vaguely the role the hormones excreted by our endocrine glands play in our sexual arousal. And we know even less about the interactions between our hormonal, neurological, and biochemical physiology and learning in sexual response. Two individuals who do not differ in their hormone level or other measurable physical attributes may differ greatly in the frequency of their sexual desire and performance. The difference may hold up even when both are exposed to comparable amounts of sexual stimuli. We asked wives how often they were conscious of erotic thoughts which were arousing. Women who reported the same frequency of sexual relations often reported frequencies of arousing thoughts that varied widely. One might report once or twice a week; another might answer "four or five times a day." Some husbands said they were aroused to erection two or three times daily; others of the same age, no more than once or twice a week. Some husbands and wives recalled their adolescence as a period of almost continual sexual arousal. Others said they were little aware of sex urges during their teens. Whether these reported differences in frequency of sexual arousal represent fundamental differences in sex drive (on a purely physical level) is not known. At present, there appears to be no way to adequately study the question. We do know, however, that the sex drive may be modified (increased or decreased in frequency of arousal and, perhaps, even strength) through increased awareness of one's body and the development of sexual responsiveness. In other words, as we learn how to sexually pleasure our own bodies, we tend to increase both the sexual satisfaction we find with our partner and the frequency of arousal.

In any discussion of the norms of frequency of intercourse, it is common for the sexologist to say, "One should never be concerned with questions of frequency. If your frequency is satisfactory to you, whether it be twice a month or twice a day, fine." We agree—with reservations. No one should look to statistical averages of a population to evaluate their performance. Quantity, first of all, does not determine quality. You may have sexual relations twice a week. Someone else may have sex twice a day. Can anyone say which one experiences the greater satisfaction? On the other hand, sex is so much at the core of marriage, meets so many needs of husband and wife as individuals and as partners, and plays such a major role in the growth of their love, that anything they can do to increase the frequency and quality of their lovemaking is more than worth the effort. Enhancement of sexual response calls for at least a basic knowledge of the sexual anatomy. Again, we cannot say it is something that "comes naturally."

WOMAN: ANATOMY AND RESPONSE

Many women interviewed showed a greater familiarity with the map of Europe than with their own sexual anatomy. This is understandable. They were never punished for studying geography. They may have learned something of their reproductive organs in a "life education" class or from a facts-of-life book read before marriage, but few wives with whom we spoke had ever received any information on the *sexual* anatomy of either sex. And even fewer men. A surprising number of the wives said they had never attempted to examine their genitals and did not recognize any reasons for doing so. As one wife protested, "I don't have to understand all about digestion in order to enjoy a meal." True, but once the meal reaches the stomach, there is little we can consciously do to enhance digestion. We can do much more with sex.

Dr. Edgar Berman, physician and assistant to Hubert Humphrey when he was Vice-President of the United States, won the nomination for male chauvinist of the decade by his contention that a woman is not emotionally fit to hold high political office, perhaps not even to pilot an airliner. She suffers, according to Berman, from an instability brought on by her "raging hormones." Once each month, he suggested, she rides a glandular roller coaster. (Then, toward the close of her childbearing years, she enters a period of hormonal psychosis: menopause.)

Without agreeing with the good doctor—and we do not—we will not minimize the role of the various sex hormones in the emotions and behavior of both sexes. The several sex hormones, plus hormones secreted by the other endocrine (internal) glands, affect our sexual functioning in several ways. They act in concert to determine our overall growth and development, distribution of fatty tissue, secondary sex characteristics, hair distribution, complexion, pitch of voice, energy level, and many of those characteristics which are physically identified as "masculine" and "feminine." The endocrine system, functioning as a complex feedback network involving the biochemistry of the entire body, is essential to our well-being. We have no reason to believe it has less effect on our personality, emotions, and behavior. If our endocrine glands were not functioning with respect to sex, we would be emotionally as well as physically sterile.

The hormones carry messages to the brain. The brain sends messages back to the glands. In sex, it is these hormonal messages to the brain which arouse us in a generalized response. That is, they act to make us receptive to external or mental stimuli which then are more directly arousing. These mental responses act as stimuli to elicit further output from the glands. As we said, it is not known how much the output of sex hormones, especially the principal hormones, testosterone (male) and progesterone (female), affect our arousal and functioning (assuming the necessary minimal level is present). We cannot explain the "highly sexed" woman or man by pointing to a high level of sex hormones. Or an individual who appears to have little interest by a low output. Physicians who in the past have treated impotence with injections of male hormones have had doubtful success beyond the placebo (suggestion) effect.

Whether this observed stimulus-response feedback cycle (hormones–brain–arousal–gland–hormones) is the dominant factor in sexual response is unimportant for our purposes. What *is* important is the fact that, however it operates, our sexual drive appears to increase with the frequency of sexual arousal and satisfaction.

In woman, there is a further interesting phenomenon: as the intensity of her sexual drive increases, the number of body areas which are "erogenous" increases. The first locus is generally the clitoris. Usually a girl discovers the response potential of her clitoris in infancy. We say "usually" because, unlike the penis, the clitoris is not as "obvious" as a seat of pleasure. Usually smaller than a pencil eraser, it is located near the frontal, upper interior of the genital "lips." It is understandable that many men fail to locate this sensitive organ. More than a few women are also not sure where it is—or how important it is. The clitoris has no known function other than sexual pleasure. In this respect, there is no comparable male organ. The penis is the primary organ of sexual pleasure in the male, but it also serves the functions of transporting urine and carrying the seminal fluid. Assuming the young girl discovers the pleasure in touching and stroking her clitoris, she is well on her way toward eventual orgasm. Of the women who were most consistently orgasmic, all had discovered the pleasure of clitoral stimulation prior to the onset of puberty. Most had engaged in "masturbatory" activity (clitoral) to orgasm in their pre-teens.

The glans (head) of the clitoris is rich in nerve endings. When appropriately stimulated, impulses are transmitted from the clitoris to the spinal cord, and from there to the brain. The brain registers the pleasure message: "I am being touched, and it feels good." To this, the brain adds memory traces, fantasies, associations, and sensory input from the other senses. If she continues her stimulation, the sexual tension (arousal) builds toward orgasm. Of the 648 women interviewed, the overwhelming majority said they experienced orgasm more often through self-stimulation than through any other means. This finding was not significantly different for the low-orgasmic women than for the high-orgasmic ones. This might seem initially puzzling. If a woman is satisfied in her sexual relations with her husband, why would she "resort" to masturbation? The answer we received from the sexually fulfilled wives was that they did not have to "resort" to masturbation. Self-stimulation was "in addition to" rather than "as a substitute for."

Self-exploration and self-stimulation are virtually essential to the growth of a woman's sexual response. This has apparently been well-recognized by highly responsive women, but it is only in recent years that the subject has been openly discussed. *The Sensuous Woman,* written under the pseudonym "J," gave rather explicit instructions in self-stimulation. Although the book was written in a nonserious, breezy style and lacked scientific validity, what the author had to say about what a woman might do to enhance her sexual response made the book worth reading. The women we interviewed who were most responsive had engaged in self-stimulation from an early age, often two or more years prior to the onset of puberty. Interestingly, they did not view masturbation (a word most women said they found "disgusting") any less negatively than did their less responsive sisters. The majority of women, whatever their level of responsiveness, said they had been raised to view self-stimulation as wrong or sinful. This attitude, most admitted, had been carried into adulthood. Those women who had been able to overcome a negative attitude, however, had discovered the importance of self-stimulation in the development of their sexual response. They found that by exploring their bodies they discovered the response potential of many areas of their body surface. The number of so-called erogenous areas expanded to include virtually the entire body. Almost any touching, therefore, which can be interpreted as erotic sends messages to the brain, which triggers responses of arousal. As the woman develops her sexuality through self-stimulation, she increases her sexual associations, which add to the sensory message carried through the body's communication network.

The body's communication network, the nervous system, is broken down into the *central nervous system*, the brain and spinal cord; the *peripheral nervous system*, the "branches" of the central nervous system that provide input from the five senses and direction for our voluntary movements; and the *autonomic nervous system*, which regulates many physiological functions of which we are not usually aware and which are involuntary. Secretions of certain glands, heartbeat, construction of peripheral blood vessels, control of the gastrointestinal muscles, and most of what happens in our sexual responses involve the autonomic system. All these involuntary and semivoluntary processes (the *visceral* activities) are controlled, directly or indirectly, by the two divisions of the autonomic system: the *sympathetic* and the *parasympathetic*. These two subsystems check and balance each other. When the sympathetic is turned on, the parasympathetic is turned off—or at least diminished. Actually, neither one is ever completely turned off. It's all relative. But this relative on and off becomes very important in sexual response. We have a lot to learn about the autonomic system, but we do know it is involved in the physiological responses associated with emotion. And what can involve our emotions more than sex?

Until Masters and Johnson investigated the normal physiology of the sexual response, sexologists relied on a great deal of guesswork, half-truths, and chance observations in describing what happens when a woman becomes aroused and stimulated to orgasm. Thanks to their research, we now know much more. And for this, we are in their debt. It provides what follows.

Just as love is not confined to one part of a mature woman's life, isolated and compartmentalized, her sexual response is not limited physiologically to the primary and secondary organs of reproduction. It involves her entire body and all systems of her body. It is all-encompassing.

Masters and Johnson chose to describe the cycle of sexual response in four phases: the excitement phase, the plateau phase, the orgasmic phase, and the resolution phase. The divisions were employed as a descriptive aid, and were not meant to imply any clear dividing lines. The response cycle might more accurately be portrayed as an ascending curve which may, at some point, level off, then surge to a peak before dropping back to its baseline. With recognition that there may be considerable overlap, the four phases can be plotted along the curve.

Excitement Phase: A woman responds to effective sexual stimulation very quickly—within ten to thirty seconds. This is true regardless of the source of the stimuli. It can be mental or physical, induced by touch, a thought, fantasy, or suggestion, something she reads, sees, or hears, or by a combination of these. It is only necessary that the stimuli be effective, that they turn her on. The first sign of response is the production of vaginal lubrication. A lubricating material appears on the walls of the vagina. Until Masters and Johnson devised research techniques to study this phenomenon, it had been thought that the lubrication originated either in the Bartholin glands, a pair of glands located in the inner lips at the entrance of the vagina, or in the uterus itself (where it passes into the vagina via the cervix). In one of their many important findings, Masters and Johnson found that the walls of the vagina itself produce most of the lubricating material. As the woman becomes aroused, a "sweating" phenomenon takes place on the walls of the vaginal barrel. It appears somewhat akin to the beads of perspiration on one's forehead on a warm day. The lubricant is not, however, sweat, nor does it result from a temperature change. Within a matter of seconds, an aroused woman may become "wet" enough to be ready for intercourse.

As the excitement stage progresses, other reactions occur within the vagina. Except during menstruation, the anterior and posterior walls of the vagina are essentially in contact. The vagina is a sheath. In fact, the word *vagina* means sheath. It is a passageway leading from the vulva to the *cervix*, the neck of the uterus. In its unstimulated state, the vagina of a woman who has not borne children is about 7–8 cm. (approx. 3 in.) in length and 2 cm. (approx. ¾ in.) in diameter. The walls of the vagina, however, are remarkably elastic. It has been called an organ of accommodation. It can accommodate the smallest to the largest penis and, during delivery, even a large baby. The vaginal walls are elastic longitudinally as well as transversely. In the excitement phase, the vaginal barrel lengthens, and there is a distention of the inner two thirds. By the latter stage of the excitement phase, the vaginal barrel is markedly expanded: to 9.5–10.5 cm. (approx. 4–4½ in.) in length and 5.75–6.25 cm. (approx. 2½ in.) in diameter for the inner two thirds of the organ. This expansion plays a special role later.

The vaginal walls also undergo color changes during the excitement phase, changing from the normal purplish-red coloring to a darker, purplish hue. This results from the vasocongestion within the vaginal walls.

Vasocongestion, the swelling of the blood vessels, is one of the most significant physical changes during sexual arousal in both sexes. Superficial and/or deep vasocongestion is present during all phases of the sexual cycle. In her breasts, the woman experiences both superficial and deep vasocongestion. Nipple erection is the first indication of sexual arousal in the breasts. This results from involuntary contraction of muscle fibers within the nipple. This response may increase the nipple length by 0.5–1.0 cm. and the base measurement by 0.25–0.5 cm. over the unstimulated measurements. Men frequently rely on signs of nipple erection as an indication of her arousal. It is an unreliable test. Not only are there individual differences within any population of women, nipple erection is frequently not a constant within the same woman. One nipple may lag behind the other in erection. Also, her nipple may become more erect when directly stimulated, then less erect when his caresses are directed elsewhere, even though her overall arousal may not be at all diminished and might, in fact, be increasing. The deep vasocongestion also brings about an overall increase in the actual size of the breasts as arousal increases. Many girls have discovered their bra becoming tight as they sat passionately involved with the boyfriend in his automobile.

Vasocongestion dramatically affects the female's external genitalia. Her external genitalia include the labia major (major lips), labia minora (minor lips), and the clitoris.

Enclosing the vulva, forming protection for the labia minora, vaginal opening, and the urinary meatus, the labia majora are two longitudinal folds of skin. They are skin-colored and are covered with hair on their outer surface. When the woman is unaroused, these lips generally meet in the midline. With childbearing, the major lips may lose this integrity. As sexual arousal increases in a woman who has not borne children (there are frequently observed changes in women who have undergone pregnancy and delivery; generalities are difficult), the major lips thin out and flatten against the perineum. They also become slightly elevated in an upward and outward direction away from the vaginal opening.

The labia minora meet at the front of the vulva and are thinner than the labia majora. This makes it possible for them to be protected within the folds of the large lips. These smaller lips are more pronounced in front, lessening in size toward the rear until they disappear in the posterior portions of the larger lips. In appearance and texture they resemble the inner surface of the labia majora. Both are soft and smooth. Both are about the same color, and both are slightly moist, becoming moister with arousal. During the excitement phase, however, changes in the minor lips are more marked than those in the major lips. During excitement, the labia minora expand considerably in diameter. By the time the plateau phase is reached, the diameter has increased as much as three times. With this expansion in diameter, the labia minora protrude through the thinning major lips. They also become increasingly sensitive. During sexual intercourse, they serve to guide the penis into the vagina. Color changes with arousal are even more vivid in the labia minora than in the labia majora. For this reason, the minor lips have been called the "sex skin."

Bartholin's glands, mentioned earlier, are located on the inner surface of each of the labia minora. During the late excitement phase or early in the plateau phase, the Bartholin's glands secrete a small amount of fluid, but as noted previously, this plays little part in lubricating the vaginal barrel.

The clitoris can justly claim to be the only truly sexual organ. It is the only organ whose sole function is the initiation or heightening of sexual arousal. There is no comparable organ in the male.

In most writings, the clitoris has been described as a homologue of the penis. The similarities are apparent. Both have a shaft and a glans (head) rich in nerve endings. The penis has a passage running the length of its underside which transports the urine and semen out of the body, while the clitoris is solely a sexual organ. But there are other significant differences, making the clitoris other than a "miniature penis." Like the penis, the clitoris may react to direct stimulation, to erotic thoughts, or to stimulation of other erogenous areas. Also like the penis, the clitoris becomes distended with vasocongestion, the so-called "clitoral erection." Here, however, the homologue should not be carried too far. The first observable physiological response to arousal in the woman is vaginal lubrication, not clitoral erection. The average clitoris, in fact, never becomes "erect" in any way resembling the penis. Not only is the clitoris much smaller (as small as 1 cm. transverse diameter), it does not react the same as the penis. In the male, the penis reacts to an arousing stimulus, whether mental or physical, by almost instant erection. Clitoral response is not equally rapid, and response time depends upon whether the stimulation is direct (i.e., manipulation of the clitoral body or adjacent area) or indirect (i.e., stimulation of other erotic areas or sexual fantasies). Reaction to direct stimulation is much faster.

With sexual arousal, the clitoral glans increases in size, but this increase may not be significant enough to be observable without magnification. Size of the clitoris and extent of increase, however, are no indication of sexual responsiveness, despite the myths of pornographic writing. Parenthetically, it should be noted that half of the Masters and Johnson study subjects did not develop clinically obvious tumescence of the clitoral glans. Hence, the husband looking for clitoral "erections" as proof of his wife's arousal is on the wrong track.

While the clitoris is not a perfect homologue of the penis, the glans of both are the same in their sexual responsiveness. They are by far the most sensitive to tactual erotic stimulation. The glans of the penis, however, is many times larger. A woman does not need specific instruction in finding the head of the penis. The clitoris, however, is not so easy for the man to locate. Anatomical diagrams are seldom of much help. The wife who is intelligently concerned with her own sexual gratification recognizes this and shows her husband exactly where it is and how to stimulate it. Hopefully, she has discovered this herself in self-exploration. And self-gratification.

As her sexual tension increases and the woman enters the plateau phase, several changes present themselves. Pulse and respiration rate increase, and there is a rise in blood pressure. The sex flush, a measles-like rash which may spread over the abdomen and breasts, may appear if it has not shown itself during the excitement phase, or it may spread if it has already appeared. Contraction of the voluntary muscles, both specific and general in character, often shows itself or is increased during the plateau phase. These contractions may, of course, be voluntary, intended to increase sexual response.

No one needs to tell the sexually responsive woman that physical changes take place as her arousal increases. She can feel them. But some of them may not be identifiable.

Most pronounced during the plateau stage is what Masters and Johnson call the "orgasmic platform." This is an engorgement and swelling of the tissues in the outer one third of the vaginal barrel. This vaso-congestion acts to reduce the diameter of the outer third of the vagina by as much as 50 per cent over what it was during the excitement phase. This serves two purposes: one, it serves to aid in retention of the seminal fluid at the time of the male's ejaculation, and two, it may in-

crease the "grip" on the penis, enhancing the pleasure of both partners. The name "orgasmic platform" may be misleading. Its presence
does not necessarily indicate that orgasm is imminent, or even that it
will ultimately occur. Many women who experience difficulty achieving orgasm are, nevertheless, capable of reaching high levels of arousal,
a condition which makes the failure to find ultimate sexual release all
the more frustrating. During the plateau phase, an elevation of the
uterus and a ballooning of the inner two thirds of the vaginal barrel
also occur.

With the onset of the plateau phase, there is a change in the color of
the labia minora, the inner lips. They change from a bright red to a
deep, dark-wine red. (The color change varies, depending on whether
the woman has borne children.) This color change is a signal of im-
pending orgasm, but its importance seems limited in terms of the man's
observation and response. How is the man to become aware of such a
response, and what is he to do if he is aware? The significant changes
during the plateau phase are an increase in engorgement of the sexual
blood vessels and an increase in muscular tensions. These build up to the
point of readiness for orgasm. Masters and Johnson (p. 119) describe
the plateau phase as follows: "The female gathers psychological and
physiological strength from the stockpile of mounting sexual tension,
until she can direct all her physical and mental forces toward a leap
into the third or orgasmic phase of sexual tension expression."

Late in the excitement phase or early in the plateau phase, the areola
of the breasts become significantly engorged. The tumescence becomes
so pronounced it may create the illusion that the responding woman
has lost nipple erection. During the plateau phase, there is a
physiologic reaction in the clitoris which occurs with universal consistency to effective stimulation. The entire clitoral body retracts from its
normal pudental overhand positioning. This finding was one of the
more significant of the Masters and Johnson observations. They found
that any portion of the clitoral glans that normally projects from the clitoral hood is withdrawn deeply within the clitoral foreskin during this
period of arousal. This amounts to at least a 50 per cent overall reduction in the length of the total clitoral body.

What brings a woman to this height of arousal, this brink of orgasm?
There are no simple answers to this question. If it were a simple matter
of physical, tactual stimulation, sex could, in fact, be reduced to a cook-
book formula, devoid of human emotion. Here we confront the psychological "turn-offs" which block the acceleration of sexual tension cul-

minating in orgasm. Without such inhibitory turn-offs, we should expect appropriate (nonpainful) tactual stimulation of the clitoris from whatever source to result in orgasmic release. Psychological stimuli might be enhancing but not essential. The psychological stimuli, however, are important. They are important in both arousing the woman and, when negative, in turning her off. Developing her response potential, therefore, entails a threefold approach: working to rid herself of the "turn-offs," increasing her tactual erotic response through self-stimulation, and working to increase the "turn-ons"—the fantasies, memories, associations, and positive attitudes which provide the all-important psychological component of sexuality.

A majority of women interviewed said they found it difficult to practice self-stimulation. Even when they were able to accept the benefits intellectually, they felt that time spent pleasuring themselves was somehow wrong. Some said they didn't have time. Others said they felt that sex, in any expression, should be with their husband. And still others felt that self-stimulation was immature or selfish or neurotic. The reaction is especially puzzling if we consider that these women are finding actions which are intensely pleasurable difficult to engage in. We would be hard pressed to find stronger evidence of the power of nonrational, emotional attitudes in defeating what our intellect tells us. The importance of overcoming these inhibitions, however, is underscored by the finding that every woman in our sample who was consistently orgasmic considered self-stimulation "very important" in the development of her sexual response.

Many of these wives used their daily bath as the opportunity to explore and pleasure their bodies. It gave them an extended period (during a long, leisurely bath) in which to move their hands over thighs, abdomen, arms, shoulders, buttocks, breasts, and genitals, not striving simply for an orgasm, but working to discover the pleasure areas. One wife expressed her experience this way: "I learned to like my body. Before, I had always been kind of unaware of it, of the sensitivity that was there. I found out how important touching is. It's like coming alive. Now my husband can run his fingertips over my forearm or just about anywhere and I get turned on."

What about self-stimulation to orgasm? Many wives expressed the concern that self-stimulation to orgasm during the afternoon would lessen their desire for lovemaking that evening. And although, as we have indicated, this is in no way necessarily true, many employed it as their explanation for avoiding *any* self-stimulation. Without playing

down the satisfaction found in orgasm, we must say that the importance of the orgasm is, in many respects, overemphasized. If orgasm is
achieved, nothing is lost, nor is anything other than pleasure attained;
if there is no orgasm, no pleasure is lost—and sensory/sexual responsivity is enhanced. A woman is able to judge where she is sexually. She
is in the best position to know what will add to or detract from her response with her husband.

Since the lovemaking of which we are talking takes place between
persons of "opposite" sexes, there is the important question of how one
learns to satisfactorily stimulate a lover who has a very different sexual
anatomy. And there is only one answer: through instruction. If a
woman wishes to be pleasured to the fullest (and why wouldn't she?),
she will show (demonstrate) how to do it. Which means, of course, a
willingness to stimulate herself in the presence of her husband. This is
not easy for women who have been heavily indoctrinated in "modesty."
And this means most women. Breaking down these barriers, however, is
essential if the emotional freedom to love and be loved is to be found.
This, it should be noted, goes for men as well as for women.

MAN: ANATOMY AND RESPONSE

It is almost axiomatic to say that men and women differ greatly in
their sexual response. Ignoring the evidence, writers have long emphasized the differences between the sexes. Women are more compas-
sionate, emotional, peace-loving. Men are more aggressive, logical, and
dominant. Women are slower to respond to, and less interested in, sexual stimuli. Almost none of these clichés is supported by anything
which can be called legitimate research. Repeatedly, both in the reading of published studies as well as in observations of our own sample
population of couples, we have been impressed with how very much
alike men and women are. In their physical sexual response, similarities
far outweigh differences. Psychologically, the differences may be more
rhetoric than reality, more conditioning than gender.

The nervous system functions the same in men and women. Messages are sent from the senses to the brain. Impulses are sent from the
brain to the muscles and glands. Basically, this input-output system is
no different for men than for women.

Most writers of sex instruction in the past have accepted the fact that
sex is not, in a woman, solely a response of the primary and secondary

erogenous areas of the body. Yet they have assumed that sexual response in man is a relatively simple matter, largely restricted to the genitals. This assumption has led to a number of erroneous conclusions. For one, women have been led to believe that sexual stimulation and enhancement of the man is unnecessary, or at most can be limited to stimulation of the genitals. Men, so they say, have no "secondary" erogenous areas. Men are quickly aroused, in no need of a "meaningful relationship" for sexual satisfaction, and capable of rapid arrival at climax. But not women. If we accept all these supposed differences as established, it might be easy to postulate some very real—and significant —differences in the physiology of sexual response between the sexes.

Emphasis on both the psychological and physical differences between the sexes has been so heavy, it is tempting to go overboard in the other direction, as some radical feminists have tended to do, and deny all but a few relatively minor (?!) anatomical distinctions. Neither position serves our understanding. Nor does either one have validity. There are obvious physical differences between men and women, but the sexes are more alike than different. There may be emotional and intellectual differences as well, but any such differences are far from established by well-controlled studies. For the present, it seems safe to say that individual differences within the sexes are at least as great as any suggested differences between the sexes—all sexist generalizations notwithstanding.

With presentation of appropriate psychogenic or physiogenic stimuli, the woman very quickly signals her arousal by a lubricating secretion on the vaginal walls. The man's arousal is signaled by an erection. These reactions are neurophysiologic parallels. And both occur with equal facility, a fact which brings into question the long-held belief that women are much slower to respond sexually.

The penis serves a twofold function: transporting urine out of the body, and conducting semen during ejaculation. The organ forms a protective sheath for the urogenital passage through which urine and semen are discharged via the meatur, a slit opening in the head of the penis. There are three major sections running the length of the organ. Two of these, the *corpora cavernosa*, are sponge-like structures running the length of the organ and extending behind the scrotum back between the legs. The third structure, the *corpus spongiosum*, extends along the back of the penis and surrounds and protects the urethra.

Erection occurs when these unique columns, under sexual arousal, rapidly fill with blood, creating a pressure which causes the penis to swell and become erect and firm. Essentially, erection is the functioning of a physical hydraulic system. Valves, like floodgates that can be shut, prevent the return flow of blood and maintain the erection. It is the stiff, erect condition of the penis which assures the ejection of the seminal fluid, the male seed, deep within the vagina during coitus.

The gross structure of the penis includes the head (glans), the rim of the glans (corona), and the penial shaft. As with the glans of the clitoris, the penial glans is usually the most sensitive to erotic stimulation. Unless surgically removed through circumcision, a fold of skin, the *prepuce*, covers the glans. Some sex writers have suggested that the absence of the foreskin results in lessened sensitivity and hence to greater ability to prolong ejaculation. Masters and Johnson's studies failed to find any support for this notion. Circumcision, or lack thereof, in other words, apparently has no demonstrable effect on sexual performance. Nor does penis size play any major role in the woman's satisfaction in coitus. Perhaps the most widely accepted "phallic fallacy" (to borrow the words employed by Masters and Johnson) is the concept that the larger the penis, the greater the woman's satisfaction. No hard-core erotic writing would be complete without a description of the male's "massive organ" and his amazing sexual prowess presumed to follow from it. The female sex partners in these male-written fantasies are, of course, "overwhelmed," then in "ecstasy" as recipients of this over-sized phallus.

There are two fallacies involved here. First, that, to a woman, the bigger the better. Studies of sexual response in women have consistently shown penis size not to be a reported variable. Of the women we have interviewed, less than 3 per cent have expressed any feeling that the size of the husband's penis was an important factor in their dissatisfaction. And over half of that group felt they might be able to enjoy coitus more if their husband's penis were *smaller*. Although measurements were not made, and estimates by the wives have doubtful reliability, our overall impression is that any distress these women experience from the "very large" penis is probably related to either physical problems from which the woman is suffering or adverse emotional reactions to coitus. In fact, while many men are concerned that they may not be "big enough," the range of penis length and diameter among male adults is relatively small. The second fallacy, and one which feeds this concern, is that erection of the penis which is large in its flaccid state provides significantly greater increase in length and diameter than does erection of the smaller penis. Masters and Johnson found that, in general, the per cent of increase in size of a large (flaccid) penis is less than the per cent of increase of a small penis. Since most men see other men in the nude only in the nonaroused state, however, and since there is considerable variability in flaccid length, it is understandable that this fallacy is so widely held by men. With many, it is probably rooted in the uncertainties of early adolescence and the comparisons made in the shower room during physical-education classes.

The testes (testicles), a pair of oval bodies about an inch and a half in length, lie in the scrotum, a thin-walled sac with two compartments hanging beneath the penis. During embryonic life, the testes develop with the abdominal cavity. The male sex cells, however, cannot develop within the warmer environment of the abdomen. Shortly before birth, or occasionally later, the testes descend into the cooler environment of the scrotum.

During the excitement phase, penile erection is attained. This response varies from man to man and within the same man from one time of arousal to another. After full erection has been attained, the excitement phase may be very brief or extended for many minutes, depending upon the kind and intensity of the stimulation. Erection may not be constant during the excitement phase. If the period is prolonged, erection may be partially lost and regained many times. Partial, or even complete, loss of erection can result from a sudden loud noise, a telephone call, or an adverse remark by the woman. It appears to depend on the degree of arousal, the intensity (objectively and subjectively) of the aversive stimulus, and the man's emotional security.

During the excitement phase, the testes elevate. This drawing of both testes up into the crotch is accomplished by a shortening of the spermatic cords. If the excitement phase is continued for more than five or ten minutes, the testes may again descend into the scrotal sac. This is not, however, necessarily accompanied by any loss of erection.

As with a woman, there are two basic male responses to sexual stimulation; vasocongestion (both general and specific) and myotonia, muscle contraction (both general and specific). And there are other similar responses as well. The majority of men attain erection of the nipples without any direct stimulation. A measle-like rash, what Masters and Johnson call the "sex flush," appears on the chest of many men during sexual arousal, just as it does in women. Other responses—contraction of the rectal sphincter, increase in blood pressure, pulse rate, and respiration—are common to both sexes.

Sex is unique among our drives. With each of our other physical and/or psychological drives, it is the satisfaction of the drive which is experienced as pleasurable. When we are hungry, it is satisfaction of the hunger—eating—which is pleasurable, not the hunger itself. There is no pleasure in thirst, only in quenching the thirst. With sex, however, there is pleasure in arousal itself, as well as in the satisfaction of orgasm. Prolonging and increasing arousal thus has a dual purpose. It builds sexual tension to the point of orgasmic release, and it is pleasurable in itself. Even where orgasm can be attained quickly through intense stimulation, the pleasure experienced is seldom as intensely pleasurable as when there has been a prolonged period of physiogenic and psychogenic stimulation. One finding of Masters and Johnson in this regard is of interest: In general, the more prolonged the period of sexual tension in men prior to ejaculation, the longer will erection be sustained following climax. This obviously can have an effect on the sexual satisfaction of a woman who may not have reached orgasm when her husband's ejaculation is complete. If he is capable of maintaining erection and continuing copulatory movements, he may continue until she attains her climax. While our own studies confirm these findings, we have found maintenance of erection following ejaculation to be more a matter of individual differences.

The progression from introduction of effective sexual stimuli, through the excitement and plateau phases to orgasm is too often presented by popular writers as a series of actions aimed at reaching the point of climax as quickly as possible, as if orgasm is the end all and be all. Ironically, they are often the writers who most repetitively use the word "love" when describing sexual acts. But this how-to-get-from-start-to-finish-with-the-least-effort-and-in-the-least-time approach to sex is the furthest thing from love. It doesn't even place much value on sex. To a couple in love who share a full appreciation of their sexuality and are free of inhibitions which might curtail a broad spectrum of expression of sensual pleasures, lovemaking is never casual and superficial, a mere striving for orgasmic release. They raise their physical expressions to a high art. And in so doing, they develop and express to each other the best of their humanity.

CHAPTER 7

Their Orgasm

There are some experiences which just cannot be described.

A husband

I've heard that in some Eastern religions they hold the belief that heaven is a continuous orgasm. It sounds great, but I'm not sure I could stand it.

A wife

In Human Sexual Response (p. 127), Master and Johnson wrote, "For the human female, orgasm is a psychophysiologic experience occurring within, and made meaningful by, a context of psychosocial influence. Physiologically, it is a brief episode of physical release from the vasocongestive and myotonic increment developed in response to sexual stimuli. Psychologically, it is subjective perception of a peak of physical reaction to sexual stimuli. The cycle of sexual response, with orgasm as the ultimate point in progression, generally is believed to develop from a drive of biologic-behavioral origin deeply integrated into the condition of human existence." There are what Masters and Johnson call, "three interacting areas of influence upon female orgasmic attainment": *Physiologic, psychologic,* and *sociologic.* It comes as no surprise that the same three variables interact in the male orgasm.

In man, of course, the primary indication of orgasm is ejaculation. In woman, there is no comparable "proof." Ejaculation, however, is not orgasm. As ejaculation occurs, the man *experiences* orgasm. While there is no ejaculation involved in the female's orgasm, the similarities between the sexes on all three levels of orgasm are greater than the differences. In both sexes, orgasm is an experience of total body involvement. In both, there are spasmodic muscle contractions involving most of the body's voluntary muscles. In both, there is a sensation of orgasm onset. In the male this is a sensation of inevitability, a feeling that the ejaculation is coming and he can do nothing to delay or control it. In both, there are dramatic increases in respiration, heart rate, and blood-pressure elevation. Aside from ejaculation, Masters and Johnson found only two major areas of physiologic difference between male and female orgasm: The female is capable of rapid return to orgasm if she is restimulated following orgasm and before her arousal drops below the plateau level; and, the female is capable of maintaining her orgasm for a relatively long period of time.

It is far easier to investigate and discuss the physiologic, rather than the psychologic factors in orgasm. For an experience which has no analogy, one that is extremely intense, involves the total body, and carries associations to self and others, it has not wanted for descriptions. Writers have used phrases that would embarrass a Hollywood publicist. "Like going over Niagara Falls in a barrel." "A series of beautiful rockets bursting." "An angelic choir." "Being caught in a giant wave." We collected a number of these descriptive phrases and asked women if they would check those with which they could identify from their personal experience in orgasm. Most said, "None." Masters and Johnson collected the subjective descriptions of 487 women. From them they drew a consensus establishing three distinct stages of woman's "subjective progression through orgasm." The first stage involves "an isolated thrust of intense sensual awareness, clitorally oriented, but radiating upward into the pelvis." During the second stage, a "suffusion of warmth" pervades the pelvic area first, then spreads progressively throughout the body. With the third stage, there is a feeling of involuntary contraction with a "specific focus in the vagina or lower pelvis, a 'pelvic throbbing.'" There are contractions of the orgasmic platform which are experienced subjectively as throbbing within the vagina.

The subjective reports we collected cannot challenge the Masters and Johnson consensus. Nor do they provide substantial support. The problem has to do with the words used. We heard many descriptions which we could say were similar but not the same. And some which were almost the same—but not quite. The description which seemed to come closest to what Masters and Johnson reported was the "suffusion of warmth." Every orgasmic woman we interviewed said they felt the feelings spread throughout their body. It was a total body experience. A wife spoke for all others when she said, "It radiates. I can feel it flow all the way to my fingertips."

The "throbbing" was also consistently reported by our interviewees. One wife said, "When my husband comes, I can feel the pulsations in his penis and it seems to cause me to match him. I can feel it in my vagina." This might be interpreted as an attempt to achieve simultaneous orgasm. We don't know if this was her intent. If so, it may be unfortunate. It could diminish her chances of reaching orgasm at all. Many sex authorities have attacked the emphasis which, in the past, has been placed on the importance of simultaneous orgasm. Dr. Alex Comfort has said it "doesn't matter a whit." This, we feel, is the pendulum swinging to the other, perhaps absurd, extreme. Of course, simultaneous orgasm is not essential to marital satisfaction, but if it "doesn't matter a whit," why does Comfort then go on to suggest how a couple may achieve it? Simultaneous orgasm can add a plus to the orgasmic experience. How much of a plus is up to the individuals. If it has enough value, the two can work on timing their orgasmic response, slowing one to match the response pace of the other.

The subjective reports of the men interviewed yielded more confusing results. Few men we interviewed were willing or able to verbalize their subjective experience in orgasm. It may be that men do not experience the nearly overwhelming reaction that women do. Or, more probable, that men are not comfortable expressing emotional reactions. If we could identify any consensus, it would be a feeling of "total release." It is the ejaculation of seminal fluid which apparently provides the peak experience. With each spasm of ejaculation there is an emotional surge, however indescribable. Most men could describe the orgasmic experience only as intensely pleasurable. Some, however, said they experienced a feeling of "power" at the point of ejaculation, especially in a male-superior position. For most, however, tension release seemed to be the dominant feeling. The difference in descriptive adjectives employed by men and women in their subjective descriptions of orgasm seemed to us to confirm what is known of the differences on a physical level: that orgasm in the female is a more intense, profound, peak experience. All evidence argues that woman is more sexually responsive once she has freed herself of the fears and inhibitions laid so heavily upon her by our society.

In recent years, much has been written in popular books on sex about multiple orgasm. Some self-proclaimed authorities have made multiple orgasm the ultimate goal of every woman. One such author, without citing any authority, reports a "scientific" investigation in which a female volunteer copulated with fifty men in succession, reaching orgasm with each one. If anyone took such literary trash seriously it could give science a bad name. Far worse, it could contribute to the sexual problems of many women who are already insecure about their responsiveness. We can only hope the readers of this best-seller granted the author no more authority than he deserved. Kinsey and his associates found that only 10 to 16 per cent of women were multi-orgasmic. They were not, it should be noted, reporting the *potential* for successive orgasms within a limited period of time. They were speaking of the average number of orgasms in each coital experience reported by the women in their sample. The potential average may be considerably higher. A smaller percentage of women in our sample reported more than a single orgasm during average coitus. What strikes us as a more significant finding, however, is the number of women who said they did not usually *desire* more than one orgasm. Others said they felt they should be multi-orgasmic and were disturbed that they did not meet this criterion of a "sexual" woman. Many women, it seems, feel under a pressure similar to what some men feel when reading "pornographic" novels that portray the "hero" as a sexual superman. Live up to the model or consider yourself as inadequate! Some husbands contribute to the problem in no small measure by urging (virtually demanding) a wife to have several orgasms (apparently as proof of their outstanding ability to satisfy a woman). Orgasm is a personal experience. One doesn't have an orgasm *for* someone else, or as a *gift* to someone else. "Did it happen for you; did you have an orgasm?" is not a question a gentleman lover asks a lady. Whether she reaches one orgasm or fifty is no one's business but hers. Sex can be a delightful, fun-filled game between lovers. But not if someone is keeping score.

The physiology of the male and female orgasm has been extensively studied. We know much less of the emotional experience. A number of writers have attempted to put into words what a woman feels at the moment of that reflex reaction. Much less has been written of the male experience. The reason has to do with the argument which raged for years, touched off by Freud, over whether there is more than one type of female orgasm. The Freudians contended there was a "clitoral" orgasm, qualitatively different from the more "mature" orgasm centered in the vagina. The opponents argued that female orgasm is always and only "clitoral," and that a lack of nerve endings in the vagina make any so-called "vaginal" orgasm physiologically impossible. Now, except for some diehards, the argument has passed into psychosexual history, not because of any clear findings one way or the other (even the physiological studies of Masters and Johnson left the questions of subjective response unanswered), but because most therapists and investigators have recognized that the problems inherent in individual variability, plus the extreme difficulties encountered when one is called upon to verbalize an emotional response, make any conclusions highly suspect. We suspect many of our colleagues also reached the point of muttering, "Who cares?" If so, we share their feelings. If the woman experiences orgasm, is she likely to care whether another woman might describe orgasm in the same words or attribute it to the same locus. We

asked the women interviewed to describe the experience of orgasm, and
to compare their experience with words used by other women (including those of novelists and professional sexologists) in describing the experience. Very few said they could identify with the descriptions given
by others. "I suppose someone might describe it that way, but . . ." was
the most frequent response. In some cases, the respondent even doubted
that the woman whose description they read had ever experienced orgasm. And there was general agreement that no man could possibly
succeed in describing what a woman feels in orgasm.

Men were no closer to agreement when asked to describe their feelings during orgasm. Most said they had never given the matter much
thought. (The majority of women, on the other hand, had spent time
analyzing nearly all their sexual reactions, perhaps encouraged by the
numerous articles dealing with female sexuality which have appeared
in periodicals in recent years.) Many men reacted somewhat defensively when asked to talk about these subjective reactions, either passing the question off with a short, superficial answer (e.g., "It's just a
great feeling"), or borrowing the clichés of hack fiction writers (e.g.,
"It's like a gigantic rocket bursting"). Overall, we could not escape
finding, in the answers given by those of both sexes, confirmation of
what has been suggested by many writers: that the subjective experience of orgasm is a less profound experience in the male than in the female.

In their efforts to de-emphasize the importance of the orgasmic experience, an approach which has made the orgasm virtually the totality of
lovemaking, some writers may have gone too far. It is a mistake to
imply that orgasm is little more than a bonus to lovemaking, pleasant
but not greatly important. To tell men and women, "Don't worry about
it, you can enjoy sex even if you never reach an orgasm," as a syndi-
cated advice columnist did, is no help at all. Orgasm is too powerful an
experience to be so lightly dismissed. Physiologically, it is very similar
in men and women. It is a neuromuscular, reflexive reaction, accompanied by an increment in myotonic tension, contractions within the genitals, and dramatic peaks in respiratory rate, cardiac rate, and blood pressure. Little wonder it is so difficult to describe the feelings. There is
simply no comparable human experience. A few women said they were
not sure whether they had ever experienced orgasm. Others said they
had, yet when they described the experience, their descriptions indicated they had not (e.g., "It's a warm, pleasant feeling like when he
puts his arms around me and tells me he loves me."). It is doubtful that
any woman who has ever experienced orgasm would have any doubts

about it. During the moments just preceding orgasm and during the orgasmic release, the individual experiences a feeling of vulnerability. The lovers are never more open to one another. Psychologist Oswald Schwarz has called sex the only function that cannot lie. He means that while we may successfully hide behind facades and deceptions in other areas of our life, in sexual relations we reveal ourselves to our partner as we really are. And this can be a threatening thought to one who wishes to remain hidden.

In the total body experience of orgasm, the pleasure is felt at the moment of release of tension and continues in the gradually ebbing waves. Yet moralists have for centuries been fond of repeating their "wisdom": *post coitum, animal triste* (after coitus the animal is sad). In so doing, they have turned a sexual neurosis into a natural law. If there are unhealthy guilt feelings or hostile reactions, then we might expect sadness or other negative feelings following sexual relations. But for the couple free of unhealthy attitudes and very much in love, it is a feeling of peace and exhilaration. Ecstasy.

A number of wives complained of their husbands frequently "breaking the spell" following coitus by words or actions which conveyed the message: "Now that that's over, let's get on with the day-to-day business of living." (A smaller number of husbands complained of this in their wives.) "It's just as if he forgets all about it as soon as he pulls out," said one wife. "If we make love in the afternoon, he is likely to reach for the phone to call a business associate a minute afterwards. I'm left with the feeling it's all sort of meaningless to him." This may, however, be more a reflection of a sexual difference in the "profoundness" experienced in orgasm by women and men than a difference in degree of loving or meaning found in lovemaking. Which does not, however, excuse husbands. The loving husband strives to be aware of his wife's feelings, to know where she is emotionally. It has been said that the sexually fulfilled woman wakes up singing. As her lover, her husband will do nothing to put a damper on her singing.

It has been found that the physiological intensity of the female orgasm is greatest in a climax induced through masturbation. Yet no researcher, to our knowledge, has claimed that masturbatory orgasm is a superior experience. The feeling of oneness and *joie de vie* which accompanies and follows the orgasm of coitus when lovers share their vulnerabilities cannot be reduced to physiological measures. It is the ultimate psychophysical act in the drama of sexual love.

Man: *I have conquered you!*
Woman: *No, my love, you have won me.*

CHAPTER 8

Sexual Loving

A long, long kiss, a kiss of youth, and love,
And beauty, all concentrating like rays
Into one focus, kindled from above;
Such kisses as belong to early days,
Where heart, and soul, and sense, in concert move,
And the blood's lava, and the pulse a blaze,
Each kiss a heart-quake . . .

Lord Byron (1788–1824)
Don Juan, Canto II, CLXXXVI

*W*here do we find the essence of a rose? In its color? The shape or texture of its petals? The flower's delicate fragrance? Perhaps in what stirs within us when we behold it. A rose *is*. We can describe its color in wavelengths. We can analyze its structure, examine its petals under a microscope. And we can extract its perfume. But none of these give us the essence of the rose.

The love that men and women are capable of expressing is much the same. When it is at its finest and most ennobling, their love is physical, emotional, and intellectual. It is whole. It cannot be dissected. If we are to avoid the distortions of mind/body dichotomies, we must explore the varieties of physical expressions of love while not losing sight of the emotional responses, the generosity husband and wife bring to their lovemaking, and the beauty of commitment to a relationship which is repeatedly bonded and renewed in their sexual encounters.

We asked husbands and wives to describe a good lover. The majority of both sexes, understandably, talked of what a man might do to give pleasure to a woman. None described a lover in terms of what a woman might give to her man. The title "lover," by common usage, is masculine. And this is indeed unfortunate. It helps perpetuate the attitude that man is the aggressor in lovemaking, the partner charged with the responsibility for the sexual overtures. Woman is the recipient. It is a chauvinistic attitude for which both sexes pay a price. The attributes and actions of a lover are essentially no different for women than for men. We are all potential lovers.

Loving doesn't start with the one loved, it starts with the one loving.

To be worthy of the title *lover*, one must *love*—freely, unconditionally. With awareness and sensitivity. The ability can be found only in the mature (what some have called "self-actualized") man or woman. To grasp the nature of this relationship, we must understand what loving is *not*. Not some basic emotion or desire for sexual gratification or possession. Not dependency. Not a reaction. Not egocentric. Not sacrificial.

We love through our actions, not our reactions. The young woman who said, "Love is when a man makes me feel special" is setting herself up for frustration. She is seeking ego satisfaction while calling it love.

Sexual loving is giving, yet it is not sacrificial. It is self-interested, yet not egocentric. It is the adult in each of us in the service of the child in each of us. These paradoxes in loving make it the challenge it is. In loving, as Masters and Johnson so succinctly put it, one must "give to get." This is not easily understood. Many of our couples initially misinterpreted it. They saw it either as self-sacrifice or bartering ("I'll do this for you in anticipation that you will do that for me"). Some even interpreted it as "giving in," a capitulation for the sake of some unspecified payoff.

"What's in it for me?" is so much a part of the thinking of most of us, it is little wonder we are confused when faced with the proposition that giving is its own reward. As children we are told it is better to give than to receive, but never *why*. As adults we teach it to our children, perhaps still without knowing why. We may not understand fully the "why" where sex is concerned, yet more than sufficient evidence supports this truth. Example: We polled a number of husbands and wives on their reactions to a variety of sexual acts—strongly arousing, arousing, mildly arousing, not arousing, repugnant. The acts could be divided into those in which the respondent was the actor (caressing her breasts, manually stimulating his penis, giving him/her a backrub) and those in which he or she was the recipient (stimulating *her* clitoris orally, giving *him* a bath). Without going into a detailed analysis of the findings, we can say that, in general, those who were at least as strongly turned on by actions designed to pleasure their spouse as by actions accepted from the spouse, were those individuals of both sexes who reported the greatest sexual satisfaction in their marital relationship. We have questioned whether this might be a reflection of the strength of a person's basic sex drive, and we have concluded it is not the most important factor. Those who were most egocentric in sex were generally egocentric in other areas of their relationship. Those husbands who were turned on by being treated as the passive recipient of the "favors" of the wife, but not aroused by "giving" pleasure to her, were those who proved to be self-centered in other areas of their lives. It seemed to express itself in a gradient: the less the strength of arousal in "giving" sexual pleasure, the greater the overall egocentricity of the individual. And conversely: the stronger the arousal from actions designed to arouse one's partner, the less the overall egocentricity, and the greater the individual's own sexual satisfaction.

The *lover* who can lay claim to the name and the satisfactions of the title is one who is strongly aroused by performance of all those actions intended to arouse and pleasure his/her loved one, as well, of course, as accepting pleasure from the ministrations of the partner. The pleasure —*and arousal*—the lover experiences in "pleasuring" the loved one is not an ego reward (as with the husband who needs reassurance of his manhood: "Did you climax, darling?"). Nor is it solely the pleasure we find in seeing someone we care for made happy. There may be elements of all of these in the lover's arousal and satisfaction, but overriding all else is the pleasure derived from the actions of loving.

To be a good lover, one has to *like* the other sex. To be a *great* lover —physically, emotionally, intellectually, hormonally, romantically, and totally "turned on." It can be argued that this sexual "chemistry" reaction can be separated from loving. And it can, but we would argue with force that the two cannot be separated in the definition of *lover*.

One may, however, have a strong sex drive, a genuine liking for the other sex, a freedom from hangups and fears, and a desire to give the best of oneself to one's lover, yet not qualify as a great lover. There is more. As much as men and women have in common, physically as well as otherwise, there are differences between the sexes as well as between individuals. The man who would be a great lover must understand women, their feelings and sexual responses, and he must learn the particular feelings and responses of his special woman. And a woman, of course, must do likewise where men, and her special man, are concerned. In what will be said in this and the following chapters, the reader should keep in mind that we are speaking in generalities. The statements carry qualifications (whether stated or not): "Most women," "The majority of men," "Many wives enjoy . . . ," "Very few men . . ." The statements may or may not be true for you or for your spouse. Individual differences are a mark of our humanity. Without them, we might be robots or Barbie dolls. We can err as much in overemphasizing individual differences, however, as in giving too much weight to norms. Most of us are pretty much alike in most respects. We like to see ourselves as unique, but if we were each very, very different, we would find relationships almost impossible to establish. It is the similarities between men and women that make marriage work. If the sexes were truly *opposite*, living together would be a running battle. While we prize our "uniqueness," we often, paradoxically, pass judgment on those who do not share our preferences and attitudes. If we have no taste for cauliflower, the person who enjoys cauliflower is "strange." The wife who prefers sex only at night in bed with the lights off may view her husband as "kinky" when he expresses a desire for sex in the afternoon in the woods. There is a danger, therefore, in reporting any norms of behavior and preferences in sex, that readers may use the norms to "prove" the "abnormality" of their spouse. Norms are norms, nothing more. They do not, in themselves, indicate good or bad, healthy or unhealthy. They may be of help in reassuring some people that what they feel or do is not abnormal or perverted. And they may help us learn about the other sex in general, and set a foundation for communication aimed at learning what we need to know to sexually love that one special person.

HIS OVERTURES

Since sexual relations are still most often initiated by the man (and for no other reason, certainly not because we feel this traditional role structuring is desirable), we begin with his initial lovemaking actions.

Ideally, lovemaking doesn't begin at 10:30 in the evening when the couple turn off the television and climb into bed. It starts when they wake up in each other's arms, continues over breakfast coffee, gets a lift when he phones her during the day just to say he is thinking nice thoughts of her, and grows steadily in words and touches throughout the evening. Feeling loved and being made to feel desirable are perhaps the most important factors in the woman's arousal and ultimate fulfillment. So much of sexuality is psychological. And the husband who can keep his wife feeling sexually desirable and very well loved has several points up to support the claim of great lover.

As the sexual stimulus for women (and one frequently slighted by husbands), kissing must be ranked very high. It is one of our first boy-girl sexual acts, expressing affection as well as desire. Most women never lose the thrill of a lover's kiss. It is, then, sad to hear so many women speak of "a typical husband's kiss" with a shrug of boredom. A hurried peck on the cheek is not a lover's kiss. It is, to many wives, even anti-erotic. As we have said, acts of loving should never convey a "contractual message" that says, "I'm in the mood for sex and want to go to bed—now." The husband who kisses his wife passionately only when he wants sexual relations doesn't express a desire for her, only for what service she can provide at the moment. The kiss of lovers should always express desire. It should always say, "I find you exciting and desirable: I love you."

We have never read a good description of the erotic kiss. There are some things which defy words, and we don't claim success where great novelists and poets have failed. Many women, however, have shared their complaints, and perhaps much can be gained from them. Here is a sample:

"*He kisses me too fast. He just grabs me and pushes his tongue into my mouth. I feel choked.*" The lover's kiss should be a seduction, not a rape. It is a homologue of the coital act. The husband who is a lover does not grab his wife and, with no preliminaries, force his penis into her vagina. With his lips and tongue, he *builds* her desire. If the genitals are the organs of sex, the lips, tongue, and hands are the organs of sexual lovemaking. With lips and tongue touching and circling her lips, he coaxes her to part them to admit his tongue. He penetrates and withdraws, arousing her with his "teasing."

"*I find kissing a real turn-on. I like a lot of it, and I like it to last a long time. He kisses me for about twenty seconds, then it's 'let's get at it.'*" Kissing, like all loving, should have a timelessness to it. To hurry it, giving it a "strictly a means to an end" feeling is inexcusable. It tells her he finds no enjoyment in kissing her. It is only something he goes through in order to attain physical release. "What's the rush?" is a question which can frequently be asked.

"*I feel like I'm being slobbered on, or as if he's trying to swallow me whole. He doesn't know how to kiss.*" The erotic kiss is a learned skill. The fact that he has not developed this skill may be owing to her reluctance to instruct him in what she wants, or it could be his fault for not listening—or caring. If the wife wants the greatest arousal and satisfaction in her husband's kisses, she will, with loving concern, tell him what she desires. If he is concerned with pleasuring her, he will try his best to discover her wants. With both motivated to *give* to each other, it becomes solely a matter of communication and practice.

Judging from the expressed desires of most wives, kissing is one thing the lover never abandons in his lovemaking. He may leave it from time to time as he pleasures his spouse in other ways, but he returns to it at each opportunity. The praise of the lover's kiss bestowed in poetry and song is no mere metaphor to loving. The lips and mouth are a primary area of erotic stimulation and response.

As we have said, there seems to be no clear line between sensory pleasure and that which is sexually arousing. For one thing, what might simply feel pleasant to many of us (e.g., a foot massage) could be highly arousing to some. For another, there are subtle differences, both qualitative and quantitative, which can spell the difference. And, of course, how turned on we may be initially is an important variable in predicting how we may respond to a sensory stimulus. With women, the line between pleasurable touching which is not sexually arousing (at least not strongly so) and that which is highly erotic is even harder to draw. Most women said that being held in their lover's arms, stroked, and caressed was very important to them. Most said that it was arousing, at least sometimes, but the degree of sexual arousal did not play a major part in their expressed need. With some who could not find being embraced by their husband arousing in itself, direct sexual stimulation (e.g., clitoris or nipples) was far less arousing if unaccompanied by the "closeness" experienced in being held. The desire to be held, embraced, cuddled (all terms used by wives) is probably as close as we can come to a unanimous desire expressed by the women interviewed. It is also one of the most often reported frustrations when it is lacking. Before marriage, most couples spend as much time as they can steal kissing and embracing—in automobiles, theaters, doorways, and elsewhere. Husbands admit they enjoyed it then, but may have slacked off since marrying. The main reason may be the suppression of our need for physical intimacy and the masculine, nonromantic role so well conditioned in most males. Whatever the explanation, men who hold back from embracing are missing much. So are their wives.

In the classic marriage manuals, actions designed to arouse one's partner to readiness (and, hopefully, eagerness) for sexual intercourse were called *foreplay*. We strongly object to what it implies. As it was generally described, *foreplay* was strictly a technique of preparation—a means toward the end. It wasn't lovemaking, which is its own reward. Rather, it was closer to a warm-up period in sports, which has as its only rationale the game to follow. Our other objection is to the roles it assigns to the sexes. Foreplay is something a man *does to* a woman to "ready" her for intercourse. He is active, she remains passive. He stimu-

SEXUAL LOVING 125

lates, she responds. Since in the views of the writers of these how-to-do-it books, women are slow to respond while men are almost always aroused on a moment's notice, the wife has no reason to do anything to arouse and pleasure the husband. Typically, the books inform the husband of the "primary erogenous areas" of a woman's body (e.g., the nipples, clitoris, and external third of the vagina), and a list of less generally agreed "secondary erogenous areas" (e.g., throat, nape of the neck, buttocks, inner thighs, abdomen, small of the back, earlobes). One such text even included a drawing, front and back, of the nude female with the erogenous areas designated in shading! It looked like patches of some horrible skin disease. Worse than that, it was very misleading. In response to this long list of "turn-on" areas, we found ourselves asking, "For *what* woman, under *what* conditions, *when,* and *by whom?*"

To say, "A woman responds to stimulation of her earlobes" is ridiculous. First of all, there are sense receptors covering the entire surface of the body, including the earlobes. Some transmit stimuli of cold, some heat, some pain, and some touch. What type of stimulation arouses a woman? The answer, of course, is that only that woman can say. One woman may find her husband's earlobe nibbling a bore. Another may be driven frantic with its tickling. Still another may find it turns her off. And there are undoubtedly some who find it mildly to highly arousing. No man makes love to a statistical average. He makes love to a particular woman. And it is that woman he must look to for his answers. Nothing beats verbal communication in this as in other areas when we are attempting to learn how best to love, but this is one area in which talking is not enough. She may not be able to tell him ahead of time what she likes and dislikes. Even if she remembers that when a former lover stroked her thighs it drove her wild with passion, she might wisely judge it would not be discreet to share this knowledge with her spouse. Besides, it probably would not communicate exactly what and how this previous lover did it. Was it a light or heavy touch, rapid or slow? She can only suggest, either in words or by taking his hand and placing it where she wants it, that he stimulate her thighs. She then can help him by her encouragement and/or further requests ("Will you do it a little lighter, and up a bit higher?"). Said with loving concern, not critically, her husband is not apt to feel he has failed or that he is being "ordered about."

Probably every man thinks of a woman's breasts and genital area when he thinks of where to touch her sexually—to arouse and be aroused. From early adolescence, he has been instructed in the locker room that those are the "hot spots" on a girl's body. Stroke, rub, squeeze, or insert your fingers *there* and the girl—any girl—will passionately surrender. After a series of panting sessions in parked cars, most males become virtually conditioned to this one-two approach. But they don't deserve the criticism heaped on them by so many women. They were taught the approach, and no woman has taken the time and effort to correct the situation. Like so many other things we learn about ourselves and others, there is enough truth in what a boy is taught about the sexual anatomy of a woman to perpetuate the misinformation from one generation of adolescents to the next. It is true that the average woman, with a man who turns her on as a person (and not just in what he does physically), at a time and place when she is generally responsive, is capable of becoming highly aroused by appropriate and sufficient stimulation of her nipples and/or clitoris. Obviously, the husband who is to make use of such a highly qualified statement must learn much about the special woman he hopes to love well. Lovemaking is an art which can only be developed through practice—and negative and positive feedback. Just as a deaf mute cannot develop skill on the violin because he is incapable of hearing the tones he produces, and a blind painter cannot develop his technique with the brush since he cannot see the canvas, so a husband who aspires to become a great lover must continually seek and rely upon feedback as he practices his art. He must stay tuned in to her desires.

If there are two general rules that bear repetition and emphasis, they are the following: (1) *Never hurry your lovemaking.* (2) *At all times, in words and actions, strive to communicate your desire to give pleasure to her.*

You can be sure no woman ever invented the "quickie" in sex. Even in those rather rare times when she virtually tears the clothes off her lover as he walks in the door, her arousal began some time before. She may have had it on her mind from the time he left that morning for the office, or it may have started when he phoned in the afternoon and told her how much he missed her and of how he wanted her. It may even have been triggered by an erotic story she read while she had her afternoon coffee. It is not that women are slow to arouse, only that unless a woman is so highly aroused she is willing to forego the pleasure of prolonged lovemaking in order to get sexual release as quickly as possible, she will try to make the lovemaking last. Like a gourmet, she savors each subtle flavor of sensuality in an artful timelessness. Her lover expands and enriches the experience. And of such hours, memories are built.

As he makes love to his wife's body, the lover *plans* his actions. The word *plans* may give the impression of a cold, calculated series of moves designed to attain some desired response. This is not the intended meaning. Loving is never cold. Nor is it exploitive. The planning in lovemaking is goal-directed toward ever increasing the sexual pleasure of one's spouse. Her initial sexual response may be to his kiss or the touch of his hand, or even to a word he whispers. A positive response is twofold: the pleasurable feelings of arousal, *and* the desire for *more* stimulation. As her sexual excitement increases, more areas of her body become responsive. When fully aroused, it would not be a great exaggeration to say that her total skin surface has become erogenous. As he moves his hands and lips over her body, the lover plans his moves to respond to the longings she expresses for his further touches. He follows her developing desires; he doesn't attempt to force them. While we feel the word is poorly chosen, this should be what is meant when we speak of a lover "teasing" his loved one in lovemaking. As he moves his lips and hands over her body, he leaves her always wanting more—not in frustration, but in yearning. In his caresses, he entices her responses, building the physical appetite within her.

One of our findings which may surprise many husbands is that the wives interviewed almost unanimously admitted finding themselves strongly aroused when their lovers made a "sensual ritual" of disrobing them. Where the kisses and caresses started while the partners were both clothed, even if the wife was covered by only the sheerest negligee, the subsequent lovemaking actions were enhanced. Here is the description given by one woman:

> I walked into the bedroom just ahead of him. We had just returned from a movie—and incidentally, it wasn't one of those sex films which send you home ready to make it in the entry hall; it had been just a fun, kind of romantic, evening. He took my arm and turned me around toward him. It may sound silly, but it was like something out of one of those old romantic movies. You know, where "their eyes met, and then their lips." Instead of putting his arms around me right away, he took my face in his hands and kissed me ever so lightly; his lips brushed mine like a feather. I'm not kidding. It was pure fairy-tale romance. Then he ran his fingertips through my hair at the temples. Maybe you'll say the

scalp isn't a turn-on area of the body, but believe me, it was for me that night. About then, I expected him to say, 'Let's get our clothes off,' but he didn't. I was wearing a high necked, long-sleeved, dress, and would you believe it, he began moving his fingertips over my shoulders and arms very slowly and lightly. It was like being on a first date. You know, very tentative. You don't expect to get goose bumps from that sort of thing after you're married, but I sure felt chills up and down my spine. He was like a handsome stranger who had fallen passionately in love with me. His hands were fantastic. Slowly down my back, then up the outside of my thighs. He didn't try to touch my breasts. Not then, although by that time I wanted it more than anything. I wanted our clothes off, and I wanted to be touched all over, and to touch him. I don't know how long he kept it up. Maybe five minutes, although it seemed like hours. Then you know what he did? He unzipped my dress. My God, I couldn't believe it! I never would have thought just having my zipper pulled down could have made me that aroused, but it did—and how! I swear it took twenty minutes to get that zipper all the way down to my hips. Why it was such a turn-on I don't know. But it was. And how! It was like a movie in slow motion. Every inch that zipper went down got me more and more aroused. And it didn't stop there. He undressed me in a way every woman deserves to be undressed at least once in her life. It was only later he started doing things you might expect him to do to arouse me, and by that time, I was so hot I could have raped him ten times in a row.

Lovemaking does not have to start with clothes on. There are no hard-and-fast rules. It depends entirely on the circumstances, one's partner, and the mood of both. But the prolonging of the loving which results is, in the evaluation of most wives interviewed, a decided plus. It builds response potential to its ultimate.

Lovemaking which creates an anticipation for the next step in arousal gives support to the proposition that the most important sexual organ is the brain. Nothing else would explain why the descent of a zipper would be an erotic stimulus. In a recent movie, the male lead says, "Love is in the erection, not the climax." It is a truth we believe is better understood by women than men. To a woman, satisfaction in lovemaking is like they used to advertise in the tour brochures: "Getting there is half the fun." Men, on the other hand, too often act as if the "destination" is the only thing that counts. In an effort to be the ultimate lover, the husband will try to become tuned to what his wife's mental turn-ons are. And if they include a slow unzipping of a dress, he will develop the skill. He may not be able to identify with her feelings, but he will accept them.

Three modes in lovemaking most frequently desired by wives interviewed were: slower pace, prolonged foreplay, lighter touch. When their husbands were independently interviewed, most of them, interestingly, were not aware of these desires. Furthermore, the majority felt they spent more than sufficient time in "foreplay," at a very slow pace, and with a very light touch. This establishes once again how *relative* words can block communication. How slow is slow? How light is light? We do not feel we can give an answer. Minutes, seconds, or other units of time are inadequate. When making love, who watches the clock? Who measures the intensity of a touch? There is only one sure answer: The one being pleasured is the only one qualified to evaluate the quality of the pleasuring. She has to let him know. And he may have to ask her to let him know. Words are seldom of much help, however, since what she means by "touch me lighter" and what he interprets it to mean may be very dissimilar. It is in her self-interest to show him, both with her own hands caressing herself and by guiding his hands, what will give her pleasure. It is also up to her to let him know what she means when she says she would like him to spend more time in lovemaking. We found many husbands who echoed the complaint of one who said, "There is no satisfying her. No matter how long I spend caressing and kissing her, it is never enough." When we spoke with their wives, we found the complaints were often unjustified. Obviously, if the wife is sexually unresponsive to her husband, bitter and hostile, no amount of lovemaking will arouse her. Many wives we interviewed, however, were responsive, and it was precisely *because* they were responsive that they desired more prolonged lovemaking. They were in no hurry to have something so enjoyable come to an end. The husbands felt that ten to twenty minutes of such "preliminary" lovemaking was more than "sufficient." Many wives said they desired a half hour or more of just touching and being touched—all over—with lips, tongue, and hands before coitus, not simply to arouse them sufficiently for orgasmic coitus, but because of the intense pleasure they experience and wish to prolong. The consensus was that they preferred a long, sustained period of lovemaking in which they could reach a high plateau of arousal and remain there while the lovemaking continued, rather than being brought to the peak of climax as quickly as possible. Since many women can reach orgasm more than once during lovemaking, and an orgasm during precoital lovemaking seldom precludes another during coitus, many husbands could not understand why a woman might prefer *not* to be brought rapidly to orgasm. (The men found this capacity for multiple orgasm highly enviable; we so often envy the other sex what we don't have but mistakenly view as desirable from the perspective of our own sexual nature.)

When the man's lovemaking progresses to include what for the majority of women are the most erogenous parts of the female body, the "teasing" of approach-withdraw, approach-withdraw becomes even more important. He brings her level of arousal up to a high point, then stops and briefly backs off. This may be repeated a number of times. When he first touches her breasts with his fingertips or lips, he doesn't go at once to the nipples. He may run a fingertip lightly over the underside of her breast, or brush his lip and tongue between the breasts. His touches increase her desire for him to go further, to stimulate the nipples. With each action, he leaves her wanting more. He circles her areola with a fingertip or the tip of his tongue, but still doesn't go to the nipple. It's not that he is trying to frustrate her. Delaying and holding back is, especially to women, a means of increasing pleasure. It is the *making* of love. Men might do well to think of it as a symphony. It has delicate, barely audible phrases played perhaps by a single cello, and it has shattering fortissimos with screaming brass and exploding tympani. It rises and falls in crescendos and diminuendos numerous times; it doesn't hold at one pitch and volume; that would be boring. Nor does it leap from the introductory bars to the climax of the final movement.

In making love to her nipples and clitoris, the husband can time his pauses to her response. When he sees signs of her arousal rapidly approaching a peak, he stops what he is doing long enough to permit her tension to subside, making love during the pause by kisses and caresses to less erogenous parts of her body. Throughout the lovemaking, communication remains important. She is the only one who knows what she is feeling and desiring *at that moment*. The couple may have made love hundreds of times in the past, but we humans have variable moods. Our feelings and desires vary from time to time. Hence, we are limited in how much we can rely on prior experiences. We found that many wives were reluctant to express their desires out of vague feelings of embarrassment or fear of not appearing "feminine," yet they expected their husbands to somehow intuitively know what they wanted in lovemaking. There is only one answer to such a wife: It's up to *you*. This seems especially true where intensity of his touches are concerned. Most women prefer a much lighter touch than men do. The husband, understandably, caresses his wife as he likes to be caressed by her. She in turn caresses him as she enjoys being caressed. Consequently, his touches might be too "rough" and/or heavy. Her touches so light they tickle. The answers are found only in recognizing that sauce for the goose is *not* necessarily sauce for the gander. They can then demonstrate to each other exactly the type of touches they most enjoy. She can, for example, demonstrate how she touches her clitoris when she stimulates herself. Then, if he is an attentive lover, he will make an effort to closely copy her example.

A husband becomes a great lover *not* through the development of a variety of physical techniques. The techniques are employed *because* he loves her; they are not, in themselves, the totality of loving. In his sexual loving, he *cherishes* her body. There might be other words, perhaps better ones, to describe it, but the word *cherish*, a word we said on our wedding day, seems to best define the essence of true lovemaking. We cherish—protect and care for—that which we *value*. Through each touch, each caress, each kiss, he communicates, "I value your body, I value you."

HER OVERTURES

The art of lovemaking is not taught in our schools and universities, but if it were, we doubt that classes would be offered to both sexes. Girls would be excluded, victims of sex-role discrimination. It is an art expected of men, but not quite proper for women. In light of the scores of best-selling books on sex—several authored by women—we were surprised to discover a general persistence of the attitude that the husband is the initiator and aggressor in sexual love, the wife is the recipient, "seduced" into surrender. As he pleasures her, she "responds" by permitting him to pleasure her further. The erroneous dictum, "Men are aggressive, women are passive" is apparently still with us. When asked what they would like most in their lovemaking that they were currently not experiencing as much as they desired, the greatest number of husbands answered, "I would like my wife to initiate sex more often."

With most of the couples, the wife made the overtures less than one time in fifteen.

It goes further than that, however. The majority of wives not only admitted they seldom initiated lovemaking, they also admitted they only infrequently shared equally in precoital lovemaking actions. The usual role was, as one wife put it, "to lie back and enjoy it." This is the role they were taught, and learned well, from the time they first started dating. And it is the role most husbands more or less accepted. A dozen or more articles have appeared in women's magazines in the past two or three years asking if men are turned off, or even made impotent, by aggressive, liberated women. The answer given by our couples was a very qualified, "It depends upon what you mean by aggressive." And, of course, it does. The "aggressive," demanding and uncaring husband is also not likely to succeed in turning on his wife (unless she is a masochist).

The many husbands who longed to have their wives initiate sex more frequently were certainly not seeking a female rapist, only a wife who shows she enjoys making love, that she has feelings of sexual arousal when he is around, that she is not reluctant to express them. The socially conditioned inequality in sex roles which keeps so many women from initiating lovemaking cheats both sexes, but we suspect it is women who lose the most. Since the individuals of both sexes who appeared to us to consistently experience the greatest satisfaction in their sexual relations were those who reported strong arousal when caressing and otherwise stimulating their spouse, women who maintain the passive-recipient role in lovemaking can be expected to stand less chance of total sexual fulfillment.

"How will he see me if I'm the one who makes the overtures? And how will I see myself?" In varying degrees, these two questions have disturbed the majority of wives, and understandably so if we consider the often conflicting "messages" conveyed back and forth between the sexes. Girls are taught that boys like girls who are "feminine," and that femininity is displayed by modesty in dress and actions, by unquestioning acceptance of the leadership and natural superiority of the male, and by a childlike naiveté in all matters sexual. She is taught to be a "sweet little girl." And little girls don't know anything about sex, do they? Certainly "nice" girls don't. At the same time, she is learning how to convey sexual desirability, even a subtle seductiveness, to elicit sexual overtures from boys, all the time appearing unaware of the effect her actions are having on the object of her attentions. She might spend hours talking about sex with her girlfriend, but on a date she would seem to have never had any such thoughts in her life. A girl who talked about such things with boys or who openly showed she was interested was "cheap." She wasn't the type a man would marry, at least not the *right* kind of man.

The majority of husbands expressed attitudes which supported these views. Male chauvinism came through stronger in this area than in all others. Most husbands saw themselves as more sophisticated and sexually dominant than their wives. And as the "natural" sexual aggressors. There is, therefore, an obvious contradiction in their expressed desires for sexual advances by the wife. If the wife is to make the overtures to sexual relations, she must feel secure, confident she will not be rejected or scorned by her husband, or seen as lacking in femininity. It is up to the husband to convince her he no longer subscribes to the sex-role stereotypes, and that he sees her as embodying all that is best in womanhood when she shows by her words and actions that sexual love is important to her.

The mature woman is *sexual*. She enjoys her frequent feelings of sexual arousal, and she is not at all embarrassed to admit to them. She is not ashamed of her sexual thoughts and fantasies; she welcomes them as a normal part of her everyday thoughts. She likes her body, the things she can do with it, and the response she enjoys when her lover does things to it. She approaches lovemaking with joyous anticipation. In her view, sex is good—*very* good when it is loving. She is not reluctant to verbalize her desires or to take the initiative in lovemaking. In doing so, however, she proceeds with caution. What she knows is what every woman knows: A physically normal woman can have sexual intercourse at any time; a man can have intercourse only when he has an erection. And she is aware that his erection is not "willed," nor can it be demanded.

It is this accepted fact which lies at the core of the uneasiness some, but not all, men feel when sexual overtures are made by their wives. If the husband feels his wife is making a demand which he must meet at the risk of appearing unmanly, he may react defensively. Several popular women's magazines have run articles recently proclaiming, in the name of equality of the sexes, the *right* of women to *demand* sexual performance from their men. This may seem equitable, but we cannot change our psychobiology: A penis cannot become erect on demand— no matter how much a man may desire it. Contrary to what some wives

believe, husbands do not fail to attain erection as a conscious choice in
an attempt to spite their wives. A man may be emotionally aroused, but
physically unresponsive. As a lover, therefore, the wife attempts to
be aware of her husband's emotional and physical state whenever she
is in the mood for lovemaking. And if he is not in the mood for sexual
love, she knows what every woman who loves a man knows: that love
is not a one-night (or one-day) thing. If not now, then another time.
And as far as suffering frustrations? She knows lovemaking offers
many varieties leading to satisfaction. They don't all require an erect
penis.

How the wife makes her desires known will depend on what she has
learned to be effective in arousing her husband—and the means she has
found to communicate her feelings. "I didn't know *that* was what she
had in mind" is a not uncommon plea of husbands. The wife may drop
hints ("Don't you think it's time to go to bed?") or play a flirtation
game reminiscent of first dates, but the cues are often far from obvious,
and such cues are frequently missed.

Most husbands said they preferred hearing direct "I want . . ." statements in sex as in other matters (but only so long as they didn't sound
like demands). Subtlety, it seems, is not the male forte. Many wives, on
the other hand, told us they felt uncomfortable being verbally direct.
Some felt it was unfeminine; others feared being demanding; and still
others feared possible rejection. These problems were resolved when
spouses worked out their communication, agreeing upon ways they
might express desires with security. One couple agreed to the coded
message, "Remember the evenings in Nassau?" as the wife's means of
expressing her desire for lovemaking. We personally believe greater
candor—"saying it like it is"—is preferable, but if it works well for
them, fine.

Since what a husband looks for are signs of his wife's arousal, the
wife who shows a desire to make love to her husband, rather than a
strictly self-centered desire to be made love to, meets with the greatest
success in her approaches. "I'd like to give you a long, slow, sexy bath."
"Let me tell you how I would like to make love to you tonight." "I
want you very much; may I undress you?" These tell him she wants to
give pleasure because it pleasures *her*. "I want you to make love to me,"
says something quite different.

To say that men are basically voyeuristic while women are basically
exhibitionistic is too broad a generalization, although it has been
repeated by many sexologists. Judging from the popularity of the cen-

terfolds in the men's magazines, we can say that the majority of men enjoy looking at the nude female body of a certain age and attractiveness. Until some women's magazines started running photographs of athletic men in the nude, it might have been easier to cling to the other half of the generalization. No longer. We now know that women also can be turned on by looking. And some men, we have found, thoroughly enjoy posing nude for their wives, and seeing the pleasure it elicits. It is true, however, that the sexes differ in the conditioning they undergo in childhood. Girls are taught to "show off" for boys. Boys are taught to girl-watch. (Until recently, few girls would admit they boy-watch.) As a result, most men are more responsive than their wives to visual stimuli. Knowing this, a wife can use it to her advantage in making overtures. She can, in a word, display her body to her husband to show her desire, and arouse his. Every woman knows how to dress—and undress—provocatively, if she will only admit it. Most women have wardrobes of "erotic" clothing—a sheer negligée, bikini panties, a form-fitting dress he likes—which they learn to slip on when they want to communicate arousal. The woman who loves and desires her husband has also studied her makeup and hair style with an eye to sexual appeal. In her movements and voice—in the total image she projects—she strives to communicate the message, "I want to make love to you." This isn't something she turns on only at those times when she is aroused and in the mood. She may increase it at those times, but just as lovemaking doesn't start when the lights are turned off, but is going on in their words and touches throughout the day, her communication of desire is present at all times when they are together.

Very few husbands interviewed said they enjoyed a "cute," teasing approach on the part of the wife. It seems that nibbling a husband's earlobe while he reads the paper, or running fingertips over the nape of his neck, are not arousing to the majority of men. The coy little girl jumping up on Daddy's lap mussing his hair is not a sexy image. As with verbal expressions of desire, most men prefer somewhat more direct physical approaches by their wives. Stroking and kissing should not be seen as a man's way of loving a woman but not a woman's way of loving a man. Many women interviewed assumed there was no "necessity" for them to make love to their husbands. If he had an erection, they felt, there was no reason to further arouse him: he was already "ready." It is a narrow view of both men and lovemaking, as lacking in humanity and the meaning of sexual *love* as the concept of "foreplay," defined as the actions a man goes through to arouse his wife to the point of readiness for intercourse. Unless the husband is experiencing difficulty achieving erection, or is simply not aroused initially, the wife does not make love to her husband's body to get him "ready," but because she thoroughly enjoys it. She finds it highly arousing, and she finds joy in his obvious enjoyment.

Most men could not identify any strong erogenous areas on their bodies other than their genitals and anus, at least none comparable to, say, the female thighs. This point is generally noted in marriage manuals. Unfortunately, many wives have the impression that there is nothing arousing to men in caresses and kisses (except those to the penis). They refrain from doing what they believe their husbands don't desire. The husbands interviewed, however, unanimously admitted to feeling erotic pleasure in being touched, caressed, and kissed over most areas of their bodies. The finding was hardly a surprise: Massage parlors enjoy great popularity.

The touches a husband may find most arousing will no doubt vary from one time of lovemaking to the next, just as they will vary from one man to the next. The intelligent, loving woman will do her best to discover what actions will be most effective in pleasuring her man *at the moment*. In general, however, most men prefer a firmer, stronger touch than do the majority of women. Japanese massage girls pleasure male customers by walking barefoot up and down their spine. It may not be a common sensual diversion, but in any case, we have not heard of it being preferred by women. In touch as in words, most women prefer their men to "try a little tenderness." Most men find a very light touch more annoying than arousing. What is gentle and what is firm, fast or slow, however, cannot be put into words. Try it. Then ask. Then adapt.

The tendency of many men to hurry things in lovemaking results, as every woman knows, in less than the most fulfilling sexual experiences for their wives. But more than that, the men cheat themselves. They miss the opportunity to fully develop their sensual and sexual responsiveness. The majority of wives interviewed said their husbands lacked "patience" when it came to accepting caresses. Typically, the husband would "tolerate" only a minute or two of his wife's caresses to a nongenital area, then, with a "let's get down to business" attitude expressed either in words or by guiding her hand, he let her know he wanted penile stimulation (followed almost at once by coitus). He might have found pleasure in her caresses had he permitted them in a *timeless* loving. But in denying himself, he lost. He lost the sensory enhancement which might come had he permitted her to pleasure him over his thighs, back, nipples, and, yes, even feet. The male nipples are an interesting example. We all accept the fact that the nipples of the adult woman are (in most women) highly erotogenic, yet it is seldom suggested that this may also be true, or potentially so, in men. While we know of no studies which have investigated this potential—no attempts, that is, to discover if the male nipples can become highly sensitive to erotic stimulation if exposed to "sensitization" by a sexual partner—there is at least anecdotal evidence that this may be so. Certainly we know our responses, both negative and positive, are often learned or conditioned. We may have a strong aversion to cauliflower, but with repeated exposure we might learn to savor it. There is no reason to suspect that sexual responsiveness should be different. If men can be persuaded to give up the male image which demands a "let's get down to business" approach, and can learn to accept sensory pleasuring from a wide spectrum of tactile stimulation, fulfillment for both sexes might be a more common experience.

Stimulation of the male genitals, manually or orally, is a problem for many wives. Some, of course, suffer from aversive reactions born of their own early training. They are simply turned off to sex and, consequently, to the male sex organs. A greater number, however, are apprehensive. They enjoy touching and otherwise stimulating their husbands' genitals, but fear stimulating beyond the "point of no return"— ejaculation. A number of women told us of reading the words of caution given in a marriage manual: "Since this is intensely arousing to a man, a woman must be careful. More than a slight amount of such stimulation can cause him to 'come.'" Such books have overstated it. While it is, of course, true that sustained stimulation of the sort which is highly arousing (to that particular man) will usually result in ejaculation, unless the husband has a problem with premature ejaculation, there is a considerable amount of stimulation which is not ordinarily ejaculatory. Here, as in so much else, communication is all important. A man must tell a woman when the danger point is approaching, or she may not find out until it is too late. In time, of course, after the couple have made love a number of times, she will learn what she *can* do, and for how long, yet still be on the safe side. Generally speaking, the scrotum, anus, and penis shaft are less responsive than the glans, just as the small of the back is less responsive than the buttocks. Every man, from his experience with self-stimulation (if not with other women) knows what is most stimulating to *him*. And every man can, if he is willing to do so, communicate this to his wife. It is then up to her to make use of the information. Her caresses should follow a pattern of pleasuring her lover's *total* body, including but not concentrating exclusively on, those areas which will bring him to the highest point of arousal. Neither should she avoid them. It is not the length of time she spends in caressing his genitals, but the intensity over time, which will determine how long she can continue before triggering ejaculation. With periodic backing off when the feelings become too intense, she may find she can continue her pleasuring for as long as an hour or more.

One more word should be said in this regard. If, despite everything, ejaculation does occur in response to her caresses when it is not desired by the partners, it is hardly a calamity. Those wives we found to be most sexually responsive (and who were most in love with their husbands) were not in any way distressed or frustrated by such an occurrence. On the contrary, a number of them said they found the experience of watching the ejaculate spurt from the penis an intensely exciting experience. Parenthetically, these wives found seminal fluid —in appearance, texture, odor, taste, and warmth—an erotic stimulus. They did not feel it was "messy" or repulsive. Several, in fact, said they were brought close to orgasm when they felt ejaculate spray over their breasts, abdomen, or face. Moreover, the sexually mature woman knows the love affair never succeeds or fails on the basis of a single experience, and that, in any case, her satisfaction (and orgasm) can be brought about through a variety of means.

In initiating sexual relations, the wife proclaims her equality. She breaks down the division of the sexes. Could it be, then, that the reason so many women are reluctant to make sexual overtures has to do with their reluctance to declare their equality? That they are by nature as responsive and sexually capable as men is a fact which cannot be refuted, but to accept this fact and implement it through their actions with a man calls for an acceptance of vulnerability, an admission that they, as women, desire—crave—sex at least as much, and maybe more, than their husbands. They must then give up a control factor, i.e., the role in which they "bestow" their sexual favors. Once a wife admits she genuinely enjoys and is aroused by the appearance and feel of male genitals, she can no longer take credit for being "loving" in engaging in sexual relations.

At some point in the orchestration of their lovemaking, husband and wife will usually desire to climax their experience in orgasm. (Note: We said climax the experience, not conclude it. Lovemaking should always convey an aura of no beginning/no end.) As we emphasized previously, the goal need not always be orgasm, and orgasm should *never* be the primary goal. Usually, however, the intensity of their mutual arousal makes orgasmic release imperative to the couple. It is not the release of orgasm, however, which is important. It is the quality of love mutually given and received which is paramount. In love, the sexual embrace finds not only its meaning but its greatest sensory pleasure. And in the initiative and giving of sexual love, the wife has both the obligation and the privilege—equal to the husband—of sharing her humanity, her vulnerability, and her sensual satisfactions.

CHAPTER 9

The Coital Bond

If anything comes naturally to man without
any prior learning and experience, it is
not sexual intercourse.

Albert Ellis
The Art and Science of Love

We need so little room, we two . . . thus on a single pillow—
as we move nearer,
nearer heaven—until I burst inside you
                    like a screaming rocket.

Walter Benton
This Is My Beloved

. . . and the two shall become one flesh.

Genesis 2:23–24

*T*he relationship of lovers has not and cannot be explained. If it could be, would it hold its attraction for us? Isn't it, in part, the always new, ever mysterious component which imparts the excitement? It cannot even be adequately described. This mystery has led some to fear—and expose—any explicit description or representation of sexual acts. They fear the mystery may be lost, and human love with it. They are wrong. The astronomer can chart the galaxies, measure the distance to the stars, analyze the composition of the planets, without losing his sense of awe at the majesty of the universe or his belief in a Supreme Being which created it. Sexual acts retain the same ability to inspire awe in lovers who are free from fear and ignorance.

In the coital act, sex presents its greatest mystery. We can explain the physiology of the act and its reproductive function, yet we can never understand what it is that happens in that union of lovers. They *become one.* Yet he cannot know what she feels. He can never comprehend or identify with it. He is a man, and she is a woman. In a paradoxical way, they are never so far apart as when they are physically closest. Many writers have described coitus as a paridigm of battle in which man is the victor, woman the vanquished. At the same time, it is an act of love. It is egocentric, yet selfless.

Ideally, the husband enters the wife when the sex drive of both is near its peak. Not so close as to bring an orgasm before it is desired by both, but certainly at a height. And at this intensity, sexual actions become very self-centered. They are imperative. His overwhelming desire is to penetrate her fully. Her desire is to be penetrated. At that moment each becomes an almost totally *sensual* being. Nearly all sensations are concentrated in—or related to—the aroused genitals. We may not, as Thomas Aquinas, philosopher of the Middle Ages, asserted, lose our faculty of reason, but in the flood of sexual sensations we tend to shut out everything else. Even what would be uncomfortable or painful under other circumstances goes unnoticed in those seconds. It becomes, then, doubly difficult to remain aware of one's partner and his/her feelings and desires. We might say there is a psychosexually induced egocentricity during coitus which may give rise to much misunderstanding. Many women (and some men) told us they felt "used" in sexual intercourse. "He seems interested only in his own satisfaction" was a fairly common complaint. It is a complaint which in part only verbalizes what is normal in both sexes. The woman who said, "When he enters me, all that exists for me is that penis. It isn't lovemaking. It isn't even him. It's just that first glorious stroke of a penis," was simply reporting with honesty the sensations of a sexually mature woman. Or man. They may both, to a degree, strive to increase one another's pleasure during coitus, but the concern and awareness which were dominant during the preceding lovemaking give way, in large part, to the imperious demands of self-satisfaction.

There is only one answer to the question, When does the couple proceed from other acts of lovemaking to coitus? When both strongly desire it. Mutual arousal to the heights makes this a very natural transition. It is not something demanded by the husband, or a compliance by the wife. And it should never become merely the final step in a routine. Boredom, as we have said, is the ever-lurking cancer threatening sexual love. Because of what in many women is a greater variability in state of arousal from one time of lovemaking to another (although this is *not* an indication that women are biologically "slower to respond," as claimed by so many popular sexologists), it is generally up to the woman to signal when she is ready to be entered. Despite signs of "readiness"—vaginal secretion, body movements, panting, moans, or whatever—there is no way the man can be certain the woman is experiencing a strong physical demand to be entered unless she tells him. If she does not communicate her physical readiness and desire to be entered, she is asking him to read her mind—and no amount of awareness, concern, or experience give either spouse this ability. He cannot *see* her feelings and desires. Only she can know her sensations. She has the responsibility to communicate them. How she does so is not important. It may be done by a variety of means—verbal or nonverbal, direct or indirect. The only requirement is that it be clear, unambiguous. Lovers, in time, develop their own "language of love." The wife may tell him in words she is ready to receive his penis. She may tell him by taking his penis in her hand and guiding it toward the entrance of her vagina. She might even do it by a code word or a facial expression. It isn't a matter of *how* she does it, but *how well.* Every husband and wife should, however, be aware of the ambiguity inherent in "subtle" messages. Ambiguous messages can be misunderstood, and they can wound deeply. Especially in sex. The wife who feels reticent to clearly express her desires should recognize the price she may pay in not doing so. She cannot, in justice, blame her husband ("If he loved me, he would know . . ."). If both husband and wife have worked to develop the *individual* freedom to express their desires and feelings (tempered always with awareness and concern for one's lover), they will then develop a mutually satisfactory *method* of doing so. Then, and only then, will they initiate coitus.

Whether it is the wedding night or a Wednesday evening after a hard-day-at-the-office and a hectic-afternoon-with-the-kids in the twelfth year of marriage, the sexual union should always have a for-the-first-time feeling. But that statement, we feel, should be clarified. Let's take a look at what our society says about the initial experience, the "loss of virginity." First of all, virginity is not something which is "lost." It is nothing more than a state of *not* having experienced sexual relations. It is a negative condition, a non-occurrence of an event. What more can be said of it? It is the consummation of the relationship which has meaning. The first time and the thousandth time should carry the same meaning: *Love is new; love is alive; love is life.* When we say that the sexual union should always have a *for-the-first-time* feeling, we are not, in any way, implying a fearful, inhibited, sacrificial role-playing by either or both lovers. What we are emphasizing is the *romantic,* the exciting, new, *tingling-with-apprehension-and-anticipation* feeling which makes loving a *young* and *vital* experience—*each time.* The wife (and husband) who loves in a total way, loves in an *impractical*—foolish—way. *Lovers* are not "sensible," as nonlovers would define "sensible." They walk in the rain (disregarding pneumonia), make love on a beach (risking public disgrace), and pleasure each other for hours (ignoring the lateness of the hour). The consummation of the love relationship is not a one-time occurrence. With lovers, it occurs each and every time. Each day is a brand-new day in their love affair. When he enters her, plunges his penis deep within her vagina, it should be a "first night."

How an act which they have performed perhaps thousands of times is kept ever new is the greatest of challenges to the love of a couple. Yet it is not impossible. One husband expressed it rather well, we think, when he said, "I have seldom gone to bed with the same woman two nights in a row. She is always someone new. One night she may be the sophisticated call girl, the next she may play harem girl, and the next she may come on like an Oriental princess. The only roles she doesn't play—and let me say, 'Thank God'—are those of housewife, mother, and companion." We doubt that his wife went so far as to maintain a wardrobe of costumes for her various roles. She simply did not want to become boring, and she knew that talk about kids, house, and neighbors each night was not likely to keep love new and exciting. And needless to say, the same goes for her husband. Romance always carries with it an element of surprise. It always has in it that tingling, slightly apprehensive feeling of "What next?" It is never, in other words, an entirely "comfortable" feeling. To be comfortable, it would have to be predictable, and to be consistently predictable, it would have to be routine. And nothing which is routine is ever romantic, whether it be the vacation spot, the Valentine's gift, or the way in which a couple make love. Not even the locale.

Coitus can be accomplished in any of several postural positions. Some Eastern texts describe scores of positions in words which tax the imagination when it comes to trying to put the descriptions into action. It strikes us, however, that most of these are somewhat like cookbooks which give recipes for chocolate cake in a ten-inch pan, chocolate cake in an eight-inch pan, chocolate cake with white frosting, chocolate cake with chocolate frosting, and chocolate cake without frosting. All are recipes for chocolate cake. The rest are merely theme and variations. In coitus, the nature of the act and the mechanics of the body permit only a few major variations. The gymnasts among us may be able to expand on these basics to some extent, but even the most nimble have their limitations, and it is doubtful that their pleasure is increased in proportion to their agility. Husbands and wives with a strong sex drive and a lack of crippling inhibitions, do in time explore a variety of acts and positions, generally settling on one or two which are mutually most satisfying, but without discarding the others. If their session of lovemaking is lengthy, they may try several different positions before reaching their final climax in the position most preferred. Other couples, those who find sexual relations less fulfilling, may fall into one behavioral extreme or another. Some may continually search for a new, more exciting position. For them, it is not merely the fun of occasional variety; it is a quest for what they unconsciously feel is missing. The latest sex manual promising a dozen new and different ways to make love will be eagerly devoured and systematically applied, one positional variation after another. Although they still fail to find that "ultimate" position or act, it does not deter them from purchasing the next sex manual to hit the bookstores.

Couples who fall into the other extreme avoid any variety. For them, sex is bounded by rules of what is and what is not right and normal. While not, perhaps, admitting it, they generally fear any deviation from what they believe to be "normal." "If you enjoy sex, I don't see why you have to try all those other positions" is their usual argument. But unless they are arguing against the other extremists—the "variationists"—they are arguing with a straw man.

Couples who fully enjoy lovemaking never claim they *have to* try a wide variety of acts and positions. One could eat the same foods every day and, as long as the diet was balanced, there would be no reason, nutritionally, to introduce variety into the menu. Even with the most savory dishes, however, how long would it take most of us to become bored (and the food tasteless) if we were compelled to eat the same dishes day after day?

The words "normal" and "abnormal" have no place in any discussion of coital positions. Any posture the partners assume which permits penile entrance is "normal." Unless we use the word "normal" to mean the "norm" or average, the position most commonly assumed by over 50 per cent of the population, the concept of normality is meaningless. And why should any couple be concerned with the average behavior of their neighbors? Those statistics may be of interest to sociologists and sexual demographers, but what have they to do with a man and woman in love?

The most frequently preferred position for intercourse in Western culture is the so-called "missionary position," so named because, supposedly, natives of some Pacific islands had never engaged in such a position until they played Peeping Tom on the white missionary and his wife. In this position, the wife lies supine—on her back; the husband lies in a face-to-face position, his legs generally between hers (although once he has entered, he may move his legs outside of hers so that she can draw her thighs tightly together to increase the tightness and friction). In this position there is, of course, physical contact over the length of their bodies. Their faces are close together; they are able to kiss, and even to express their feelings in words, with the added communication of eye contact. Also, if the husband does not lie on the wife in a way which totally pins her down, both are able to move in various ways to increase their pleasure.

There are psychological as well as physical dimensions of the relationship which are touched on in the choice of position. The preference of one or another position often has meaning and communicates how husband and wife interact in their total relationship (although neither may be conscious of it). In our age of psychological sophistication, we can, however, become self-conscious about what we may or may not be communicating. Is the husband, by his physically superior position in lying atop his wife, expressing a desire to dominate her? If she prefers the position, is she expressing submission or feelings of inferiority? And if this is the position they most often enjoy, is it evidence that they are locked in to conventionality? As an inhibiting force in society, it would seem that psychologizing is fast replacing puritanism. Perhaps some of all of these meanings are buried somewhere in their actions. Perhaps there are other, even opposite, meanings. If their sexual actions are mutually satisfying, what difference should it make?

We sometimes get the impression that many how-to books on sex are written for people who never intend to have sexual relations, or for those who plan to engage in lovemaking once and only once and, therefore, want to be sure it will be the best possible *once-in-a-lifetime* experience. The author describes each act in detail, then goes on to inform the reader of what he/she may or may not enjoy in each act, rather than saying, "Try this, you may like it; and if it isn't your preference, well, try something else." Albert Ellis, for example, in *The Art and Science of Love,* after describing the *face-to-face, man-on-top* position, with roughly a dozen minor variations, goes on to list for the reader seven advantages of the position and an equal number of disadvantages. Not satisfied that the reader can take things from there, this writer goes on to describe the *face-to-face, woman-on-top* position (again with minor variations). He lists, by number, ten advantages and eight disadvantages for that position. The implication of such writings, whether intended by the authors or not, is that coitus (and other sexual acts) is at least as complex a mechanical skill as, say, repairing a washing machine, and that trial-and-error experimentation and exploration is to be avoided. What, we ask, is wrong with the wife saying, "Hey, my foot is

going to sleep like this; how about rolling over?" Or the husband saying, "Let's try it with your legs up over my back"? There are face-to-
face positions, positions where both face the same direction, positions in
which the husband is the more active partner, positions in which the
wife is the more active partner, etc. They may do it sitting, standing,
lying down, or in any of several combinations. They may engage in
coitus lying side by side or with the husband lying prone, his wife
astride or with the wife bending backwards over a table—or bending
forward over a table, her husband entering her from the rear; or with
the husband sitting in a chair his wife astride, either facing him or
facing away from him. They may have coitus with the husband and
wife facing the same direction, the wife lying prone or kneeling in a
knee-chest position. They may even assume positions which are almost
at right angles. Only the limits of their imaginations and inhibitions,
plus, of course, the physical limits of the body mechanics, will determine
what they may attempt.

In addition to the psychological and visual, there are other reasons
for varying the positions. In each position the penis enters the vagina at
a slightly different angle. Also, the depth of insertion may vary. Some
women may, for example, find greater satisfaction when the penis penetrates to the fullest, the glans rubbing against the cervix. Others may be
most stimulated by the head of the penis rubbing against the posterior
vaginal wall (e.g., a face-to-face position) or by the head of the penis
striking against the anterior wall (e.g., a rear-entry position). We vary
in our neurophysiological as well as our emotional reactions. It is, therefore, not unexpected that our reactions of intensity and pleasure in the
positions we choose will vary from one time to another, and from one
position to the next. Variability in preferences and desires is a mark of
our humanity.

The sexually mature and strongly motivated couples, we found, had
explored virtually any and all positions. And they had found all of
them satisfying, some more exciting than others. They had usually
found one or two positions their chosen preference, but they all felt
that the position, philosophically and emotionally, which they held toward the sexual act was more important than the position they assumed
in the act.

The sexually aroused woman feels a *hunger* for a penis. There is
nothing passive and accepting about it. It is an eager demand. Every
fiber in her body seems to scream NOW. The physical demand felt by
the aroused man is no less intense. It is in the act of coitus that their

lovemaking art is put to its greatest test. His physical demand tells him
to plunge, at once, fully within her. Her need is to be penetrated to the
hilt. They have much to gain in satisfaction, however, by holding back,
taking as much time as possible. Only the husband, of course, can exercise such control in most positions, since he is the one performing the
act of penetration. With self-control, he can insert just the glans between her labia—no further at the start. If he feels he is able to hold
back his ejaculation, he can slowly move in and out of just the outer
third of her vagina. Only when the demand of her sexual arousal
reaches its highest peak does he enter her all the way, in one sudden,
hard stroke or with slow deliberation, depending on what he interprets
as her desires *that time.*

If they both crave complete insertion, it makes sense to ask why the
husband would delay. The answer, of course, is that delay is its own reward; if something *that* pleasurable can be prolonged, who would pass
up the opportunity? In addition, by prolonging the act, the arousal of
both partners will reach the highest possible level. Almost all couples
reported a superior orgasmic experience when coitus was maximally extended.

Such holding back, however, may seem easier said than done to most
men. When fully aroused, most will ejaculate with very little added
stimulation. Less than a minute of hard thrusting will suffice. If the
wife is not close to orgasm in her arousal, his ejaculation may, in such
case, be mistakenly labeled "premature." Premature ejaculation is, of
course, a real problem with some men, but it is wise to distinguish what
is the normal expected reaction of a man in coitus and what is "premature." Where such a problem does not exist, but the husband would
like to prolong his ejaculation in order to increase the pleasure to both,
we have found two techniques to be of help. First, at the moment the
penis is inserted, the man usually experiences a sudden increase in sexual tension which may bring him close to the edge of his climax. If he
continues thrusting movements at once, there is a high probability of
imminent ejaculation. If, on the other hand, he stays almost motionless
(at least in pelvic movement) after he has fully penetrated, remaining
so until that strong flush of excitement has partially subsided, he may
then be able to go on, pacing his movements until he and his partner
are ready to bring coitus to its climax. Second, in the hard thrusting
most men associate with coitus, there is contraction of the muscles of
the buttocks and adjacent areas. Some of these muscles also play a part
in the mechanism of ejaculation itself. Hence, if the man can learn to

lessen the contraction of these muscles as he moves his penis within his partner's vagina, he may delay this neuromuscular trigger. The idea is to move the hips in the fashion of a swinging pendulum, employing the muscles of the back and legs but not those of the buttocks. Think of the hips as a suspended steel ball, swinging freely and easily, not banging against a wall like a pile driver. Where both partners are physically free to move in this pendulum fashion, it is easier to develop. This is one of the advantages offered by waterbeds, but it can generally be accomplished if the husband in the face-to-face, man-on-top position partially supports his weight on his elbows and knees. This calls on the wife, of course, to pace her movements so as to not counteract the pendulum and cause a reversion to the hard, pile-driver thrust until both are ready. A third technique some couples have found successful in delaying ejaculation involves full insertion followed by movement which does not include any thrusting in and out. In this, the husband keeps his penis in to the hilt. His movements (until ready for ejaculation) may then be lateral, in a rolling side-to-side motion, or up and down, as if rising on his toes (this is sometimes helped if there is a footboard against which he can push). These movements are often almost as stimulating to the woman, yet seldom will trigger ejaculation as fast as active thrusting. This is also true of some other positions. In the woman-astride positions, for example, the wife may derive intense pleasure from a forward-backward rocking movement, all hers alone, while his penis remains fully inserted. There are, we found, wide variations among individuals in all of this. It may be more psychological than physical. The only sound advice would seem to be to experiment: Find out what works best.

For the majority of couples, it seems, coitus comes to an abrupt, almost wrenching conclusion with the male climax. With ejaculation, it is finished—and virtually at once. Many wives interviewed accepted this as inevitable—just the way men are made. Others expressed resentment at the abrupt, and what they interpreted as callous, withdrawal. In the course of our interviews, we stumbled across an individual variation which has not, to our knowledge, been systematically studied: the length of time erection is maintained following ejaculation. The range was nothing short of remarkable. Some men reported "going soft" within a minute. At the other end of this continuum, others said they would generally still have a firm erection twenty to forty minutes after ejaculation, even if they withdrew at once. To further confound this finding, among the men who maintained erection, there was a wide range of difference in reaction to further coital activity. Some said they could tolerate no further movement ("I can't stand it; it's too painful." "If she tries to get me to go on, it drives me up a wall."). Others, again at the opposite end of the spectrum, said they experienced no discomfort in continuing coital movements to the point of bringing their partners to orgasm one or more times, after reaching orgasm. Erection is a physiological response. It is controlled by the autonomic nervous system, a hydraulic system which is not fully understood. Erection is lost when the "values" which control the return of the blood are opened and the tumescence is allowed to subside. Why this should vary from one man to another is not known. We don't know if it is primarily psychological or physiological or a combination of both. We have found, however, that it is not the maintenance of erection which is most important to the overall satisfaction of the wife. It is, most often, what is communicated in this post-ejaculatory period. Masters and Johnson (*Human Sexual Response*) and others have reported a rapid drop in sexual tension in the man following climax, a much more gradual decline in the woman. As a result, many wives feel rejected and left hanging when the husband "pulls out, turns over, and goes to sleep." Whether the husband loses erection or not, he can be aware of her needs and meet them through his lovemaking long after he has ejaculated. There is no reason for abrupt withdrawal. A number of women told us of a special feeling of satisfaction in falling asleep with their husband's softening penis within them. Others said they enjoyed being brought to orgasm (for the first or fifth time) by his fingers while his penis stayed inserted. Immediate withdrawal may leave a wife with the feeling she has been "used." This is understandable. If there should be no *beginning* of lovemaking, there should be no *end*. When the lover's body is valued—cherished—this valuing will be expressed no less after climax than before. Touches and caresses will continue. Loving does not burst like a rocket, then burn out. Lovers never ignore the opportunity to express their desires for intimacy.

CHAPTER 10

Variations

Come live with me and be my love,
And we will all the pleasures prove.

Christopher Marlowe

there are no ways to love but/beautiful/
I love you all of them

Lenore Kandel
The Love Book

Normal? I don't know what you mean when you
ask what is normal. What is normal to me?
To a Samoan? To a Trobrian Islander? I can't
be bothered with the question of what is normal,
only what is loving.

A wife

*T*here is virtually nothing in the expressions of sexual *love* which can be called "normal." Man has been called a "reasoning animal," a title which seems a contradiction in terms. If we are animals—and we are—then we may be expected to behave as other members of the animal kingdom, as what Freud called "biting, clawing, fornicating beasts." All else, all which we think of as ennobling in man, is "unnatural." And nothing could be more unnatural than loving. Harry Stack Sullivan said love exists when the welfare of the loved one means as much to you as your own well-being. This asks for us to act against our nature—that of almost totally egocentric creatures. To copulate is natural, to make love is not. Taking, even by force, what will satisfy our biological drives is part of our animal nature. We can then argue, with confidence, that *rape* is very "natural."

Strangely enough, sexual acts which are pleasure-giving—loving— are often branded as unnatural by those who most loudly proclaim the "sanctity" of sex. If their charge is not that it is "unnatural," it is that it is "animalistic." This, too, is a false charge. If we speak of animalistic sex, and we are to be honest, we describe the most *human*, the most imaginative and innovative sexual actions. This, however, makes no sense. Animals perform the sexual act in an almost rigidly nondeviating manner. The first time a dog engages in coitus, it is no different from the fiftieth or the five-thousandth time. The dog doesn't seek variety. He doesn't look for change in location or position. Physical release, nothing more, is all that is important; it is in answer to a drive state. Yet it is this rigid approach—an unvarying repetition of the act—which some would describe as the only "human" form of sexual expression. Human beings, however, with all the intelligence and creativity with which they are gifted, search for ways to increase and vary the pleasure —and ultimately the meaning—in their lives. And the area of sex is no exception. If we find sexual love exciting and rewarding, we will search for ways to enhance it, to innovate it, in much the same way we look for ways to enrich our music, expand our art forms, and increase our experiences.

The sexual union is the act by which conception occurs. It is the generative act. And it is this "fact of life" which has led some philosophers and moralists into the position of asserting that procreation is the *only* licit end of sexual relations, and any sex act which cannot result in conception is immoral—or unnatural. By their view, mutual love and pleasure are never enough in themselves to justify sexual activity. Pleasure to these moralists is inherently wrong (although they might not admit it), and pleasure in sex is to be condoned only if it stays within the boundaries of conception—at least the possibility of it. This phobia against sex-as-a-pleasure-bond has been so strong and so pervasive that some moralists have even contended that there is only one normal position for sexual intercourse. Tying "normality" to "procreative," they have branded most of what is pleasurable and loving between spouses as "perverted."

Despite the numerous explicit works on sex of recent years, many husbands and wives are, if we are to judge by our data, still apprehensive about committing acts of sexual love other than coitus. For a minority of couples the fears and/or negative reactions of one spouse had led to conflict, and even bitterness. Oral and anal sex were the two areas most often at issue.

ORAL SEX

Fellatio is stimulation of the penis by mouth, tongue and lips. *Cunnilingus* is stimulation of the clitoris and adjacent female genitalia by the lips and tongue. Both have been part of the sexual activity of men and women through the ages, but since sex has been a taboo subject in most cultures at most times, these forms of sexual activity have seldom been openly discussed. The reports of Kinsey and his associates opened the door on oral sex. It was long overdue. A sexual pleasure enjoyed by the majority of couples (who often must have wondered if they were unusual) was finally brought into the open. In recent years we have seen books and motion pictures devoted to oral sex. So many, in fact, that we have sometimes wondered whether coitus isn't being relegated to second place. Pendulums do swing, nevertheless, and perhaps it is necessary that this one swing back in order to place oral sex acceptably within the repertoire of loving.

Psychoanalytic writers, as is their obsessive tendency, have tried to explain the psychology of oral sex. In doing so, they have stretched the observable analogues to the breaking point. In cunnilingus, the man's face is buried between the woman's thighs, but must we conclude that this represents a desire to re-enter the womb? Or does the fact that she kneels before him to take his penis into her mouth mean that she has chosen to be subservient, or that—heaven help us!—she unconsciously wants to devour him? *We think not*. To the sensuous individual, the pleasure derived from appropriate stimulation of the lips and tongue makes oral sex as natural and desired as kissing. The lips and tongue are as richly endowed with nerve endings as the glans and clitoris. It would be natural, therefore, to expect stimulation of tongue and lips to be second only to the genitalia as organs of sexual gratification. Only taboos imposed by a frightened society would judge otherwise, and it is these taboos which we find (although frequently in disguised form). The strongest taboo has to do with "personal" hygiene. The bugaboo over what is "clean" and what is not is the most frequently cited block when it comes to oral sex. Most books on sex have attempted to counter this by reassuring the reader that frequent bathing will leave the genital area cleaner even than the mouth. We have doubts, however, as to how far such information may go. The husband who views his wife's vagina as "dirty" is not likely to be convinced otherwise by a bacteria count. We may assume that concerned lovers will bathe their entire bodies frequently enough not to risk "offensive" body odors. The woman who expects to make love to her husband will be sure to present him with her body in a meticulously clean state. It is a matter of presenting your lover with a most perfect gift. And it is also related to self-esteem. She will concern herself with personal hygiene before going to meet her lover. And he will do likewise. Neither of them will view the body of the other as in any way "dirty," physically or psychologically.

Cunnilingus: In modern sex manuals, oral sex has almost always been discussed in terms of what may be done for the sexual partner. It is generally presented as a technique (somewhat self-sacrificing) of increasing the other's arousal. In one particularly heavy-handed work it was referred to only as a means of "treating" a woman who finds difficulty achieving orgasm. Nothing, mind you, about the man being aroused by doing it. Cunnilingus refers to licking, sucking, penetrating (with the tongue) the entrance of the vagina, and stimulation of the labia and clitoris by lips and tongue. The man who is sexually attuned to a woman will have a very natural desire to find stimulation through his lips and tongue, not just through kissing but through the fullest possible contact with the soft, warm tissues of her genitalia. It is not something he does for her, but something he does for himself. We consistently found that those of both sexes who derived the greatest satisfaction from sexual relations were strongly aroused by engaging in acts of oral-genital sex. As one husband put it: "When I put my mouth down on her sex, it turns me on like nothing else, not even having her do it to me."

For a woman to be effectively pleasured by cunnilingus, the vulva must be spread, the labia as open as possible. There are two reasons for this: First, spreading wide the labia allows a greater stimulation of the most sensitive areas. His tongue can explore, with ease, her clitoris, inner and outer labia, and the entrance to the vagina. Second, unless her vulva is spread wide, there is a chance he may get pubic hair in his mouth or throat, a most uncomfortable situation. Some women will spread their vulva with their fingers; others prefer to have their lover separate the major lips while they remain "passive" and receptive. It would seem to us to make little difference as far as the woman's satisfaction is concerned. If both partners are satisfied, it should be of no importance.

The soft tissues within the labia are very similar to those of the inner lips and cheeks. They are sensitive and easily irritated. They are also warm, with a rich blood supply, and smooth. While some women enjoy the added stimulation provided by a man's beard or mustache, many find the rough stubble of a one-day growth of beard painfully irritating (a point husbands would do well to keep in mind). How much of the man's face will come in contact with the inner labia, clitoris, and vaginal entrance will depend on the technique he is employing at the time, but over a long period of lovemaking, including oral-genital acts, it will probably be considerable. As with other caresses, oral sex should be "orchestrated." Seldom should lovemaking start with oral-genital stimulation. The intensity is too great. The gradual building of mutual passions would be missed. And as with all other varieties of lovemaking, cunnilingus should be approached with the artistry of a musician composing a symphony or improvising jazz. The lover continually introduces changes in tone and style—at times slow, romantic, languorous, at other times light, up-tempo, playful, and at still other times, in fast bursts of crescendos which, in turn, subside like waves retreating from the shore. It has been said that the master lover plays the body of the woman as a great musician plays a violin. The women whose reports indicated the most consistently high degree of sexual fulfillment almost unanimously said they found no difficulty identifying with this poetic metaphor. In cunnilingus, perhaps more than in any other act of lovemaking, the husband has the opportunity to demonstrate his virtuosity. In muscle control, the tongue is far more versatile than the fingers—and not nearly so rough. It can be moved with great lightness and speed up and down, from side to side, and in and out. And with its remarkable set of muscles, it can be made soft or firm. In almost every respect, one could argue that it is a more efficient organ of lovemaking than the penis. This seems supported by the fact that, while many women who reported difficulty reaching orgasm during coitus were able to experience orgasm with ease by cunnilingus, not a single woman who could regularly achieve orgasm in coitus had any difficulty achieving it during cunnilingus.

Basically, the positions which can be assumed for cunnilingus are, like those for coitus, limited. Essentially, it can be performed in any position in which the lips and tongue of the man can be brought into contact with the vulva. Generally, the choice will be dictated by the physical comfort of both, by whether or not they wish to engage in simultaneous oral sex (fellatio and cunnilingus), and the extent of accessibility to the genitalia desired. In cunnilingus, comfort and accessibility are often related. If, for example, the husband lies in the opposite direction from his wife, he must bend his head down at an extreme angle in order to reach her vaginal opening, a move which cannot be maintained for long. If he lies with his face between her legs, both lying in the same direction, he will be forced to bend his head back as far as possible in order to reach any areas lower than her clitoris, unless, of course, her hips are propped up by a pillow or two (and even then, access may be limited). Unless the couple chooses to engage in mutual, simultaneous oral sex, the best positions will be those in which the wife's entire external genitalia are exposed to the husband's lips and tongue. She may lie back over the edge of the bed or table, her legs spread while he sits or kneels at her feet. Or if she is lying on her back, she can draw her knees up as far as possible, thus elevating the pelvis. And for the greatest possible access, she can kneel with her legs straddling his face while he reclines on his back. She then lowers her vulva to his mouth as she would lower herself on his penis in the astride position of coitus. The object in any case is obvious: to provide her with the maximum pleasurable stimulation. There is one further factor which may be given consideration in any choice of positions for cunnilingus or, for that matter, any sexual act: the psychological. We humans have an unfortunate tendency to read things into our actions and the actions of others which were not intended and which make little sense. This seems especially true when it comes to sex. Just as there are couples who view any coital position other than the "missionary" position with vague suspicion because "it seems like the way the animals do it," there are husbands and wives who reported feeling uneasy during oral sex undertaken in some positions. A few husbands told us they felt "subservient" when they knelt between the wife's legs while she sat on a chair or bed. Some wives said they felt acutely embarrassed in positions in which their genitals were most fully exposed. Attitudes such as these can sometimes seriously inhibit the full enjoyment to be found in sexual love. They stem from our internalized self-instructions, the things we tell ourselves about ourselves, other persons, or situations. The human body is the most beautiful of God's creations. The ways in which we employ it when we give and receive pleasure in making love cannot be ugly or less than human. Nor, for the husband and wife who share love and mutual respect, can any act or position they enjoy connote domination, subservience, or anything other than an egalitarian, mutual love.

Technique is never as important as feelings. The position *in* sexual relations is never as important as the position *toward* sexual relations. The method counts less than the meaning. There is no reason, however, why the two cannot be combined. With a motivation to love well, they will be.

In cunnilingus, the first concern is *where*. The second is *how*. The female genitalia, being far more complex than those of the male, present more of a challenge to oral loving. Most sensitive, of course, is the clitoris, and it is to the clitoris that the most prolonged stimulation will usually be given. The tongue, sometimes the tip only, sometimes the entire tongue surface, stroking up and down against the head and shaft of the clitoris will, without fail, bring the responsive woman to orgasm. That's easy enough, but it may not be objective. As we have stressed repeatedly, orgasm should never be the primary goal. Therefore, stimulation of the clitoris should not be the sole interest. The area between the clitoris and the vaginal orifice, which includes the urethra, is a highly sensitive area in most women. A slow, tantalizing licking of the area, interspersed with return tonguing of the clitoris and vaginal entrance, will provide erotic arousal and pleasure which, if desired, can be orgasmic to most women. The anterior portion of the vaginal entrance is probably second to the clitoris in erotic sensitivity, much more so than the tissues deeper within the vagina (which in any case would not be accessible to stimulation by the tongue). By moving the tongue from the area just posterior to the vaginal entrance to the anterior portion of the entrance, then along the portion between the labia between vagina and clitoris, her sexual sensations will progressively leave an always-wanting-more feeling of mounting arousal. While a number of books (a few of them serious works, most of them only pseudoscientifically disguised erotic fantasies) have been devoted exclusively to descriptions of the supposed wide variety of techniques in cunnilingus and fellatio, they seem hardly worth the reading effort. Lovemaking is an art, and, as in all arts, imagination is indispensable. With imagination and sufficient experimentation, the attentive lover will master those techniques that pleasure his loved one.

For those who have not yet explored the pleasures of oral sex, it may be appropriate to say a few words about vaginal secretions. As the sexually responsive woman becomes increasingly aroused, the "sweating" secretions from the vaginal walls (so ably documented by Masters and Johnson) increase significantly. This secretion, as most women know, can thoroughly soak the woman's panties and wet her thighs. It can also wet the cheeks of her husband during cunnilingus. Some wives (more than husbands) expressed uneasiness over this. They feel their vaginal secretions may be offensive to their mates. In our discussions with wives, it became clear that many women have a negative reaction to their own bodies and the functions of their bodies. They have been taught, directly or indirectly, that the female body in its reproductive cycle is repugnant. It is "smelly and messy." It may be that some wives have had this view reinforced by their husbands. For reasons probably buried deep within the unconscious, and explored in depth by psychoanalysts, some men do have a phobic reaction to the female genitalia and the functioning of the female reproductive organs, including menstruation, pregnancy, and the vaginal secretion accompanying arousal. In our group of sexually fulfilled couples, however, this never presented a problem. The more highly aroused the wife was, the heavier, generally, was her flow of vaginal secretion. At the same time, the greater the husband's arousal, the less he tended to experience negative feelings to the taste or odor of the secretion. In fact, the majority of such husbands found the experience even more arousing. The secretion itself is nearly tasteless and odorless, assuming the wife is careful in her personal hygiene. In this regard, it is of interest that the majority of wives in the highly responsive group made a practice of douching before retiring and/or making love. Most of them had heard or read that douching is not necessary, that the vagina has a natural cleansing mechanism and that "excessive" douching could disturb the chemical balance, etc. They chose to ignore such counsel in favor of sexual loving and a strong desire to avoid anything which might prove offensive. Their fastidiousness may have been a major factor in helping their husbands overcome what might, at least for some, have been an initial reluctance to cunnilingus.

Fellatio: It could be said that cunnilingus is less complex psychologically than fellatio. In cunnilingus the man is always the active partner. The woman (except when she is engaged in mutual oral sex) is passive. When the wife accepts her husband's penis into her mouth, she may be either active or passive or, alternatingly, both. This choice of roles may in large part account for the strong reactions—negative and positive—encountered by both sexes. Certainly no common sexual act seemed to elicit such depth of feeling. We make no attempt to interpret the psychodynamics of these feelings and preferences, other than what might be conjectured from statements of husbands and wives. Not only do we feel that statements attempting to explain one's "reasons" for desires and feelings call for far greater self-knowledge than that possessed by most of us, we believe that unless the desires are consistently rejected, and the resulting frustration leads to a breach in the relationship, such psychologizing can contribute nothing to the sexual loving of the couple, and may even create an atmosphere of self-consciousness. Whatever it may indicate, well over half the husbands interviewed, when asked what they would most like in sexual relations, said they would like their wives to perform felatio on them. Of course, this may only indicate a desire for a form of sexual relations which, because of the reluctance on the part of many wives, they experience rarely. They crave it perhaps primarily *because* they are refused it. Some support for this premise is indicated in the finding that those husbands who reported *no* reluctance to engage in fellatio on the part of their wives (in fact, an eagerness for it and enjoyment of it) overwhelmingly preferred coitus as their final orgasmic experience in lovemaking, with fellatio (except as an occasional variation) as only one part of the preliminary scenario.

Without making any attempt to explore the psychology of men, there does seem to be evidence that *some* husbands view the act of fellatio as a sign of male superiority and female inferiority. In each instance where this seemed to be true, we found ample evidence of a battle of the sexes in which the husband felt his wife was trying her best to exercise dominance. Fellatio, where the husband could succeed in getting the wife to acquiesce, apparently gave the husband the short-lived feeling that he was the master, she the slave. For the sexually fulfilled couple, however, this is not true. The sexually mature woman pleasures a penis with her mouth *because it pleasures her.* She is not so lacking in self-esteem as to see herself as a slave; he has no reason or desire to see himself as a master. Sexual love always involves an equality of giving (and receiving). Some students of sex have asserted that it is the wife who receives greatest satisfaction in fellatio, and the husband who gets the most from cunnilingus. For those couples with the most satisfying relationships, we are persuaded by this argument. Statements of our most fulfilled couples bear it out. Those husbands who verbalized a repeated demand for fellatio were invariably the same ones who appeared to feel in danger of emasculation by their wives. We feel, however, that this does not in any way mean that all—or even most—men who enjoy fellatio are sexually threatened. Most men do enjoy oral sex, both fellatio and cunnilingus. And so do most women.

Some authors have chosen to employ different words to indicate whether the man is active or passive in oral stimulation of the penis: *fellatio* when the man remains passive (or relatively so) while the woman actively stimulates his penis with her lips, mouth, and tongue; *irrumation* when the man moves his penis in copulatory movements (active) in and out of the woman's mouth (passive). We do not feel such a distinction should be necessary for anything other than, possibly, description. It seems to smack of the "dominance/submission" dichotomy. If the act is pleasurable to both, does it, or should it, need more than one label?

It is easier to describe what most women find pleasurable techniques in cunnilingus than to describe techniques for fellatio. A surprising number of husbands reported some degree of dissatisfaction in their wife's technique. We found three explanations for this: (1) *unrealistic expectations; (2) unsatisfactory technique; (3) evident lack of desire on the wife's part.*

Part of the male mythology, exchanged in the locker room and in the pages of porno novels, presents the fiction of the supreme orgasm of fellatio. Adolescent boys hear tales of super-skilled prostitutes (often Oriental or Middle Eastern) who can "drain a man dry" or "blow the top of a guy's head off" with their oral techniques. Somewhere, the stories would have us believe, there is that woman with an agility of mouth and tongue (and even throat) who can transport her lover into sexual Nirvana. Classical Eastern works such as the *Kama Sutra* of Vatsyayana devote lengthy chapters to detailed descriptions of fellatio techniques. The woman who masters them will, it is implied, enslave her lover with her oral charms. It is no wonder some men find the real thing to be something of a letdown, somewhat like the wife who told us she had expected to hear choirs of celestial voices burst into the Hallelujah Chorus the first time she made love. Fellatio is one of a variety of sexual acts. For most men it is most frequently chosen as a preliminary to coitus or an occasional change of pace. To make it sound like the ultimate experience is absurd.

A lack of satisfactory technique is also frequently the result of misinformation from many of the same sources. The popular expressions for fellatio have included "blow job" (although blowing is not the usual action) and "sucking off" (although sucking is not the primary stimulation). In fellatio, as in coitus or manual stimulation, the pleasurable sensations come from friction to the nerve endings, primarily in the glans. The friction can be applied by the lips, tongue, or by the glans rubbing against the roof of the mouth or the inner cheek. The tightness of a woman's vagina is praised as a sexual asset (This is often a matter of muscle control). It is increased friction which makes the tightness desirable. And it is the same friction which accounts for the pleasure in fellatio. How a woman can most effectively apply the friction, by licking, moving her lips on the glans, or pressing the penis between her tongue and the roof of her mouth or cheek, is a matter of trial and error —learning—and in this she can expect advice from her man. He is, after all, the one who should know. One husband told us of a "teaching method" he employed. He took his wife's finger in his mouth, and with his lips and tongue showed her how he would like her to do it. A brilliant idea!

The depth of insertion is, of necessity, limited. If the penis is taken too far into the mouth, it will come in contact with the back of the palate and cause a gagging reflex. (It is interesting to note that several women reported that the gagging greatly decreased during their highest peaks of sexual excitement.) The motion picture *Deep Throat* starred an actress, Linda Lovelace, who demonstrated the ability to accept the entire penis into her mouth and throat. The feat is apparently not unique. A number of women said they had been able with practice in controlling the gagging reflex to master the same technique. It should be noted, however, that the positive effect on the man of such full insertion is probably more visual and psychological than physical, and that deep insertion should always be at the instigation and control of the wife, never by the husband thrusting.

Kinsey reported more husbands interested in cunnilingus than wives interested in fellatio. Our data support this finding, but more significant is the observation that a majority of spouses of both sexes are more interested in being pleasured (and loved) than in pleasuring (and loving). This egocentric approach to sexual love was inversely related to the satisfaction they expressed in their relationship. That is, the couples who expressed the greatest satisfaction in all aspects of their union, including sex, were those who found the greatest satisfaction in *giving* pleasure. Does this mean that women are inclined to be more selfish in lovemaking than men? We don't think so. It seems more probable that the traditional "passive" role which women have been taught has conditioned them to "accept" rather than "give" in sexual love. In fellatio (as opposed to cunnilingus), there is a further explanation. At orgasm, there is a sudden, somewhat powerful spurt of seminal fluid from the penis. If fellatio is continued to this point, the husband's "eruption" may come as a frightening inundation to the wife who is not ready for it. Many wives said they felt they were being drowned the first time it occurred. With experience, the wife learns the "signs," the slight movements in the penis, which tell her ejaculation is imminent. By moving her tongue close to the meatus (opening of the penis) or directing the glans against her inner cheek or the roof of her mouth, she can avoid any feeling of being "drowned." Actually, the reaction is invariably more to the unexpectedness of the spurting than to the amount of fluid. The average ejaculate only amounts to a couple of swallows.

Whether she chooses to swallow the ejaculate is a further question. It provides a psychological—ego—satisfaction to most men, probably since they interpret it as a gesture of deep love. (The majority of husbands said they saw swallowing the ejaculate as a very "giving" act. Apparently, the idea that it may be something desirable to the wife does not occur to them.) Most wives said they were apprehensive before the first time, not knowing what it would taste like, or if it would be repulsive. This is certainly understandable. Many also said they associated the ejaculate with urine, since both were emitted from the same opening. Actually, the association is groundless, but it is understandable. We are not going to attempt to describe the taste of seminal fluid. Other writers have done so. Whether they have met with success depends upon the readers' tastes. It seems to us a bit like trying to describe the taste of asparagus or veal parmigiana. It can only be done by comparisons, and always inadequately. Suffice to say the majority of wives did not find the taste unpleasant. And with the common thread we found running through the interviews, those wives who reported the greatest degrees of sexual satisfaction said they thoroughly enjoy the taste. (Many of these wives said swallowing their husband's ejaculate was highly arousing.)

Fellatio to ejaculation was, as we said, not a frequent occurrence for the majority of our couples. It was, however, a part of the preliminary lovemaking for most couples at least half the times they engaged in coitus. These data are difficult to interpret. Kinsey and associates reported a positive correlation between formal education and experience in oral sex. The percentage of college graduates who had experienced oral sex was much higher than that of the group with less than secondary-school education. Our couples were above average in formal education, and therefore not representative of the general population. Furthermore, there is no available data on the frequency with which oral sex is included as a part of sexual relations for the overall adult population. We can say only that for our sample group it is an accepted part of their lovemaking.

ANAL SEX

While the anal orifice is second only to the genitals (and the nipples in women) in erogenous sensitivity, the taboos under which we were all raised prevent most couples from discovering it. To many, any touching of this "dirty" part of the body is unthinkable. Until recently anal sexuality was not mentioned in any books other than a few on sexual pathology. There have been many changes, however, during the past decade. A number of *avant garde* sex books and several erotic motion pictures have made anal sex, if not acceptable to the majority, at least not a perversion.

The area surrounding the anus is generously provided with nerve endings. Furthermore, it is connected in both sexes with the sexual organs by means of muscle fibers. In men, it is even more directly connected with the sexual apparatus. The prostate gland is located only a short distance up the anal canal, accessible to an inserted finger. In women, the anterior anal sheath is separated from the posterior wall of the vagina by a relatively thin membrane, thus stimulation in one orifice will transfer stimulation to the other. It goes without saying that lovers who engage in any anal erotic activity will take care to present their bodies to each other in squeaky clean condition, but this should be so whatever their physical intimacies. With cleanliness as an assumed condition, there seems no reason why a couple should not expand their lovemaking to include anal stimulation. While we did not find anal eroticism to be practiced by the majority of our couples, almost half reported some experience, ranging from digital stimulation to anal coitus to analingus. Again, those couples who appeared to evidence the greatest sexual drive and satisfaction represented a much higher percentage of those who included anal stimulation in their sexual repertoire.

Digital stimulation may range from light touching or "tickling" around the anal orifice to insertion of the finger full length. Where the wife inserts her finger in her husband's anus, she will frequently move the end of the finger against the anterior wall (toward his genitals) in order to stimulate the prostate gland. Many men report an increase in pleasurable sensation at orgasm with such stimulation. A number of wives also said they experienced heightened pleasure when the husband inserted his finger in their anus during coitus. The pressure of the finger felt through the membrane wall separating anus and vagina acted to increase the friction of the penis thrusting against the posterior vagina. For some couples, mutual anal stimulation had become a usual adjunct to coitus in positions which would permit it, and they kept some type of lubricant (e.g., Vaseline) in the night table for this purpose. Many couples also included digital stimulation of the anus in conjunction with manual stimulation of the genitals as preliminary lovemaking prior to coitus.

Anal coitus presents greater problems for many couples. Wives fear the experience may be painful, and, unless care and patience are taken, it may be. Some husbands (a minority) associate it with male homosexuals (although, ironically, this is not as common a sexual expression among homosexuals as most people believe). Both reactions can be modified or eliminated with experience and/or change in attitude. But both may demand a choice of entering into an experience which runs contra taboos assimilated over many years. There is a reality in the fear of women. The muscles which ring the anal opening, the anal sphincter, are amazingly strong. They are the muscles of bowel control. These muscles are under semireflexive control. It takes conscious thought to relax them. Any entrance into the anal canal calls for relaxation of the anal sphincter if it is not to be painful, and this is, for the most part, under conscious control. Women can, and many women do, learn to relax the anal sphincter sufficiently to admit the penis. It is not a matter of anatomical variation. The anal sphincter is capable of distending enough to admit even a large penis. It is a matter of relaxation. Unless the anal sphincter is relaxed, anal coitus will always be painful—and should not be attempted. In this respect, it is a matter of trust. If the wife fears that the husband may hurt her in callous disregard of her feelings, she will not be able to relax enough to admit even his little finger. As far as homosexuality is concerned, the matter becomes one of faulty generalization. To be sure, some (but not all) male homosexuals engage in anal coitus. By the same token, kissing is engaged in by some (but not all) homosexuals, yet we don't stamp kissing with the brand of sexual inversion. Anal eroticism may be engaged in by homosexuals, heterosexuals, or bisexuals. All humans, after all, are endowed with the same erotic anatomy where anal sensitivity is concerned. One's preference for their own or the other sex has nothing to do with it.

Explaining the desire for anal coitus is more difficult than explaining the desire for anal digital stimulation. Why, one might ask, would a man desire anal coitus when he can have vaginal coitus? The answer, for most men, is that he wouldn't. It is not a matter of *either/or*. Anal coitus is a different experience just as fellatio is a different experience— for both. The anal sphincter, being as strong a muscular ring as it is, offers a tight grip on the male organ. To the husband whose wife is prone to play a very passive role physically, not utilizing her vaginal muscles, this may seem a decided plus. There is also the "forbidden fruit" aspect. Most men and women are attracted by what we have been taught is not permitted. Taboo. Sinful.

We said that satisfactory anal coitus was, on the wife's part, a matter of trust. This trust is not an isolated thing. It is related to the trust she invests in him in all other dimensions of their relationship. Does she trust her financial future to him? Enough that she wouldn't question his investments, the amount of insurance he carries? Would she trust him if he planned a surprise vacation to Tahiti without consulting her? And told her nothing of his plans until they were ready to board the plane? Those wives who said they were willing to engage in anal coitus the first time their husband suggested it, were, without exception, those who had the self-confidence to "step off a cliff" and "take a chance on living to the fullest"—to put their lives "in his hands." This is admittedly a hard concept for the uninitiated to comprehend, demanding, as it seems to, an unrealistic—even blind—faith in the good will of another, a love represented in trust in the other's love. If the husband is anything but most careful and considerate, the attempt at anal coitus can be very painful for the wife. She must be able to gradually relax the anal sphincter to admit his penis. Since she can be the only one to know what she is feeling, the entire direction and progress in anal coitus must be left to her. The penis and anus must be liberally coated with a lubricant, and it must be her hand and words which guide his insertion. Few women are able to take any vigorous thrusting, and it may be for this reason that most husbands said that, although anal coitus was an exciting "variation," they preferred to conclude lovemaking with vaginal coitus. Most authorities, however, sound a note of caution here. Since the anal cavity may contain bacteria which can cause vaginal infection, the husband should never enter the vagina after anal coitus without first thoroughly washing his penis with soap and water.

A man can, of course, reach climax and ejaculate in anal coitus, but what of a woman? The answer is that those women who are highly responsive to sexual stimuli are frequently capable of achieving orgasm through anal stimulation. One more proof of woman's sexual superiority. Some women can not only achieve multiple orgasms during a period of lovemaking, they are capable of doing so through stimulation of the clitoris, through both vaginal and anal coitus, and even through stimulation of the nipples. A very small percentage of women are even able to reach orgasm through nothing other than erotic fantasies!

BONDAGE

As researchers learn more about the sexual behavior of men and women, they are increasingly challenged in their traditional assumptions of what is normal and abnormal, healthy and unhealthy, straight and kinky. In the past, there have been arguments founded on biology, theology, anthropology, and sheer phobias. In the end, however, almost all have come down to a single argument: "What you do that is different from what I do is abnormal." It takes honesty, objectivity, and courage to accept the preferences of another person without making judgments.

Bondage is the sexual technique of tying up one's partner or being tied up during sexual relations. Despite appearances, it is not done as an acting out of dominance/submission nor to overcome reluctance through rape, no matter how symbolic the rape may be. Bondage is employed to enhance the orgasm of the one restrained. The reasons this may occur are both physical and psychological. In both men and women, there are two physiologic reactions which have total body distribution during sexual excitement: vasocongestion and myotonia. As sexual tension increases, there is increasing muscle irritability and contraction throughout the body, becoming intense and even spasmodic at the time of orgasm. These contractions of the long muscles can be so strong that it is not uncommon for both sexes to be conscious of mild muscle aches the morning following particularly vigorous lovemaking. When one of the partners is tied up while the other provides sexual stimulation, the straining of the arms and legs against the bonds may serve to increase still more the sexual tension. Thus, on a purely physiologic level, bondage may work to heighten the arousal and subsequent orgasm of the "captive." On the psychological level, the motivation for the partners is not so evident. There are simplistic explanations aplenty, just as there are for most sexual behaviors. One of the more popular theories has it that bondage is simply a form of sadomasochistic sex, that the active partner is acting out a desire to inflict pain while the passive partner is motivated by a desire for sexual pleasure through submission to pain. The theory would have greater credibility if pain rather than pleasure was "inflicted" on the "captive." The fact that a sadist may bind his or her victim before inflicting torture and that in bondage the partner binds his or her spouse does not establish any further relationship between the two sets of behavior. The other popular theory is no surprise: Bondage is an acting out of dominance/submission. The active partner has a strong need to dominate and/or the captive has a need to be dominated. This may have more substance, but considering the fact that many husbands and wives enjoy taking turns in these roles, it seems less than conclusive. In any case, if the act is entered into by mutual desire, should the couple be concerned with the psychological whys?

Bondage, like all else in sex, calls for trust in one's partner. To submit to being tied spread-eagled, hand and foot, to the bed, at the mercy of your captor can be frightening unless you have confidence in his or her love and concern. It goes without saying that a lover would never attempt to *impose* restraint on his/her loved one. Rape is not making love. Nor is pain which is imposed. Furthermore, bondage is never intended to create fear in the "captive." It is voluntary, mutually arousing, and entered into in a spirit of joy and love. Otherwise, it is perverse in the sense that sexual encounters which lack love and mutual respect are perversions of human love and dignity.

SADOMASOCHISM

To include sadism (sexual enjoyment through inflicting pain) and masochism (sexual enjoyment through experiencing pain) in a work dealing with the experience of sexual *love* of husband and wife may seem strange indeed. Surely the desire to inflict or receive pain is hostile or pathological or both. Without very clear qualifications, we agree. The husband who gets a kick out of beating his wife deserves the condemnation society heaps upon him. The wife who takes satisfaction in being publicly humiliated by her husband has serious psychological problems. And the spouses of either sex who find they can enjoy sexual relations only when pain is a principal component, are immersed in a very neurotic (or even psychotic) interaction.

Some years ago we came across a humorous(?) book which included the flip remark, "Seduction is for sissies; a he-man likes his rape." It might be true if the author chose to define a "he-man" as a male who, for some sick reasons, hates women. It has also been reported that being the victim of rape is the most popular female fantasy. Thus, by implication we might conclude that most women are unconscious masochists. Nothing in our experience supports such a conclusion. As mentioned previously, many husbands said they enjoyed feelings of "possessing," "taking," or even "conquering" the wife in sexual relations, and a majority of wives said they enjoyed feelings of being "overcome" or "taken" by their husbands. Invariably, however, these roles were acted out with mutual consent. "You chase me until I let you catch me," was most often the wife's message. The "conquest" is more symbolic than real. Between emotionally healthy lovers, the inflicting of pain during sexual relations is quite similar. Generally, we think of pain as an experience to be avoided if at all possible. Yet the fact of the matter is that we seek many experiences which can only be described as painful. We call them pleasurable. In vigorous physical exercise there is pain. Running the mile or lifting weights can be exhausting. Two men wrist-wrestling in a bar experience pain. It may be that the satisfaction of winning makes the pain worthwhile, but that hardly seems a sufficient explanation. There *are* sensations of pleasure in some experiences of pain. The pain/pleasure paradoxes in sex are not comparable to any other activity. Sex is the only physical drive in which the drive state itself is pleasurable, not just the satisfaction of the drive. In sex, the arousal itself is pleasurable enough to make us want to prolong it. Could this be seeking "pain" for its own sake?

There is much in lovemaking which is physically uncomfortable, at times even painful. The pain, however, is not only masked by the pleasure, it becomes a part of the pleasure. A woman nearing orgasm may dig her fingernails into her lover's back. He may notice the scratches the next morning but have no memory of pain. He may thrust against her with such violence that bruises result, yet she feels only intense sexual pleasure. Within limits, pain may heighten the arousal and climax in both sexes.

These limits vary from individual to individual. "Normal," emotionally healthy, "sadomasochism" between lovers is more easily described in terms of what it is *not* than in terms of what it *is*. It is *not* inflicted with hostility. It is *not* intended to degrade or humiliate. It is *not* an assertion of dominance or mastery. It is *not* sought by the "victim" out of a need to be punished. It is *not* inflicted out of any desire to inflict bodily harm.

With everything it is *not*, this "normal" sadomasochism between lovers can be seen for what it is: a contradiction in terms. The sadism of the Marquis de Sade and its popular adherents with their affection for whips, chains, and medieval torture has no part in the loving of man and woman. The sick minds of those who attempt to convince others that torture is a form of loving are pitiable, but unconvincing. The actions of lovers are loving, not cruel, and never degrading. If sexual stimulation includes stimulation of the "pain" receptors, it is administered with a knowledge of the sexuality of the one to whom it is applied—what turns him or her on.

AND OTHER PRACTICES

Concern over what constitutes sexual normality apparently touches the majority of marriages at some time. It may be no more than a passing thought, or it may be severe enough to endanger the relationship. Marriage counselors, psychiatrists, and psychologists answer countless questions concerning the normality of various acts. The variety is almost endless. There are questions on the frequency of intercourse, oral and anal sex, fetishes, dress (kinky and otherwise) and undress, spanking, masturbation, mutual bathing, voyeurism, exhibitionism, sex role "reversal," artificial aids, homosexual desires, group sex, fantasies, erotic dreams, animal contacts, mixed racial sex, sex during later years, sex during pregnancy and menstruation, and a dozen more. The problem is, in each case, the same: It is assumed that if *most* individuals engage in an act, the act is healthy and good; if most *do not* engage in the act, it is unhealthy and bad. The question is wrong. We don't ask, "Is it normal to eat caviar?", then base our answer on a poll. There should be only one criterion for any actions in the sexual loving of husband and wife: *Is it loving?* Does it express a desire to meet the needs and desires of the loved one? Lovers don't measure their loving against the yardstick of their neighbor's mores, the antisexuality of parents, pronouncements of puritans or sexual revolutionaries, or Kinsey's statistics.

In answer to the question, "What if my husband/wife wants to do something [e.g., oral sex] that turns me off?" Most counselors have stated rather flatly: "You should never do anything you don't both want to do." Unfortunately, we have heard the words used to justify unloving attitudes. If the wife wants to be kissed and the husband is not in the mood, are we to advise him not to kiss her. "Don't do anything you don't feel like doing" is a statement of pure egocentricity—a flat-out rejection of giving. Of course, one might answer, "But kissing your wife isn't comparable to engaging in oral sex." What if oral sex—just the thought of it—turns you off? Do you have to do it just to prove you're not unloving? Do you have to give in to whatever your spouse wants? Not in the least. In loving we *give;* we don't *give in.*

There are a number of sexual acts which to the uninitiated sound less than overwhelmingly appealing. Even deep kissing may seem some-what repulsive to the twelve-year-old hearing it described but never having tried it. And many sexual activities would have no appeal unless one felt a deep love for the partner. With experience, however, most of us acquire a taste for a wide variety of activities, and to say, "I tried it once and didn't like it, so I won't try it again" seems at best rigid; at worst, self-centered. Given a strong, healthy sex drive, a freedom from crippling inhibitions, and deep mutual caring and respect, lovers will find the gates of sexual adventure opening to them. Questions of "nor-mality," like questions of "duties," rights, and what others say is "proper," evaporate in the warmth of the love which forms their bond.

CHAPTER 11

Sex and Procreation

Through the child, the bodily act itself
accepts the risk of casting love into the stream
of history and society. The relationship becomes
known, a public matter. Yet the lovers accept this
vulnerability because their new being will become a
new society in the eyes of men. Thus the surrender
of the body cannot remain a simple expression of
love like a private language for only two, it must
express that love before the eyes of all, before
society.

Abel Jeanniere
The Anthropology of Sex

Only in carrying him and his love within me,
    the union of our sexual love lasts longer.
It's as if the heights of our lovemaking
    continue on in richness
        and fulfillment
            for a full nine months.

Lois Bird
Love Is All

*T*he first questions a child asks about sex are usually questions about procreation. He wants to know. "Where did I come from?" "How did the baby get out of Mrs. Smith's tummy?" "How did it get in there?" Sex education classes in the schools are not, strictly speaking, instruction in sex as much as in reproduction. At the onset of adolescence, the body undergoes dramatic changes which prepare the way for parenthood, and every adolescent girl and boy is very much aware of this new reproductive potential. Their sexuality and their awareness of their procreative potential are as psychologically intertwined as they are physically.

In recent years it has become popular to ignore reproduction in writing books on sex (except to give information on contraception). There are many who argue that sex and reproduction can, and should, be kept separated in our thinking. In the mid-sixties feminists hailed the pill as the chemical liberator of women. No longer, they shouted, would women have to be "baby machines." Several years ago we were asked to participate in a symposium titled *Modern Woman in the Contraceptive Age*. The title seemed to represent the thinking of several of the speakers: The development of easy, almost totally effective contraceptive devices has radically changed the roles of men and women and their relationships. We questioned the position then, and we do today. It seems too simplistic. To be sure, our world is changing. The roles of men and women are changing. Their relationships are being transformed by many social forces. If effective contraception is one of these relevant variables—and we feel sure it may be—it is only one. This thinking, however, coupled with the "sex as play" philosophy promoted by *Playboy* and the spokespeople for the new permissiveness, virtually removed procreation from sex.

But not quite. Thoughts of pregnancy, fears of pregnancy, desires for pregnancy, all are very much associated with the sexual love of husband and wife. Deep feelings of both husbands and wives about pregnancy and childbearing came up repeatedly in our discussions. We have found, however, that the emotional tie between sexual love and procreation is perhaps the most difficult to investigate. One can't be sure what questions to ask or how to evaluate the statements made. If we ask, for example, "When you make love, do you feel that you would like to be impregnated?" the women may answer, "No, I have no desire to have another child." But is the desire to be impregnated the same as a desire for a child? Many women seemed to draw a distinction. Are sexual feelings in any way different when conception is possible during lovemaking than when it is safe? Some husbands and wives felt they are, and not necessarily because of either a desire for pregnancy or a fear of conception. Because of the difficulty in formulating appropriate questions and attempting to interpret what was said, we are more hesitant in drawing conclusions in this chapter than in any other. Our impressions (and we do not feel we can call them anything other than impressions) were formed more from extended narratives during therapy than from specific questions and answers.

I want a baby. When husband or wife express the desire for a child, they may not be at all aware of their reasons. Most of us are not. We say, "Because I love children," and the answer seems enough, but there may be additional motives we keep under lock and key in our unconscious. A woman may feel that bearing a child will prove her womanhood. A man may hope it will affirm his manhood. An insecure wife may want a child in order to feel loved. Her husband may want a child he can boss around. Traditionally, society has rewarded couples for having children, and frowned upon those who avoided a family. Since the population bomb has been publicized, the tables have turned among some elements of society. Whatever the fashionable do's and don'ts, society has not yet learned to keep hands off the choice of husband and wife. Everyone from the next door neighbor to the butcher to would-be grandparents offers advice and applies pressures.

Not only would we expect our motives in desiring a child to affect how we respond to that child when it arrives, we would predict they will affect the relationship we have with our spouse. No one denies that bringing a child into the family unit alters the unit. How it changes the husband-wife relationship may depend on why each one wanted a child.

A small percentage of wives, and an even smaller percentage of husbands, admitted that the desire to have a child was their primary reason for marrying. Not many years ago, of course, theologians held that procreation is the purpose of marriage, and that sex is only moral when conception was possible. For these husbands and wives, however, marrying to have children was not, from what they said, tied to morality. For whatever combination of reasons, the woman or man wanted to parent a child. Marriage was the most acceptable and practical relationship in which to do so. Love and sex were, at best, of secondary importance. We asked one husband what he felt his reaction might have been if, prior to marrying, he had learned that his fiancée was unable to bear children. He said, "I would have called off the wedding. There would have been no reason to marry her." A mother of three children told us, "I had wanted a baby of my own from the time I was thirteen or fourteen. I guess I married the first boy who asked me in order to get one." It is more than possible that the initial motives were more loving than the statements would indicate and that we were hearing only a bitterness born of the scars of an unhappy marriage. We see no reason, however, to dismiss all such statements. If a woman can marry for financial security or a man marry for mothering, we feel sure a desire to give birth can be reason enough for others.

In attempting to study the relationship between husband-wife sexuality and desire for pregnancy, we again compared those couples with the most fulfilling sexual relationship with those who enjoyed sex much less. We were interested in finding answers to several questions:

Do children contribute to the happiness (or lack thereof) of the husband-and-wife relationship?

Couples with the best sexual relationships said no. Almost without exception, they felt the arrival of children neither added to nor detracted from their sexual love. "We enjoy our children," one wife told us. "It's hard to imagine what our life would be like without them, and maybe the challenge of four kids has helped each of us grow, but things were great—and that goes for sex—before we had kids, and they're still wonderful." On the other hand, many couples with less fulfilling relationships said they felt children had made a difference. Some for the better, some for the worse. One husband told us, "Things seemed all right before Kenney was born. Then it changed. She changed. I can't turn her on any more." Ironically, when we subsequently spoke with the wife, she said, "I became a new woman after our son was born. Maybe it was that I had a purpose in my life. Even our love life improved."

Was there a change in sexual relations during pregnancy?

For those with the best sexual relationship, again the answer was, no. "We made love the whole nine months," said one wife, "and it was just as good as before. Then the day after the baby was born, I wanted to have sex with my husband so bad I was almost tearing the sheets." Her husband concurred. "I don't know whether we did it any more during those months, but I'm sure we didn't do it any less. Was it good? Sure, it was great, like always. In fact, there was a special sexiness about her when she was pregnant. I loved stroking her tummy." Those in the lower-satisfaction group more often reported a change in level of satisfaction for one or both during pregnancy. Some felt it improved. This was usually attributed to being relieved of the fear of pregnancy (especially those who had adjusted—or resigned—to the pregnancy, once it was discovered) or to no longer having to employ contraceptive methods, which they found anti-erotic (e.g., condoms) or morally objectionable. Women who found a drop in desire or satisfaction during pregnancy frequently attributed it to what they believed to be a normal physical change. One told us her doctor had told her to expect the desire for sex to disappear during pregnancy. "The woman's body is totally directed toward nourishing and protecting the child; sex is turned off once conception occurs." (Unfortunately, sex education has only in recent years been introduced into the medical schools. Obviously after this physician's time.) Other women said intercourse during pregnancy was painful (although with a physically normal woman there is no reason why it should be). Fatigue was the explanation offered by some wives. "I was so exhausted the whole nine months," one young wife told us, "I just couldn't get turned on at all." A few said the same of nausea during their pregnancy. A small number said they feared the baby might somehow be injured if they engaged in active coitus, and this inhibited their response.

The majority of husbands in the lower-satisfaction group admitted a significant drop in desire during their wife's pregnancy, and less satisfaction when they did engage in lovemaking. Most of them found their wives physically unattractive. "From the time she was about six months along," a husband whose wife had recently given birth to her first child said, "she looked so deformed I couldn't get turned on at all." Some husbands in the same group said their interest in sex had diminished since the birth of their first child. Their explanations (excuses?) varied, but most complained of loss of "tightness" in the wife's vagina following delivery. A few told us they felt their desire had lessened as a result of having to "share" the attentions of the wife with the baby. One husband said the newborn was sleeping in the master bedroom. "I guess I'm just too uptight to get aroused with the baby there with us," he said.

Rivalry and jealousy between husband and baby was a common source of discord, especially for couples who had been married several years before starting their family. The husband, in his resentment, may sexually reject his wife. Reacting to his resentment, she may reject his advances.

Are you conscious of a desire for conception when you make love?

In 1967 we first described what we observed as a desire for impregnation felt by both husbands and wives in couples having very close and fulfilling marriages. It proved controversial then, and in view of the concern of many over population, it could trigger even more today. What we said then, we feel, was substantially supported by the couples we interviewed.

First, the question must be clearly understood. The question is *not* whether husband and/or wife have a desire, conscious or unconscious, for a child each time they make love. They may not. Another addition to the family may be the last thing either of them wants. The desire to be impregnated by the man you love and the desire to impregnate the woman you love is not the same as the desire to have a baby. At least not in the minds of some wives and husbands. The desire to impregnate or be impregnated is an emotional reaction to one's lover. The desire for a child may be partly emotional, but hopefully, it is largely rational, and it is centered on the hoped-for child rather than the lover. This distinction may seem more a matter of semantics than reality, but we are persuaded the distinction is valid.

Although few husbands and wives could identify with these feelings, those who did made a strong argument for the distinction. Each of these individuals was a partner in the marriage we judged to be among the most sexually fulfilling. The desire for impregnation would seem to be an outgrowth of a very deep, meaningful sexual love. If these desires do exist, they will probably be recognized by those husbands and wives who are inclined to be very introspective. Feelings being what they are, we seldom attempt to describe them; words are simply inadequate. And often we are only vaguely aware of them. For this reason, care was taken to phrase questions in an open-ended manner that suggested no desired or "correct" answers. The following is a compilation of the expressed feelings of several of these spouses:

"When I reach my orgasm I sometimes get an overwhelming feeling that I want all of him, that I want his baby" . . . "We had our last child four years ago, and we decided that was enough, but there are many times when we make love that I just feel so close to her and love her so much I wish we could make another baby" . . . "When I'm pregnant, it's like he's with me all the time. I'm carrying *him* for those nine months" . . . "I never had much interest in kids before I got married, but I wanted a baby with her—our baby. You know it's funny. Now that she's pregnant, I still get the feeling at times when we make love, especially those times when it's really fantastic, that I hope it will happen, that she will become pregnant" . . . "I certainly don't want any more children. Four is enough. But when we make love, I find myself almost hoping he'll make me pregnant. It's crazy."

Does a fear of pregnancy affect your enjoyment of sex?

In the enthusiasm which followed the introduction of the contraceptive pill, many popular writers hailed the advent of sex without fear. Now, they announced, women are free to enjoy sexual relations without the dread of an unwanted pregnancy. The voices have somewhat tempered since with findings that the pill, the most reliable contraceptive, is medically or psychologically inadvisable for many women. There are still many women of childbearing age who find themselves with no sure method of birth control. And others who for religious reasons can use no method other than periodic continence (the Rhythm method). Hence, we find there are still many couples who do not want to bring another child into the world, yet must take this risk each time they make love other than when the wife is having her menstrual period.

What, then, happens during sexual relations if this fear is present in the mind of the wife? Or the husband? Some, a small minority, said the fear caused them to virtually turn off completely. "I would turn cold all over whenever my husband came near," one wife told us. "I could relax only after he had a vasectomy, and I guess by then I had permanently lost interest in sex." Another wife said she had at one time refused to have sexual relations for over a year. "No, I didn't feel any strong desire. I think the fear was too strong." Her husband, she said, was "very understanding." He explained, "I love my wife too much to want to do anything which might make her uncomfortable. Besides, I think sex is overemphasized. It's not something you can't live without. There are other things more important in marriage." We asked them about the frequency of their relations when they had not been concerned about pregnancy. It had never averaged more than once a week.

Other wives told us of a strong fear of pregnancy but denied that the fear diminished their response. "I might be scared to death before, and scared to death after, but at the time, when I was aroused, all I could think about was having his penis in me," said one. There was a tendency by a number of these women to rationalize away these fears. "I could talk myself into believing it was the safe time of the month, no matter when it was," said one. "I'd be hotter than anything, and I would make a play for my husband. I'd tell him it was just before my period or my period had just ended or something and it was all right. At those times I didn't want my head to overrule my hormones."

When two women used the same words to describe their fears, it was impossible, of course, to tell if they did, in fact, *feel* the same. It is arguable, therefore, that those women who reported strong fear but said it did not diminish their sexual responsiveness were actually less fearful than those who were affected. Since in this situation fear and sex may be said to be competing drives, however, we might expect that those women who ordinarily had the strongest sex drives would have the least problem with responsiveness under conditions of fear. Conversely, those with low sex drive and difficulty responding when no fear existed might be expected to have even greater difficulty when an unwanted pregnancy might result. In general, this is what we found, but there were sufficient exceptions to make us question any rule of thumb except to say that the most highly sexed women were not unresponsive even in the face of what they said were great fears. And, in keeping with the law of competing drives, women reported that as they worked to develop their own sexual responsiveness, the fears they felt during periods of arousal and lovemaking were reduced.

As we listened to women relate their fears of pregnancy, we became increasingly aware that the fears were often not of pregnancy *per se.* They were a reflection of feelings held toward the husband. "Things had been touch-and-go between us. I can never be sure either one of us will stick it out. That's why the thought of having a baby scares me," were the feelings of one wife. Another said, "He's irresponsible. Sure, I'm afraid of getting pregnant. I can't rely on him. When our last one was born, he didn't even stay with me at the hospital." It is doubtful such feelings may properly be called *fear*. Hostility would be closer to it. And feelings of resentment and hostility most certainly can dampen sexual ardor in either sex. We feel there may be many cases of "fear of pregnancy" which mask a lack of trust, a battles of the sexes, and long-held resentments. When they are resolved, the "fears" may dissipate.

Contraception and sterilization: There is yet no "perfect" method of contraception. Nature is not easily foiled. Some means are esthetically objectionable, others have undesirable or even dangerous physical and psychophysiological side effects. And many are far less than reliable. Does the contraceptive employed affect sexual response? There is substantial evidence that it can.

Most of us would agree that sexual love, like the human body, has beauty, but that its beauty is affected by all that surrounds it. When the method of contraception becomes a part of the preliminaries to lovemaking, the esthetics of the method may affect response and satisfaction of either husband or wife. If they have been engaged in mutually arousing acts and are eager to engage in coitus, to pause to insert foams or jellies, or to roll on a condom, may be enough to cool their passions. Sexual love should always have a romance, beauty, and mystery to it. A husband may appreciate the fact that his wife douches daily yet not desire to see her douching. She may enjoy his clean breath without being turned on by watching him brush his teeth. Most couples who had employed contraceptives which called for such "preliminaries" to coitus admitted they were anti-erotic. For some, the effect was strong enough to cause them to lose interest.

Contraceptive pills, while they do not present an esthetic problem, may have side effects which curb the woman's sexual response. This was not initially recognized, but it has come to the attention of doctors increasingly in recent years. The effect can be subtle. The wife may find her sex drive and response gradually dropping off, yet not know why until her doctor questions her. Often the doctor will change her prescription. There are a number of similar, but chemically slightly different, pills on the market. They may not all cause the same reaction.

There have been disturbing reports of serious physical side effects of oral contraceptives appearing in the press in recent years. Oral contraceptives are not risk free. No medication is, not even aspirin. There may be serious dangers involved for some women in taking oral contraceptives. For others, the dangers may be less or perhaps nonexistent. Considerable research is in progress evaluating these possible risks. The doctor, staying informed of these research findings, is in the best position to judge whether it is reasonably safe *for his patient* to take this or any other medication. The woman for whom oral contraceptives have been prescribed should keep in mind, however, that she is taking medication, and as with any medication program, it is important that it be monitored by the patient's physician through regularly scheduled check-ups.

If oral contraceptives are felt to be physically or emotionally undesirable, the doctor may be able to suggest other methods. The intrauterine device (IUD) is one alternative. Again, however, some women have incurred serious physical problems with the IUD and each woman should check with her physician.

Periodic abstinence (Rhythm method) is not, strictly speaking, a contraceptive method, but it is a method of birth control. As more than a few couples have said, it calls for making love by the calendar. The majority of couples who were practicing Roman Catholics married ten years or more, had some experience with the Rhythm method. Almost all said they found it unsatisfactory. The spontaneity of their lovemaking had to give way to temperature charts and dates of her cycle. To make it "work," they found they had to try to avoid usual gestures of physical affection during those days when coitus wasn't "safe." Often this placed a strain on the relationship. On those days when the calendar said it was permissible, many said they felt they *had* to engage in sex, to grab the chance while they had it. It became a demand. Included among the problems attributed to use of the Rhythm method by those interviewed were premature ejaculation, impotence, orgasmic dysfunction, ejaculatory dysfunction, and acute anxiety. We felt in many cases the Rhythm method was being made too much the scapegoat. These problems seldom have a single root. Overall, however, few could find anything good to say about the effects the practice had on their love relationship.

As we said, there appears to be no "perfect" method of birth control, none which can be said to have no adverse effect on the couple's sexual relationship. Couples would be well-advised to consider the pros and cons sexually as well as physically in the selection of a method. There *are* pros—the other side of the coin—to be found in effective contraception for many couples. The sexual freedom resultant from contraception has perhaps been overpublicized, but it is a reality which was confirmed by many couples. So long as there was a strong possibility of pregnancy whenever a couple made love, as there was until recently, acts of sexual love were procreative acts psychologically as well as physically. With effective contraception, sexuality in the marriage takes its proper place as the highest form of loving. Conception of a child is then an expression of their mutual love, a desire to give living form to the love they share, not a risk they take or a price they pay. The majority of couples said they felt their enjoyment of sex would be curtailed if pregnancy stood as an ever present possibility. "If I were in my mother's position, always waiting for the next period, I think I'd be an ice cube when I climbed into bed," was the way one young wife put it. "The pill didn't come along until after Mom went through the change of life. She had seven kids and three or four miscarriages. That's a good way to lose interest in sex. If she ever had any."

We interviewed no couples with two or more children who had not employed some method of birth control. It is, therefore, not possible to discuss possible effects that nonplanning might have on a couple's sexual satisfaction. It would seem, to that extent, that we live in a contraceptive age. Surprisingly, we found that a majority of husbands and wives had given little or no thought to the question of the possibility of conception as it relates to sexual satisfaction. The reactions, as we found, vary widely. It would seem advisable for couples to examine their individual reactions to any contemplated contraceptive method. Effectiveness in preventing conception, to express it in another way, is not the sole consideration.

Voluntary sterilization: In recent years, vasectomy, an operation on the male in which the vas deferens, the tubes which transport the sperm from the testes, are severed in order to produce sterilization, has been promoted by advocates of population control. Surgically, the procedure is relatively simple, does not incapacitate the patient, generally results in little discomfort, and, if performed correctly, is 100 per cent effective. It is also, at present, rarely reversible, should the man decide at some later date that he wishes to father a child.

The psychological effects on the man and on the woman with whom he is engaged in sexual love are less understood. While in approximately 15 per cent of the couples interviewed the husband had undergone vasectomy, reactions to the sterilization were difficult to elicit from either husbands or wives. Hence, we can make no general statements other than to suggest that further study, perhaps by extensive, large-scale, in-depth interviews, might prove fruitful in understanding the relationship between sexual fulfillment and procreation. Our interviews suggested the following as some of the questions which might be considered. Was it the wife or husband who urged vasectomy? Could the relationship be described as dominated by the husband, by the wife, or as egalitarian? How satisfying was the sexual relationship prior to vasectomy? And following? How did the husband see himself (his self-image) before and after? How did she see him? Has there been any change in desired frequency of sexual relationships, since vasectomy, by husband or wife? Have specific sexual problems (impotence, premature ejaculation, orgasmic dysfunction) arisen for either spouse since the operation? Any regrets? Resentments?

Tubal ligation, a surgical procedure for the sterilization of the woman, is more complex, involving as it does penetration of the abdominal cavity in order to tie off the fallopian tubes. It is consequently less common than vasectomy. The small percentage of women interviewed who had undergone tubal ligation had had the surgery as an adjunct to abdominal surgery or childbirth. Again, we feel no conclusions can be drawn regarding the psychosexual effects. The same questions might, however, be asked.

Since voluntary sterilization must, at present, be considered irreversible, it would seem that, even more than in the choice of a contraceptive, a couple should attempt to examine their motives, attitudes, and possible reactions before taking such a step. Sometimes the end, avoiding another pregnancy, can make virtually any sure means seem reasonable. We are psychological beings, however, as well as physical organisms, and the psychology of our sexuality is as complex and finely tuned—and as easily tipped out of balance—as any in our makeup.

The love which is expressed in the desire to share with another in the creation of another life can perhaps never be fully understood, let alone explained, by any of us. When there is a deep sexual love between husband and wife, it is not having "a baby" they desire; it is having *his* baby or *our* baby. They share the love and responsibility for the child just as they share the joy in the sexual love in which the child is conceived. It is for this reason, we feel sure, that so many couples we have counseled with troubled marriages—once their marriages again began to grow and reach fulfillment—have felt the surge of desire to "make a baby"—together.

CHAPTER 12

And Others

No matter how perfect—or practically perfect—
a wife may be, she always has to watch out for the
Other Woman. The Other Woman, according to my
definition, is anyone able to charm my husband,
amuse my husband, attract my husband, or occupy
his wholehearted interest for more than 30 seconds
straight.

Judith Viorst
Yes, Married

Erotic love excludes the love for others only
in the sense of erotic fusion, full commitment
in all aspects of life—but not in the sense
of deep brotherly love.

Erich Fromm
The Art of Loving

The best thing ever for our marriage was divorce.
We divorced my parents, her parents, and the
neighbors.

A husband

Come fly with me—to Acapulco, Tahiti, Costa del Sol, the Casbah. Just the two of us, without phones, neighbors, relatives, friends, kids, or door-to-door salesmen. Away from obligatory cocktail parties, bridge games, and business lunches. The two of us, loving and laughing together, leaving the world behind. A dream all lovers share.

There are those who claim the dream must vanish in the confrontation with reality. We live in a real world, they say; you can't live in an ivory tower; you can't shut people out of your life. They may be right. We have walked that beach in Tahiti only to come home to the social morass with its pressures and temptations. Few, if any, of us can fly away to a haven for two.

Is the answer then, "If you can't fight 'em, join 'em?" Become a full member of the social circus? If we do, what happens to the love affair? Do we try to love one another—everyone—to include them in our mutual love? Sexually? Does all love have a sexual component?

The sexual relationship, we found, was threatened by interference, influence, and infidelity. Very few couples escaped the negative effects.

Interference and influence are hard to separate. Often they come from the same sources. The influence of parents may interfere without sexual development. It also may continue, overtly or covertly, after marriage. A sizable majority of husbands and wives said they had experienced some degree of problems with parents of one or both. The interference was seldom in the area of sex, at least not directly. Any interference, however, almost inevitably touched the sexual relationship of the couple. Some marriage sages have said that when we marry, we don't just marry a single individual, we marry his or her entire family. For most couples, this seems to have an unfortunate truth to it.

Infidelity, it would seem, is not, for many couples, limited to matters of adultery. Husband or wife can be unfaithful to their commitment through involvement with a job, hobby, organization, friends, or relatives. A husband can make a mistress of his job or his golf game. A wife can make a lover of her career or her bridge club. And both can get so wrapped up in children, their love affair suffers. Parents most frequently fall into this role of the "third party." This is understandable. The parent of the opposite sex is ordinarily our first sex object, our first introduction to heterosexual love. Mothers and sons, fathers and daughters. The relationships are unique. And they are sexual. Not usually in any overt, obvious way, but sexual nevertheless. Almost half the couples reported feelings of rivalry and jealousy involving a parent of one of the spouses. Many wives reacted to their husband's mother as if they were women with designs on their sons. "If she were some little typist with hot pants in his office, I'd pull her hair out, but what can I do when it's his mother?" one wife told us. A husband said, "At times I think she would be happier if she had married her father. To listen to her, he's everything a woman could want." In a large number of cases, it was the spouse's parent of the same sex who caused the trouble, particularly the wife's mother. If the mother has experienced sexual dissatisfaction in her own marriage, the interference may come in the form of bitter advice ("Don't give in to him every time. A man is only interested in one thing.") and dire warnings ("You can't expect a man to stay interested in a woman once she loses her youth.") A cynical father, unhappy in his marriage, may try to steer his son toward the same mysogyny ("You've got to let her know who's boss. Give a woman half a chance, and she'll cut your balls off.").

Most of the influence and interference, however, was not so openly hostile or negative. In growing up, we spend perhaps twenty years or more playing the role of child to our parents. There is no magical age at which the role ends and is replaced by adult-to-adult roles. We cannot play the role of child-to-parent for those many years without it becoming a part of us which we continue to act out whenever we are with our parents. A number of husbands and wives said their spouses were not the same when their parents were present. "It's as if he becomes her son and stops being my husband," was the way one wife described it. "I can't put my finger on it. A lot of little things. She raises an eyebrow and he responds. I know it's awfully hard for me to be turned on to him when she is staying with us." A husband told us, "When my mother-in-law visits, sex comes to a halt. Her bedroom is next to ours and my wife gets uptight about the chance of her hearing us. You'd think we were breaking the law." We concluded that it was more often the mere presence of the parent rather than any direct interference which had an undesirable effect on the couples in their sexual relationship.

For most such couples, the solution to the problems raised by the presence of parents of either or both spouses did not lie in any psychological restructuring of the parent-child relationship, but in curtailing the frequency of contact. For many, this meant virtually severing the relationship until such time as the husband/wife relationship had strengthened and become more fulfilling. This was, of course, particularly difficult in those cases where parents lived in close proximity, and it was made more difficult when the parents (and frequently the other spouse) had problems accepting the necessity of such "drastic" action. It is apparently not easy for any of us to admit the extent to which we are influenced by those around us, especially when they are our parents. (We like to believe that in growing up we left all such influence behind.)

Friends can be almost as strong an influence as parents, and in some cases, stronger. Generally, however, the influence of friends served primarily to reinforce the influence of the parents and the previously well-ingrained attitudes of the husband or wife. Repeatedly, we were reminded of the saying "water seeks its own level." Friends of a wife who, for example, held negative attitudes toward sex would most often hold similar views. The "macho" husband who views women with disdain will usually select friends who share his male chauvinism. Even when we are not involved with friends who hold negative attitudes, we are virtually surrounded by neighbors and coworkers who take a dim view of marriage and marital sex. It permeates our entire society. How many novels portray the erotic love of husband and wife? Are there any? Haven't we all heard how sex loses it excitement with the passing years of marriage?

The late Eric Berne, founder of transactional analysis, spoke of the situation which exists when wives get together. A wife can gripe about her husband without the other wives challenging her. Another wife can make fun of her husband. That's acceptable. A wife may remain silent and, by her silence, give support to complaints of her "sisters." The one thing a wife cannot do in such a gathering is to profess to being deeply in love with her spouse. If she does, she will be pinned to the wall. They will exclude her from their group. The only exception is when she has been married less than a year, and then only to patronize her ("You just wait until you have been married five years. Or, just wait until you have a couple of kids. Men are all alike, He'll start chasing other women.").

Men are no less subject to such pressures. If one man, at the close of the workday, should suggest to his coworkers that they stop at the corner bar for a drink, the pressure is on. If one of them declines, saying, "Count me out. I'm anxious to get home to my wife," he will be nailed to the masculine wall. "You're really tied to her apron strings!" "She's got you by the balls!" They will not accept the possibility that he may sincerely *want* to be with his wife. (Again, they may make an exception if he is newly wed. Then they will make his desires the subject of sexual jokes.) A mistress, yes. A wife, forget it. Such is the stature of marriage in our society. And of marital love.

Many couples found it necessary to avoid friends and neighbors, and their cynicism, once they set out to build a love affair in their marriage. It is not that they became antisocial. They became "wrapped up" in each other, not really different from the way it was for most of us when we were going together during the engagement period. This is not an easy choice to make. Developing a "circle" of friends is considered as important to marriage as joint bank accounts and life insurance. Husbands and wives give up dating. They go out to dinner with other couples. They even vacation with friends. The wedding turns the couple into a group. Friends are his, hers, and theirs. No man and woman can develop and maintain a close, romantic love in that kind of environment.

Friends and relatives threaten the relationship in any of three ways: (1) negative attitudes toward sex, members of the other sex, or marriage, (2) involvements which demand time and an investment of emotional energy which lessens what they have to give to each other, (3) infidelity, whether passing flirtations or adultery.

In recent years infidelity has become fashionable. It doesn't always carry the label. Under the aegis of liberation, husbands and wives have close "friends" of the other sex. He takes his secretary to lunch and goes out with a female colleague for a night on the town when away on a business meeting. She meets a male friend for dinner to discuss their mutual interest in a charity drive or tennis, spends an afternoon on the ski slopes with her husband's best friend. All in the name of being "just friends." Over 50 per cent of husbands and wives interviewed married five years or longer had been involved in extramarital relations—adultery. (The figures were slightly higher for women, but not significantly so.) In the majority of cases, the partner in adultery was either a friend of both husband and wife or someone with whom the errant spouse was involved professionally or in common interests. Adultery, it seems, seldom happens "by accident." The husband or wife may not start out with the intention of starting an affair. "I didn't plan it; it just happened," was the explanation we heard repeatedly, and we are persuaded it is true. The goal was social, not carnal. We are all of us, however, human beings, subject to the same sexual drives and weak will. Given an environment of sufficient provocation, and a normal sex drive, few of us can resist indefinitely.

Even overt adultery, beyond cocktail-party flirtations, has been condoned by some self-proclaimed sex authorities recently. The advocates of "swinging," the mutually accepted adultery which passes for sexual sophistication, claim that the practice can enhance marriage by adding variety and relieving boredom. We know of no study which has provided reliable evidence on the incidence of "swinging" in our contemporary urban and suburban society. Estimates in the United States have run as high as twenty million couples. Since such high estimates have been given by advocates of mate-swapping, however, we suspect they may be tinged with more than a modicum of proselytizing—"Why not try it? Everybody does." We doubt that the actual incidence is anywhere near as high as they claim. More important, we feel, are the effects it may have on the participants and on the marital relationship. Of the couples interviewed, only a small percentage had engaged in mutually agreed-upon extramarital sex. We do not suggest they are representative of all or most "swinging" couples. We don't know. In none of the cases, however, were we able to conclude that the relationship of husband and wife had deepened and grown closer as a result of the extramarital sex. Nor did this appear in any way to be the motive of either spouse. Most frequently, it was suggested by the husband. Once the wife agreed, however, she was generally as enthusiastic a participant as the husband, sometimes more so. While homosexual acts between the wives were common, almost universal among the experienced "swingers," none of the couples reported homosexual activity between the husbands. The other couple or couples involved were generally close friends of long standing, often neighbors or "old school chums."

Typically, these couples liked to see themselves as broad-minded, liberal, well-educated, and above average in sexuality. Compared with all couples interviewed, however, the sex drive as well as sex experience of both husbands and wives in the sample were lower. The "swinging" husbands averaged less sexual experience prior to marriage. The majority were, in fact, virgins when they married. Some explained their interest in extramarital sex in terms of "making up for what I missed before marriage." These husbands were above average for the entire sample in incidence of sexual dysfunction—premature ejaculation, impotence reactions, and ejaculatory dysfunction. Although none of these husbands said they had sought sexual "variety" in hopes of overcoming their problems, we feel this may have been a motive for some (e.g., "This other gal had a great body, huge tits, but I'll be damned if I still didn't have trouble keeping it up.").

If a number of these husbands are motivated by the desire to stimulate their sex drive or improve their sexual performance or overcome boredom or find a partner who will engage in acts which their wives will not, what motivates the wives? Although almost every wife said she had "gone along with it" in order to please her husband or "because if I didn't join him, I think he might go after something on his own," the interviews revealed other motives. These included a need to feel desirable, homosexual desires, opportunity to act out fantasies, a desire to rebel against parental values, relief of boredom, and even the desire to win in competition with the other wives. A few said they were not sexually satisfied by their husband and felt perhaps they could be with another man. One wife said she wanted to find out if all men were built alike!

Whatever the motives of these spouses, was there indication that the "swinging" experience improved their marriages, as claimed by advocates? We have no clear answer to this question. The answer lies in the reactions of each husband and wife, and in their goals for the relationship. In this, swinging does not differ from adultery under any other name or form. Some couples said the experience brought a crisis to their marriage which brought them close to dissolving the marriage, and, facing this, to re-evaluate their goals. One wife told us, "The morning after we got involved with the other couple—it only happened that one time—I felt my world had come to an end. I didn't want to look at my husband, and I couldn't stand myself. I thought seriously of leaving, just walking out. Then a couple of days later we talked, and we both cried. That's when we decided to start over at the beginning and build what we both had wanted when we married. Maybe we had to climb down into that awful cesspool before we could come to our senses." Other couples said the experience served as an escape from what they had found to be an almost intolerable boredom. "We had gotten into a dreadful rut," a twelve-year-married wife said. "Changing partners with another couple blasted us out of that rut. Sure, I guess it was traumatic. I hadn't been raised to handle anything like that. But if it hadn't been for our experience in swinging, we might have split up. Did it help our marriage? How do you answer that? It may have kept us together. It may have kept both of us from screaming. After all, we have three kids."

We have counseled many couples who sought help because they were facing the painful crisis of discovered adultery. In almost every case, this was a traumatic discovery. For many husbands and wives, adultery is still the "unforgettable sin." Yet there is a difference between the sexes. The reactions were usually as follows: If the husband had been unfaithful, the wife felt she might never be able to forgive him. The husband, if he was repentant, took the total blame on himself. If the wife was the one involved in adultery, she felt she had been "driven" to it by the lack of affection and romance exhibited by her husband. And, surprisingly, her husband usually agreed. In other words, if the husband had an affair, he was to blame; if the wife had an affair, he was to blame. The husband carries the culpability in either case. It would seem these attitudes are based on a position held by both sexes: Men are unfaithful by nature; women, having less interest in sex but a greater interest in love and romance, stray only when they feel rejected. A double standard built on distortions! We know of no evidence which would support the notion that any difference exists between the sexes either in their temptation to adultery or their culpability. Adultery is a manifestation of infidelity—a failure to remain faithful to the commitments made in the marriage. The effects of adultery will thus be a reflection of the seriousness with which these commitments are made and received. Adultery, however, is not the only act of infidelity. We can be unfaithful to our commitments in many ways. Anytime we place something or someone ahead of the one we have chosen, we are being unfaithful. It could be hobby, friends, occupation, or even television. It seems that, to most people, only adultery breaches the commitment.

The data in the Kinsey report indicate one or both spouses in the average marriage engage in extramarital relations one or more times.

What happens to the marriage when it is discovered by the "betrayed" spouse depends upon several factors: the desire to "save" the marriage on the part of both, the emotional reaction they may have to adultery, and the state of the relationship prior to the adultery. Overall, most couples who had been through the problem of adultery had found they could use what they had learned from the experience to build upon. It was not the end of the marriage. Adultery, we are convinced, is almost always a symptom of either the sexual problems of the adulterous spouse (e.g., doubts of sexual adequacy), or emotional frustrations and strong and unfulfilled ego needs. It is neither inevitable nor is it a solution—even for those swingers who claim it "helped" their relationship.

We feel sure that few couples contemplate adulterous relationships when they enter marriage. They love each other and desire each other ⌐exclusively. It is only later that infidelity may shatter their bond. Despite the gloomy statistics and the media popularizations of adultery, however, most of the husbands and wives we interviewed had not been unfaithful. The reasons given for *not* having an affair were what we had expected. The majority of both sexes admitted they might have had an affair, given the opportunity, but had not, either out of fear of the consequences or inability to attract a partner. The consequences feared might have been moral, based on a belief that adultery is a serious sin punishable by eternal damnation. Most often, however, it was a fear of what an affair might do to the marriage. "I've thought about it a lot of times," one husband told us, "but I know my wife would leave me and take the kids with her if she found out. It's not worth taking that kind of risk." A wife said, "I'm too much of a coward to try anything like that. I live in a small town. There's too much chance of being caught." The largest number claimed simply a lack of opportunity. This may seem surprising in view of the freedom of movement enjoyed by so many husbands and wives. Many husbands interviewed made frequent trips without their wives to business meetings and conventions. Most wives were free during the day to take shopping trips or pursue recreational interests with no one to check up on them. The "lack of opportunity" was, in reality, a lack of self-confidence. A distinguished-looking, well-to-do executive with an electronics firm explained: "I couldn't just start talking to some gal on a plane or in a cocktail lounge and expect her to end up in my hotel room. I don't know how some guys do it. I wouldn't know what to say." Ironically, his wife told us, "I never learned how to give a man a 'come on.' I had this instructor in a ceramics class I took. I could have gone for him, but I didn't know how to let him know it. Flirting is not my long suit, I guess."

Are we forced to conclude that monogamy is, at best, *tolerated* by husbands and wives, and that those who remain within the bonds of marital fidelity do so not out of love and sexual satisfaction but out of fear and/or feelings of obligation? We do not think so. Those couples who had worked against boredom in sex and toward a close, exciting, romantic relationship, remained faithful to each other out of preference, nothing else. They also chose to spend their free time together rather than with friends. They were not turned off to others, just very much turned on to each other. It is not that they do not find others sexually desirable, only that they find each other even more desirable. The majority of couples either denied the possibility that such a close relationship could exist or condemned it as unhealthy.

"Any husband and wife who want to spend all their time together must have some kind of neurotic dependency on one another," one husband said. "My husband and I go out with other couples quite often," said his wife. "We have gone on vacations with this one couple we like very much. It seems normal to me, and a lot more fun." They admitted they had not wanted others along on their dates before they married, and never would have considered having another couple go along on the honeymoon, but "that was different; after a while you run out of things to talk about." Since their marriage had not remained a love affair, they found it impossible to comprehend how any couple might have kept what they had lost—or never had.

Overwhelmingly, the interviews pointed to an inverse relationship between social involvement with others and fulfillment in the marriage. The more the husband and/or wife were involved with friends or relatives, the less they were likely to report their relationship as being fulfilling or even satisfactory. Which is cause and which effect may not be as important as the question of how the effect is to be overcome? And the further question. Does the couple *want* to build and maintain a love affair which is emotionally, intellectually and sexually exciting? If they do, and they are willing to pay the price to achieve it, they will continually evaluate their priorities and put "first things first." Facing such an *either-or* alternative may not be easy. We live in a cultural climate that tempts us into the belief that we can have *both*, that we don't have to choose between desirable, but incompatible, alternatives. We are seduced by the myth that we don't have to give up *A* in order to achieve *B* when *A* and *B* are both desirable, yet mutually exclusive.

None of us likes facing the harsh realities of the world in which we live. We have no choice, however, if we are to make sense of our own lives, if we are to reach our chosen goals, and if we are to find happiness in an all too often unhappy world. If we live in a germ-ridden environment, we cannot expect to remain free of illness. The couple in love have but two choices: They can enter into and become members of an unhealthy, anti-love society, or they can build a wall against those "significant others" who would, through pressure and influence, erode their love.

CHAPTER 13

The Problem Areas

*After all the erring and meanderings, impasses
and false starts, heroic enterprises and sweaty
efforts—that it should come to this! And should
a man be able to land on the moon, and worry less
about his return than whether, once returned, he
can satisfy his wife?*

Wolfgang Lederer, M.D.
The Fear of Women

*What does this mean? With everything gone wrong:
My bed hopeless and hard,
coverlet and blanket fallen to the floor—
no sheet at all throughout the endless night
while every bone in my poor twisted body
cries out in pain?
Am I attacked by Love before I know it?
The subtle sickness?
That's it: invisible arrows in my heart;
merciless Love is here to tear my breast.*

Ovid
Love Poems of Ovid

*W*hen one reads how-to sex books, the impression comes through that some authors view sex as a series of physical and emotional hurdles to be surmounted, a succession of struggles to overcome "problems." And loving is more or less an oasis in our forced march through the marital desert. We cannot minimize the pain suffered by couples who experience severe problems in their sexual relationship. We have found, however, that the emphasis given to these problems is, for reasons not easily understood, far greater than that given to lack of communication, verbal and even physical abuse, and an overall absence of mutual love. Frequently, the couple fails to recognize a relationship between their sexual response and their mutual respect and love.

Sexual problems can be the result of physical problems, unhealthy sexual attitudes, or difficulties in the husband/wife relationship. They can also stem from ignorance of the basic facts of sex, although when this is present it is usually, we have found, associated with unhealthy attitudes.

In the vast majority of cases, no demonstrable physical problem is present. Some physical conditions can, it is true, result in sexual dysfunction, but this is, fortunately, rare. Once the question of physical pathology has been ruled out, we can look to the emotional psychological factors responsible. This does not mean that the approach toward overcoming the problems is through a strictly "mental" process— psychotherapy or other "talk therapy." Attitudes and action must be combined, and actions must usually precede any change in attitudes.

The question of what is adequate sexual functioning for either sex has never been satisfactorily answered. And this, in itself, creates a problem. What constitutes a sexual problem? Does the man who is able to achieve an erection with his wife but not with a prostitute have a sexual problem? Does the husband who desires to make love only once a week have a problem? Or does his wife, who would like to make love once or twice a day? If a wife cannot reach orgasm during coitus without some type of direct stimulation of her clitoris, is she suffering an "orgasmic dysfunction"? At what point and under what circumstances can a man's ejaculation be said to be "premature"? It is tempting to follow the lead of some writers and say the individual has a problem whenever he or she thinks a problem exists. But this is no answer at all. The adult male who is chronically incapable of achieving an erection has a problem—even if he has convinced himself it is "nothing to worry about." Sexual problems do exist. They are prevalent. And they are a major cause, directly and indirectly, of marital discord.

FEMALE ORGASMIC INADEQUACY

In 1953, Alfred Kinsey and his associates published their study of the sexual behavior of nearly eight thousand women. They collected data on virtually every conceivable factor affecting orgasm: age, educational level, parental occupational class, decade of birth, age at onset of adolescence, religious background, age at marriage, length of marriage, techniques of marital coitus, orgasm in marital coitus vs. premarital orgasm, orgasm in marital coitus vs. premarital experience, orgasm in marital coitus vs. premarital petting to orgasm, orgasm in marital coitus vs. premarital experience in masturbation, multiple orgasm, the intrinsic capacity of the female for orgasm, and the incidence of female orgasm. Almost every factor—but not all. Freud had theorized about the female orgasm and, although his theories have been roundly criticized in recent years, established the distinction between the "vaginal" and "clitoral" orgasm. Dr. Marie Robinson, a Freudian psychiatrist, in 1959 published a self-help book for women suffering from "frigidity" which followed the Freudian doctrine and which is still selling briskly. Then, in 1966, Masters and Johnson published *Human Sexual Response*, followed in 1970 by *Human Sexual Inadequacy*. Findings presented in the 1966 work answered many questions about the physiology of the female response. They didn't completely lay to rest the "clitoral" vs. "vaginal" orgasm controversy; they simply made the argument unimportant. In the work on sexual inadequacy they described a therapeutic technique they have employed in the "treatment" of orgasmic dysfunction. While not ignoring the psychological aspects, the focus of their treatment program is on behavioral techniques with husband and wife as a "unit."

Despite the correlational data of Kinsey and the theoretical formulations of Freud and other psychotherapists, only recently has systematic, controlled research been applied to investigation of orgasmic inadequacy. Psychologist Dr. Seymour Fisher sought to study the psychological aspects of the sexual behavior investigated by Kinsey and his associates and Masters and Johnson. Following thorough examination of prior research and speculations concerning woman's sexual responsiveness, Fisher presents findings of his own based upon extensive questionnaires and psychological test data (as well as some physiological data) of multiple groups of married women. For the reader seriously interested in studying what variables have been investigated by Fisher and others—and the results of these investigations—we recommend Fisher's work, *The Female Orgasm* (pp. 223–38). Even listing the large number of variables which have been investigated is beyond the scope and purpose of this book. The most significant variable found by Fisher to separate the high—and low—orgasic women was the way in which they depicted their fathers. He found, "A majority of the low-orgasm consistency women described their fathers as unavailable for a substantial or consistent relationship." They indicated an absence of a meaningful relationship with their fathers. The majority of a high-orgasmic women, on the other hand, depicted their fathers as being available for a substantial relationship. Further, the high-orgasmic women more often described their fathers as men who valued morality, honesty, and strictness in adhering to rules. Their fathers were less "casual" and more "demanding." As employed by Fisher, the description refers "to modes of behavior that have to do with setting definite standards and expecting conformance to certain values." These findings were related to overall findings that a "the greater a woman's feeling that love objects are not dependable (that they are easily lost or will disappear), the less likely she is to attain orgasm." Fisher theorized that "the woman who feels that objects are undependable and who fears their loss finds the blurring of her relationships with objects that is produced by sexual excitement so threatening that she has to 'turn it off.'"

Many sex-manual writers who have lacked professional qualifications (or who have ignored the available data) have said there is no such thing as a frigid woman; only inept lovers. The implication is that if the husband is skilled in technique, or endurance in "foreplay" or coitus, or variety of romantic gestures, he will bring the most unresponsive woman to orgasm. There has been no research which supports this old sexual myth, including the Fisher findings. Our findings are not at variance with those of Fisher or his predecessors. We, too, have not found "technique" to be a significant variable in the wife's attainment of orgasm. We have not been able, however, to dismiss the husband's actions during sexual relations and otherwise as unimportant in the orgasmic response of the wife.

The percentage of women in our group who reported difficulty in attainment of orgasm during sexual relations with the husband is higher than the percentage of nonorgasmic or "occasionally" orgasmic women reported by other investigators (e.g., Kinsey *et al*, Fisher). This, it seems is explainable in terms of the fact that a high percentage of our couples had initially sought help for their marital problems (including, of course, sexual inadequacies). We feel, however, that this does not invalidate any findings regarding the etiology of the orgasmic inadequacy of these wives, or the possibility of its general application to an overall population of women. Investigators have found, on the average, that almost two thirds of married women fail to achieve orgasm *consistently* during intercourse (although, on the average, they experience their sexual encounters positively). Most women enjoy intercourse and consider their sexual life to be important to their overall satisfaction in marriage. Still, we find many women who, unable to achieve orgasm with consistency, feel "cheated" in their marriage.

While not refuting the findings of Fisher, our findings raise further questions. The low-frequency-orgasmic women in our sample reported, on the average, a relationship with their fathers similar to those in the Fisher groups. Their fathers were, by their descriptions, "easygoing," "detached," "passive," "uninvolved," "permissive," "a little boy," "easily manipulated," "weak," "sweet," and "nice guy." Supportive of Fisher's findings, many of the women in our low-frequency group had feelings of "distance" in their relationship with their fathers. Some had lost their fathers through death or desertion. Others were raised by mothers following divorce. A majority said they had little (or less than the desired amount) involvement with their fathers due to the father's absorption in business pursuits. As Fisher found, the majority felt they had been unable to establish a "meaningful" relationship with the father. We asked the women in our sample for detailed descriptions of their husband's personality as well as behavior during sexual relations. Two principal findings emerged. The first finding shows a striking similarity between the personality characteristics of the fathers and the husbands. The low-orgasmic women employed many of the descriptive terms used above in describing their fathers when describing their husbands. They saw their husbands as lacking strength and firm convictions, as being indecisive, and as "distant" and "uninvolved." A majority said they had at times felt their husbands were less than "manly." It is not surprising, of course, to find that the descriptions were often close to those of the fathers. Our first love object of the other sex is most often our parent of the other sex. The girl's father becomes her model of the desirable husband. Often, this is not conscious. She may, in fact, hold strong conscious resentments toward him, and may insist her husband is nothing at all like her father. Careful inquiry, however, including elicited descriptive adjectives, reveal the perceived similarities. The second finding is, perhaps, not unrelated to the first. A very high percentage of women in the low-orgasmic group described a pattern of sexual performance on the part of the husband which evidenced a lack of self-confidence and/or a lack of strong sexual interest in women (i.e., weak arousal state when engaged in sexual relations).

This latter finding was of considerable interest, since, to our knowledge, it has not been previously investigated in relation to the female sexual response. While the husband's "technique" has not been found to be related, his general evidence of arousal has not been studied. While no one would probably question the suggestion that a husband's impotence could have a dampening effect on the wife's response sufficient to inhibit her orgasm, what of the husband who is not clinically diagnosable as impotent but is nevertheless often not "powerfully" aroused in lovemaking? The majority of low-orgasmic women said the sexual self-confidence of the husband did have an effect on their response—including orgasmic response. Among women in this group who denied any impotence or premature-ejaculation problems in their husbands, almost all, when questioned, described his sexual response as less than consistently and strongly potent during sexual relations. The following are typical:

> He has an erection, I would say, only about half the time when he starts making love to me. Maybe less than that. When I work on him with my hand, or sometimes with my mouth—if you know what I mean—he gets hard. But when I stop, he often goes soft. I

don't mean that he has a problem keeping it up. He usually gets an erection again pretty quickly when I go back to stimulating him.

There is only one thing that bothers me. When I ask him to do something for me, like kissing my breasts or going down on me, he doesn't seem very aroused by it. Unless I'm masturbating him or going down on him at the same time, he doesn't stay hard.

Sometimes I wonder if I don't turn him off. We usually have sex in the woman-astride position. It's what he wants. I wonder if he doesn't like the passive role rather than having to make love to me. Even then he sometimes starts to go soft when he's in me. And then I start to worry that he may get hurt if I'm on top and coming up and down on his cock when he starts to lose it. A couple of times it sort of bent. It hurt him, and he got angry.

He's never had any problem with impotency that I know of. At least not with me. I start to play with his penis and he is usually erect within a few minutes. If I have any complaint in that regard, it is that it gets him too aroused. As soon as he gets hard, he wants to put it in. Then when he does, he comes almost right away. He can't hold back. I guess his sex drive is just too strong.

What might their sexual response be if their husbands were consistently and strongly potent and self-assured enough not to experience anxiety-induced premature ejaculation? Would they then be orgasmic? There are no data which can give us an answer to this question. If the fathers of the low-orgasmic women tend to be "weak" and "passive" and lacking in strength and self-assurance, and these women marry men similar in personality to their fathers, we have no way of determining what their responsiveness *might* be if they were paired with men very different (i.e., more self-assured, more consistently potent). As has been noted many times, in second and third marriages, the partner chosen most often is very similar in personality to the first mate. If strength of the husband's potency and his self-assurance in sex are important factors in the consistency of the woman's orgasm, we can then ask whether this is related primarily to the husband's ability to perform *physically* in a more satisfying manner—i.e., is it the "hardness" and "stiffness" of his erection which provide more intense feelings during intercourse, thus bringing her to an orgasmic response level? If so, we would expect to find these low-orgasmic women equal in consistency to the high-orgasmic women when stimulated by their husbands manually or orally—

that is, when the penis is not "involved," or when the husband stimulates her with an internal, "phallic," vibrator or dildo. Our data, however, do not support any such hypothesis. Nor do the data of Fisher or
others. The low-orgasmic women were lower in consistency than the
high-orgasmic women, whatever the form of stimulation administered
by the husband. We cannot, however, reject the possible importance,
psychologically, of the husband's sexual response.

Many wives, we found, viewed their husband's sexual response, as
measured by the strength and sustenance of his erection, as an indicator
of their own desirability. Here are some of their reactions:

> I'll fondle him. He'll get a hard-on. Then if I ask him to do
> something for me, like kissing my breasts or playing with my clit,
> he'll do it, but he goes soft while he's doing it. I think my body
> must turn him off, and that, in turn, makes it hard for me to get
> aroused.

> We were on vacation, staying at this really groovy hotel. We
> had showered together and I had played with him a lot, really
> working him up. He wanted to do it with me on top, but before
> he even entered me, he started to go limp. I had to go back to stim-
> ulating him with my mouth to get him hard again. This happened
> three times. How can I believe I really excite him?

> I sometimes wonder if there is anything about me that turns
> him on. I bought this pair of crotch-out bikini panties and a real
> sexy half-bra. Then I waited until one evening when I knew he
> wasn't tired and was in a mellow mood to model it for him. Noth-
> ing. I had to work his cock for a good twenty minutes. And even
> then it was only half hard. I don't think I have a bad shape, but
> what difference does it make if your husband doesn't give a damn?

None of these women considered their husband impotent. Almost all
said they had often wondered if he would have the same "half-hearted"
response to another woman. "I've never thought I was a slob," said one,
"but I'm not a *Playboy* centerfold either. And maybe that's what it
takes."

An equal number of these wives said they felt "pressured" and "distracted" and "the one with the whole responsibility" in the lovemaking.
Many marriage-manual writers have placed great emphasis on the
woman's responsibility in maintaining the man's erection. Apparently
the message has not been lost on a sizable number of wives—and, we
might add, on many husbands. "I feel if I say the wrong thing or do

something not right and he starts to lose his erection, then it's my fault. It keeps me tense," said a wife in the low-orgasmic group. Another said, "Whenever he starts to go limp, he gets angry. He'll say I moved the wrong way or did something too much or not enough or not fast enough or slow enough or whatever. It's like walking a tightrope. And I'm supposed to get passionate feeling like that?" Still another complained, "When he's ready to put it in, I feel I have to be ready. I can't say 'I'd like some more of this or that first.' He might start to lose it. So I go along with it whether I feel ready or not, and I'm often not."

There has been almost universal agreement among psychiatrists and psychologists that a woman must be able to "let go" emotionally in order to reach orgasm. She must be free to accept her own feelings as she enters what is, in reality, an altered state of consciousness. Many women have described it as "stepping off a cliff." She cannot be "carried away" in orgasm, however, unless, as Fisher found, she is able to feel that love objects are dependable, that they will not easily be lost or disappear. "Treatment" of orgasmic dysfunction has, in the past, focused on either the psychological or the physical, seldom on both equally. Masters and Johnson (*Human Sexual Inadequacy*) have reported in some detail the program they have employed with considerable success in treating women with orgasmic dysfunction. While the program does not, itself, include any form of traditional psychotherapy (it is an intense, two-week program), it is solidly rooted in sound principles of psychology, particularly behaviorism and the psychology of learning. The emphasis is on sensate focus. Treating husband and wife as a marital "unit," the wife is aided in developing her sexual feelings unhampered by demands and the frustration which follow the cycle of "failure" so much a part of the history of so many low-orgasmic women. Masters and Johnson write (p. 298):

> Every nonorgasmic woman, whether distressed by primary or situational dysfunction, must develop adaptations within areas of perceptual, behavioral, and philosophic experience. She must learn or relearn to feel sexually (respond to sexual stimuli) within the context of and related directly to shared sexual activities with her partner as they correlate with the expression of her own sexual identity, mood, preferences, and expectations. The bridge between her sexual feeling (perception) and sexual thinking (philosophy) essentially is established through comfortable use of verbal and nonverbal (specifically physical) communication of shared experience with her marital partner. Her philosophic adaptation to the

acceptance and appreciation of sexual stimuli is further dependent upon the establishment of "permission" to express herself sexually. Any alteration in the sexual value system must, of course, be consistent with her own personality and social value system if the adaptation is to be internalized. Keeping in mind the similarities between male and female sexual response, the crucial factors most often missing in the sexual value system of the nonorgasmic woman are the pleasure in, the honoring of, and the privilege to express need for the sexual experience. (Roman type ours)

To become consistently orgasmic, a woman must be able to accept sexual feelings as a right, joy, and natural component of her total being. As Masters and Johnson say (p. 298), "The freedom to express need is part of the 'give-to-get' concept inherent in the capacity and facility for effective sexual responsivity." It is in recognition of this oft-substantiated finding that women who are nonorgasmic or low-orgasmic are often encouraged to explore their bodies, to discover the touches which give them pleasure—sensually and sexually. For many women, this is not easy. It means taking the suggestion that they do something—masturbate—which they have been taught to view as dirty and immoral. The word itself—masturbate—is emotionally "loaded" for most of us, associated, as it is, with immature behavior (or the refuge of the frustrated, lonely, old maid). If the woman can accept the goal of sexual fulfillment as being worthwhile and very much to her benefit, she will not hesitate to explore what pleasures her. A goal-directed wife told us: "When I married, I was really dumb. I had never had sex before. I used to play with myself some when I was in high school, but when I got married—I was nineteen—I gave it up. It didn't seem right for a married woman who loved her husband. But I was wrong. I read *The Sensuous Woman* and it turned my head around. If I didn't know what felt good to me, how could I ever let him know?"

Our experience has raised a more significant justification for self-stimulation. The majority of women (as well as men) confirmed that the greater the frequency of arousal and orgasm, the more often they desired sexual relations and the more they found satisfaction in lovemaking. Self-gratification did not substitute for, or detract from, sex with the husband. It added to the desire for it. When asked if self-gratification to orgasm a few hours previously diminished the gratification of subsequent sexual relations, the majority of orgasmic women said that rather than diminishing the probability of high response, it actually enhanced it. "In the afternoon before my husband gets home I usually take a bath and, to tell the truth, I sometimes, well, I guess I would have to say, frequently, masturbate while I'm bathing. It makes me even more eager for sex when my husband gets home," was the statement of a typical wife.

The sensate-focus program of Masters and Johnson is primarily a program of sensual self-discovery within the context of nondemand sex (see Chapter 5) with the partner. In addition, during the two-week program the couple meet daily with the co-therapist (a man and woman) to go over the couple's emotional reactions to the tactual experiences. The husband's role is crucial. He must provide warmth, understanding, and, above all, an absence of sexual demands. The encouraging results of their program (approximately 80 per cent initial success rate in treatment of coital orgasmic dysfunction) underscore the importance of husband and wife—as a unit—working toward the achievement of their sexual potentials.

Since publication of Masters and Johnson's *Human Sexual Inadequacy* in 1970, therapists, some qualified, many with no credentials other than exposure to a "sensory awareness" group and the reading of a book or two, have claimed to practice "M & J" therapy. Few have been trained by Masters and Johnson, nor do they follow the program of the St. Louis group. Unless the therapist is qualified to diagnose and evaluate the problems faced by *both* spouses (and seldom does only one have a sexual problem), the results may be worse than ineffective. William Masters and Virginia Johnson have achieved encouraging results with their treatment programs. They are the first to admit, however, that they have still recorded a disappointingly high "failure" rate. And for some couples a different approach, or a modification of the Masters and Johnson technique, may yield better results.

We suggest that every couple read *Human Sexual Inadequacy*. (The statistics and other research data can be skimmed.) Not just couples who have recognized a problem. Every couple. Sensate focus should be incorporated into the sexual loving of every husband and wife. To reject it because "we don't have any sexual problem" is tantamount to a musician rejecting the practice of scales and finger exercises because he has no "problem" in playing. We can all improve our artistry in loving. And anything which increases the fulfillment we find in sexual love is worth the effort.

How much of a problem failure to achieve orgasm may be to husband and wife will depend upon their mutual love, maturity, and willingness to approach the problem together. If, after reasonable time and effort (devoid of blame, guilt, and demands) in application of sensate focus (nondemand sex), a husband and wife still face sexual frustration, they should not hesitate to seek professional counseling. We cannot stress this too much. In Appendix A we outline the qualifications of professional counselors in the fields of psychiatry, psychology, and social work. Beyond the "paper" credentials, however, there is more to look for in selecting someone to help in sexual matters. We discuss this in the preface to Appendix A.

IMPOTENCE

Like much else in the area of sex, *impotence* is subject to differing definitions and interpretations. Masters and Johnson break it down into two subcategories: *primary impotence* and *secondary impotence*. Primary impotence they define, arbitrarily, for research and clinical purposes as the "inability to ever achieve and/or maintain an erection quality sufficient to accomplish successful coital connection." As for secondary impotence, they say: "If a man is to be judged secondarily impotent, there must be the clinical landmark of at least one instance of successful intromission, either during the initial coital opportunity or in a later episode. The usual pattern of the secondarily impotent male is success with the initial coital opportunity and continued effective performance with the first fifty, hundred, or even thousand or more coital encounters. Finally, an episode of failure at effective coital connection is recorded."

Primary impotence is rarely reported by couples seeking marriage counseling. No husband among our sample fell into this diagnostic class. Of the 32 primarily impotent males whose treatment is reported by Masters and Johnson (213 men were treated for secondary impotence), only 11 were married at the time they sought help. Since we are concerned in this book with the sexual interaction of husband and wife, we will limit our discussion to secondary impotence.

We feel that the above description of secondary impotence, while a good "operational definition" for purposes of research, is of little help in discussing what may be an ongoing problem for John and Mary. How often does John experience difficulty in attaining erection? Does he usually reach erection early in lovemaking, then lose it on intromission? Does he lose erection during certain acts or positions but otherwise experiences no trouble? Does he experience impotence with his wife but not with other women? Or with other women but not his wife? Is his erection generally very firm or often only partially so? Does the firmness come and go during lovemaking? How does John react to a "failure"? How does Mary react to it?

Only a very few men in our sample claimed to have never experienced at least partial loss of erection during lovemaking. Most accepted it as something which occasionally "just happens." The majority of wives had a similar philosophic attitude. Erection is not a voluntary action. A man cannot turn it on or off at will. No man has to be told this, but we have frequently found it to be a physiological fact not fully understood by even long-married women. Some wives were hurt or angered by what they viewed as his intentional rejection. "I know he does it just to spite me—and after he has gone and gotten me all aroused," said one wife. She is obviously ignorant of how the mechanism of erection in the male operates. Penile tumescence (erection) involves the endocrine, circulatory, and nervous systems plus, of course, anatomically sound genital organs (see Chapter 6). While it is often a response to a combination of external and internal stimuli together with sexual thoughts and associations, one cannot *decide* to have an erection. It happens or it doesn't. So much for fact one.

Fact two is that erection (and loss of erection) is primarily determined by the individual's thoughts and emotional reactions. While physical conditions (certain illnesses, drug reactions, and injuries) can cause impotence, this is rare. In an overwhelming majority of cases, the cause is psychological. These emotional or attitudinal causes may be rooted in a number of antecedent events in the man's life. For the purposes of this chapter, however, examination of childhood interactions with parents, influence of religious orthodoxy, and other factors which may be relevant but which are "water under the bridge," will not be detailed. Suffice it to say, in the *mind-emotion-autonomic nervous system-penile tumescence* network, in order for the man to be consistently potent in his marital sex encounters, he must be free of negative attitudes toward sex and/or women, free of intense anxiety or anger, sexually turned on to women (and his wife, in particular), and confident in his ability to perform.

In matters of sex, men are amazingly suggestible creatures. Tell a man he may not be able to achieve erection in this or that situation, and chances are he will not. The man who doubts his ability to maintain an erection has set himself up to fail. We have spoken with a shocking number of men who have been "conditioned" to impotence by misinformation dispensed by physicians, counselors of varied "qualifications," and hack writers of sensational how-to-do-it sex manuals. Several years ago, a man in his mid-forties sought counseling for his marriage. He told us he and his wife were on the brink of divorce. "It's everything. We're at one another's throat. There's no communication. We fight at the drop of a hat." On questioning, he said it had gotten increasingly worse "since I've gotten too old to get it up." We learned that he had experienced his first loss of erection three years before. He and his wife had returned home from a late-night dinner party. He was tired and had consumed more than his usual two or three drinks. Earlier in the evening, he had hinted to his wife that he planned to make love to her when they got home, so despite his fatigue he went ahead with it. He achieved only a partial erection, then lost it entirely. As it happened, he had an appointment for his yearly physical checkup the following afternoon. Concerned about his reaction the night before, he asked the doctor if he might have something physically wrong with him. After assuring him he was in excellent health, the doctor gratuitously added: "At your age, you have to expect to have that happen. It's something which happens to every man when he passes forty. From then on, you have to pretty much live on your memories." The man has been unable to attain an erection since! That may be as close as any situation could come to proving that *suggestion* can be *causation*.

Most often the man himself gives the "suggestion." What we tell ourselves about a situation or person (or about ourselves), what Dr. Albert Ellis had called our "self-sentences," can act as a self-fulfilling prophecy. The following is typical of how this operates in impotence: Harry, a thirty-seven-year-old sales manager of an insurance company, arrived home from a business trip. After a twelve-hour workday and a two-hour flight, he is in no mood for conversation. It was a tension-filled trip. Company sales were off and he had been compelled to terminate one of his salesmen. To top matters off, his wife met him at the door with the news that the hot-water heater had sprung a leak and the plumber had said it would have to be replaced. Since he had eaten a meal in flight, Harry skipped dinner. He had a couple of scotch and waters while he listened to the tale of the water heater. When he fell into bed after midnight, he was aware of his clenched teeth and the tightness across his shoulders. He began sexual overtures to his wife, but even after she had stimulated him manually and orally for a lengthy period, he remained limp. He had intense feelings of frustration and anger. The following evening, eager to prove he was "still a man," he again tried to make love. He attained erection, which he sustained until he attempted intromission. Then he lost it. Within moments of attempting to enter his wife, the thought crossed his mind: "What if it happens again? What if I can't keep it up? God, it will be awful! She'll think I'm less than a man!" As expected, the thought sent a reaction of acute anxiety through his body, and anxiety is the kiss of death to male arousal. From then on, the die was cast. Each time he tried, he failed. The self-sentences had become a part of his sexual overtures. He had conditioned himself to impotence!

The husband and wife willing to approach the problem in good faith must be willing to take a two-pronged approach: emotional and physical. Potency can be achieved and maintained *only* in an atmosphere free of tension and hostility. And free of even the implication of demand. The husband who feels he *has* to perform is dooming himself to failure. The wife who *demands* (if only by expressing her "expectations" or "disappointment") her husband's impotent performance is either ignorant of male sexual physiology, or she has not confronted the possibility that she *wants* to keep him impotent! If he fears her rejection, hostility, or manipulation, or if he fears the dominance of women, or if he fears the ridicule or disdain he may incur if he is seen (or feels he may be seen) as less than masculine, he may react with impotence. Hostility is an underlying element in many (*but not all*) cases of impotence. Most men encounter difficulty performing in an atmosphere in which they feel anger and resentment toward the woman. It is a sad irony that it is in just such an atmosphere that coitus is most often attempted by some couples. Instead of resolving the flare-up before making love (or, in this context, "having sex"), they will attempt to sweep it under the rug by going to bed and engaging in sex. The command "kiss and make up" reverses the rational order and makes the kiss a hypocritical gesture. "Make up, then kiss" (or then make love) draws the couple back together. There is first a reconciliation, then an encounter in loving infused with mutual affection and respect. When differences have not first been resolved, the couple may turn off their verbal assaults while they engage in sex, but the resentments remain, one or both of them may feel "used," and sex will lack the fulfillment which can only result from love freely given and received. They will also risk impotence reactions. The hostility may, of course, prevail throughout the relationship, not just in periodic flare-ups. We all know many couples who live in what can best be described as an "armed camp." They quite simply don't like each other. They may have negative feelings toward all members of the other sex, or hostile feelings only toward their spouse. They stay married for reasons other than caring for and valuing each other, and they engage in sex in response to a physical need or contractual obligation. Living in such an atmosphere, it would be surprising if we did not find problems of impotence and other sexual dysfunctions. If the couple, or either one individually, has been able to identify negative feelings—hostility or fear—which might be playing a part in the impotence, they may, through patient, honest, and sustained communication, resolve the sources of conflict and hence the roots of the sexual dysfunction. It is most important, however, that any feelings of demand be removed from their sexual interactions. In this regard, we have found that impotence which has not been long sustained has been "cured" by giving the order in therapy that they engage in protracted periods of nondemand sex but that they *not* attempt coitus—regardless of how firm the husband's erection may become or how strong their desire. In following the prescription, husband and wife not only take the demand out of sexual performance, they establish a paradigm which, in a "reverse psychology," can be effective in breaking the failure cycle. Just as attaining an erection cannot be consciously willed, *not* having an erection cannot be consciously willed. Since the husband has been "forbidden" to engage in coitus, there is no necessity to have an erection. Sexually stimulated, he is now free to reach erection and maintain it. The erection-anxiety-impotence cycle is broken.

Masters and Johnson have also developed a program of exercises for the husband/wife unit which has proven highly effective in the treatment of secondary impotence. We urge readers who have encountered such problems to study the description given in *Human Sexual Inadequacy*. If the problem has been of short duration, and there are no serious underlying difficulties affecting the relationship, they may be able to work together to nip the problem in the bud. If, for any reason, however, either of them feels this may not succeed, has difficulty discussing it, or does not feel capable of such a co-operative program, we strongly urge them to seek professional counseling *without delay*. The longer the problem is allowed to continue, the more difficult it may be to treat.

And sexual satisfaction is too important in the love of husband and wife to risk losing it for even the shortest time.

PREMATURE EJACULATION

Emotionally and neurologically, what can be said of impotence can, in general, be said of most cases of premature ejaculation. Frequently, the same cycle of "failure" exists. Early in the marriage the husband may have "come too soon." In subsequent encounters, he fears another "accident." The anxiety triggers another premature ejaculation. Continued for several successive times, the problem may become chronic.

But before it can be discussed as a "problem," we must understand what we mean by "premature." The definitions usually refer to the duration of intravaginal containment of the penis. How long can the man delay his ejaculation after entering the woman? Some experts have described the premature ejaculator as a man who cannot control his ejaculation for at least thirty seconds after penetration. Others have suggested one minute. Still others, three minutes. Masters and Johnson consider a man a premature ejaculator if he cannot control his ejaculation for a sufficient period to satisfy his partner in at least 50 per cent of their coital encounters. While saying, "At least this definition does move away from the 'stopwatch' concept," they admit, "if the female partner is persistently nonorgasmic for reasons other than rapidity of the male's ejaculatory process, there is no validity to the definition." And either-or, black-and-white definitions leave a large gray area. What of the woman who, although not nonorgasmic, requires five or ten minutes of penile thrusting or manual stimulation of her clitoris before reaching climax? If her husband cannot delay that long, as many men cannot, is he a "premature ejaculator"? We think not. Rather than join in the definition controversy, however, we prefer to leave it to the reader's sound judgment. We have found that the husband is generally able to diagnose accurately his premature ejaculation He knows the feeling of not being able to "hold back," and the embarrassment and frustration which follow. Almost all husbands interviewed admitted to at least one such occurrence during their marriage. The majority felt it had been (or was) a problem at least some of the time.

It is important to note that the majority of wives of premature ejaculators were low in orgasmic consistency. Does the wife's difficulty in achieving orgasm result in the husband's diagnosing himself? Does his problem of premature ejaculation negatively affect her orgasmic potential? Or are there factors which both brought to marriage and which played a part in their choice of each other which are evidenced in the sexual difficulties of both? In the absence of clear evidence to the contrary, we lean toward the latter explanation. Whatever the possible psychological interactions may be, the problem of premature ejaculation, like the problems of orgasmic dysfunction and impotence, is best approached by husband and wife functioning as a "unit."

Although some premature ejaculators will ejaculate with the slightest genital stimulation or during the attempt at intromission, the majority do so during the first few full strokes in the vagina. With almost all such couples interviewed, the problem existed from the first. The husband ejaculated rapidly during the honeymoon. It became a "problem" only after it had become persistent and the *wife* had verbalized her frustration. As with impotence, the wife frequently saw the premature ejaculation as "deliberate." Except in those few cases in which the husband knows the actions that will hasten his orgasm and deliberately engages in them in order to achieve his satisfaction while disregarding his wife's, this is never the case. Male pride being what it is, almost every man would like to "hold back" until his wife is satisfied. If in other respects the wife feels used, however, she may assign to her husband an egocentric motive in his inability to delay ejaculation. The first step toward elimination of the problem is, therefore, examination of the entire husband/wife relationship. As with impotence in which the wife may, by her verbal or nonverbal reactions, place a demand for performance upon her husband, or female orgasmic dysfunction in which the husband compounds the problem by asking each time, "Did it happen?," any reaction by the wife which increases the pressure on the husband to "hold back" will act to increase the probability of another "accident."

The first step in reversing the premature-ejaculation syndrom is a recognition by both husband and wife that it *can* be reversed. Actually, we have found it to be the sexual problem most amenable to marital-unit therapy.

As every husband knows, there is an interval immediately preceding orgasm when the man feels the approach of ejaculation and can do nothing to control it. When this stage is reached (what Masters and Johnson term "ejaculatory inevitability"), the man loses voluntary control of the ejaculatory process.

In other sensate-focus approaches to the therapy applied to sexual dysfunction, orgasmic inadequacy and impotence, the partners are dis-

couraged from direct stimulation of the genitals initially. In a therapeutic approach to premature ejaculation, the wife is encouraged—
directed—to stimulate, by touch, her husband's genitals. But within the
limits of the therapeutic instructions.

Masters and Johnson suggest (pp. 102–103), "When the male is approached pelvically, stimulative techniques are best conducted with the
wife's back placed against the headboard of her bed (possibly supported
by pillows), her legs spread, and with the husband resting on his back,
his head directed toward the foot of the bed, with his pelvis placed between her legs, his legs over hers, so that she may have free access to
his genital organs." The idea is for the wife to use her hands to stimulate the husband to erection. When erection is complete, she employs a
technique introduced by James Semans. It is a "squeeze technique."
She places her thumb on the frenulum, the small strip of skin on the
underside of the penis which attaches to the glans. Her first and second
fingers are placed side by side along the upper surface of the penis immediately behind the coronal ridge (the rim at the base of the glans).
She applies pressure by squeezing the thumb and first two fingers together for three or four seconds. With application of sufficient pressure,
the husband at once loses his urge to ejaculate. The wife then waits for
a period of fifteen to thirty seconds before resuming active stimulation
of her husband's penis. Applying this stimulation-squeeze-stimulation-
squeeze technique, the wife can continue her nondemand sexual
caresses for a lengthy period without ejaculation occurring. Through
the squeeze technique, the husband and wife attain confidence in his
ability to delay ejaculation. Aside from this obvious advantage, the
technique, as Masters and Johnson point out, leads to improved communication both at verbal and nonverbal levels. The wife learns the
sexual reactions of her husband—first from what he says, later by his
physical responses.

Following the squeeze technique, the couple, with their new-found
confidence, engage in nondemand intromission. This is accomplished in
a woman-astride position. Once she has inserted his penis, she concentrates on retaining the penis in her vagina in a motionless manner, initially avoiding further stimulation by pelvic thrusting. There is an absence of demand and/or threat. Since the greatest degree of sexual
stimulation for the man occurs during the first few seconds following
intromission, the wife, by remaining motionless, does her best to minimize this ejaculation-producing stimulation. If the husband feels ejaculation approaching, he at once communicates this to his wife. She lifts

off his penis, applies the squeeze technique for a period of three or four seconds, and reinserts the penis. There is, of course, much more to the program, and we again urge the reader to read the Masters and Johnson description in Chapter Three of *Human Sexual Inadequacy*. The role of the wife is emphasized. She is not involved simply as a sympathetic partner assisting her husband to overcome *his* problem. They are working together to increase their mutual satisfaction. As they progress from one phase to the next, she can expect to discover new dimensions of her own sexual response. It is yet another example of the satisfactions to be found in a give-to-get approach to loving.

Couples troubled by problems in sexual performance and/or response are in the majority in our culture. We do not live in a society which teaches healthy sexual attitudes. We are raised in ignorance and fear and we may have to struggle to overcome their effects. Mere learning of the true facts is seldom enough to dispel early conditioning firmly implanted in our unconscious. Before any functional or response problem can be approached therapeutically, however, the relationship of the husband and wife must be examined in total honesty. How many diagnosed sexual problems would vanish if husband and wife developed a relationship of genuine love and mutual respect, if they valued and cherished each other? Perhaps the majority. One might also ask how much marital love is motivated by and dependent upon the development of a free, healthy, and fulfilling sexual relationship? Much more, we feel sure, than is admitted by those who claim that sex is overemphasized in marriage (and who themselves, sadly, have never found it particularly rewarding in their own marriages). The two go hand in hand. A couple cannot build their sexual relationship before building their mutual love; they cannot grow in love while living in an unsatisfying sexual relationship. If we see the two as inseparable, then we must concede that we all have "sexual" problems. Loving is never consistently easy. Nor is it "natural." It is the product of many major and minor choices of giving—to get the rewards of happiness and the ultimate in fulfillment.

CHAPTER 14

Age and Sexual Love

Thus, with love, did five and twenty
Years race into nothingness, and thus
Swiftly sped the days and the nights,
Falling from the roadway of my life
And fluttering away like the drying
Leaves of the trees before the winds of
Autumn.

Kahlil Gibran
Secrets of the Heart

I long to believe in immortality . . . If I am destined to be
happy with you here—how short is the longest life. I wish
to believe in immortality— I wish to love with you forever.

John Keats
Letters to Fanny Brawne

I hate the thought of getting old and losing the fun of sex.

A young husband

When you are twenty or twenty-five, sex is pretty much a matter
of glands. It takes twenty years or more to develop it into an art.

An older husband

And my husband is an artist.

His wife

*W*hen you are sixteen and in love, you hope you'll never grow old. When you are forty, and the parent of a sixteen-year-old in love, you fear he/she will never grow up. When you are sixteen, you are sure your fortyish parents have long since forgotten what sex is all about. If you are the parents, you are sure your sixteen-year-old hasn't yet found out what it is all about. Between sixteen and forty, most of us fight hard to deny the aging process. After forty, we may fight hard to bury our fears of it. Aging is a part of living from the moment of our conception, yet we seldom seem to adjust to living with it in comfort. We surround it with misinformation, myths, fears, and misunderstandings between those of different ages.

Our obsession with age, whatever age we may be, is largely associated with sex, manhood and womanhood. At a certain *age* we undergo dramatic physical changes marking sexual maturity. At a certain *age* we begin the social-sexual ritual of dating. And we date those within a certain *age* range. We engage in romantic activities "appropriate" to our *age*, and finally marry at the "right" *age*. And most significantly, what we expect of ourselves, even demand of ourselves, and measure ourselves against, in sex is a function of our *age*.

Since Masters and Johnson broke the news that some of their sexually active research volunteers were far past the age of expected infirmity, it has been popular for sex authorities to reassure men that they can look forward to an active virile life during their sunset years. It has needed to be said. Sex during later years, however, is only one issue related to age. The twenty-year-old also has self-expectancies. Kin-

sey provided us with frequency tables for age groups. We will not repeat them, since to do so, we feel, might add to the very problem of age
expectancies. The twenty-year-old hears of the norms and, understandably, compares himself. The forty-year-old reads the figures and
compares himself not only with his peers but with the twenty-year-olds.
This obsession with self-evaluation, employing some group norms as
our criterion of "success," catches almost all of us. We read tables of
income/age, education/age, and weight/age, and measure ourselves
against them, taking satisfaction in being "above average" or finding
discouragement in "not measuring up."

It has been said that our society pays homage to youth. No one needs
to supply supporting evidence. The television commercials, fashions,
and sex-oriented magazines are sufficient. We graduate from the Pepsi
generation at twenty-five, even earlier if we marry. Sex—sex appeal,
sexual drive, and sexual activity—belongs to youth, so the message
goes. And to the single. The screenwriters and novelists attempt to
seduce us to the conclusion that sexual love blooms in the spring of life
and withers in winter.

Age-related sexual behavior and attitudes are, we would expect, present in teen-age marriages. Since our couples did not include this age
sample, however, we will not comment on what these effects might be.
For those in their twenties, there was considerable variability (as was
also true of the older groups). Hence, we are reluctant to state any generalizations. Furthermore, without a much larger sample, we could not
control for the relevant variable "number of years married." Much of
what follows, therefore, is in the nature of tentative observations and
impressions.

The young husbands were considerably less experienced in sex than
either the editors of *Playboy* or wives of the same age believed, and to
many of these men, their inexperience was an acute embarrassment.
The super-stud image would seem to have influenced this group more
than the older groups. It may be, however, that men in their thirties and
older have more often "outgrown" the influence. It may have been
equally important to them when they were younger. We should not
find it surprising if, in fact, the super-stud image has more significantly
affected the younger husbands. They have been exposed to it through
the pages of men's magazines and James Bond sexual exploits throughout most of their lives. The image creates two pressures or demands: to
perform with great frequency, and to be skilled in a wide variety of sexual acts. A number of these young husbands confessed that they felt

they *should* have sexual relations at least once each day, even more than once a day if on vacation or away for a weekend, and that they felt somewhat less virile if they failed to perform up to these expectancies. Some said they had felt this demand when they were dating prior to marriage. "If you went out with a girl," one young man told us, "she expected you to go to bed with her—or at least to try." Several psychologists and sociologists have commented on this social phenomenon, an outgrowth of the highly publicized "sexual revolution" and the proclaimed sexual rights of women. A number of single men have told us they felt they had to try to "get her in the sack." Otherwise, they feared the girl might doubt their masculinity. One said, "If I don't, she might wonder if I'm queer." In one case, a young wife in her second year of marriage told us her husband had to have sex twice each day— "almost, I think, like eating his three meals a day." Later, her husband privately told us he was "getting ulcers" keeping up with his masculine role. "We've only been married a year," he told us. "I don't want her to think I'm bored with sex or not much of a lover."

The sex-oriented magazines, including those published for women, have turned sexual innovation into an obsessive search for many men. The young husband may conclude that his "manhood" can be proven only if he is knowledgeable in every offbeat sexual technique. A "great" lover, he feels, knows every way to pleasure a woman—and employs them all—each and every time he makes love. He may never before have experimented with oral sex. He may be uneasy about trying it. No matter. He must establish himself as a sophisticated man by trying everything and anything. And at least act as if he is enthusiastic and unruffled.

The young wife, we discovered, frequently faces a similar challenge. While her mother may have felt it was feminine to be naive, the young wife of today may fear she will be considered stupid or neurotic if she is ignorant of the complete role of the "sensuous woman." There is sometimes an irony in this. The wife may feel she should be educated (and experienced?) in all dimensions of sex when she marries in order not to be a "disappointment" to her husband. Then, after marriage, she finds that her husband either lacks similar experience and knowledge or is reluctant to express it. She has no way to tell him without the risk of threatening his masculinity. Does she buy him a copy of the latest how-to book? Or tell him what she has learned? Most wives wisely choose not to take such a risk, despite what some feminist writers advise in the name of the new liberation and candor. There seems to be no easy answer to the problem. The emphasis on variety in technique, it would seem, can block the freedom to enjoy sexual love for both of them.

Imagine someone replying to the question, "Do you enjoy eating?" with "Yes, of course. I eat six meals a day and never have the same dish more than a once a month." Absurd. Yet this is the criterion many young couples feel they must meet in measuring their sexual relationship. Once they become convinced that quality (measured in terms of love and enjoyment) is more important than frequency and variety, they can explore the true joy of sex—free of demands.

A number of writers have spoken of the tendency toward premature ejaculation in young husbands. Some have suggested that this is owing to the high sex demand of the young. Others have attributed it to the nervousness and/or overeagerness of the young husband. Our interviews did not support a relationship between age and premature ejaculation.

Actual problems with premature ejaculation, as well as occasional times when the husband couldn't "hold back" long enough, were as common among those in their thirties and forties as among younger husbands. Many men reported having a few failures in control during the first days of their marriage, but we could find no relationship to their age at the time. Parenthetically, some men who entered a second marriage in their thirties or forties said they had the same "honeymoon" problems. Ability to control ejaculation is primarily a matter of emotional control (see Chapter 2), and we find no reason to assume that young men are more troubled in sex than their elders. We feel, however, that we should repeat the qualifications in our findings. We do not suggest that they can be accepted as representative of the general population of married men.

The husbands in their twenties and those in their forties shared a deficiency reported by their wives: They lacked in romantic gestures and the lovemaking preceding coitus. This came as a surprise. Since the younger group has been exposed to so much information on the role and techniques of the lover, and is in the honeymoon period (as popularly defined), we might expect them to be the most attentive and imaginative lovers. Most wives felt otherwise. "He just wants to get it in as quick as possible," was a typical complaint. Not of all wives, of course; many described their husbands in the most glowing terms as lovers. The majority, however, felt their husbands were not interested in spending the time and giving the attention in lovemaking that they needed. Possible reasons emerged in our conversations with the husbands. Some seemed to feel their sexual prowess had to be established each time they made love, and that they could prove it only by aggressively *taking* the woman. They were embarrassed by romantic gestures, and considered preliminary sexual lovemaking a waste of time. It would seem that romantic poetry is not a thing in which the twenty-year-old places much stock. A young husband, married less than two years, told us, "On Valentine's Day she got all out of joint because I didn't bring her flowers or candy or something. But that seems like something out of my grandparents' day. I'd feel like a fool." Despite the fact that the macho image is more frequently identified with an older generation, the young husbands verbalized many hypermasculine views when questioned about their precoital lovemaking. "She wants a lot of kissing and caressing," one young husband told us, "and she doesn't understand that a man wants *sex*, not some kiss-on-the-hand routine." It would seem that some young husbands are still trying to "score" as they did when they picked up a girl on a Saturday night. Husbands in their thirties and forties frequently drew similar criticism from their wives: too little romance, not enough foreplay. With the older husbands, however, it was more often a matter of neglect (taking things for granted) than a threatened masculine ego.

If a couple marry in their twenties, the pattern of their sexual activity is apparently established by their mid-thirties—to their satisfaction or dissatisfaction. For most, the honeymoon stage is remarkably short-lived. Most of our couples in their thirties, married over five years, admitted that their lovemaking had changed little since the first year of marriage. Where they made love, the time of day, and even the days of the week for lovemaking had become habits. Whatever variety there was in their sexual relations had generally been introduced during the first year or two; very little was added in the ensuing years. Although most denied being bored with their sexual relations, they did admit that the excitement of the first year had waned. The most frequent explanation for the rut in which they found themselves was a lack of time together. Wives complained of fatigue and the demands of children. Husbands talked of business pressures and long working hours. In fact, however, it was usually a matter of priorities and interest. Our interviews with these couples gave support to the old saying, "Where there's a will, there's a way." The majority of couples married over five years, we found, attempted little that might add (or sustain) excitement to their sex life by way of variation in time, setting, actions, or gestures of romance. Remarkably, many of these couples have resigned themselves to what they accept as the inevitable rut of married sexuality—attributed to children, job, and numerous "pressures."

The pattern of what can only be described as monotony in sex continues into the forties—and worsens. Not for all, of course. Boredom is not inevitable in sex any more than it is in any other area of human activity. But it can only be avoided through effort and a denial of its inevitability. *Most* couples in their forties and older had apparently succumbed to the social pressures—the dictums—which said that sex is for the young (and is somehow obscene in middle age and older). In the forties group, however, as opposed to the thirties, the rationale (excuse) was more often one related to age itself rather than pressures and activities.

Forty, it would seem, is a symbolic age for many. It marks the crossover into old age and the end of sex. This may seem an extreme description, but this was what came through in the interviews with many of our couples. Since sexual functioning in men demands a physiological response (erection), it is understandable that husbands were more prone to evaluate sexual performance in terms of age. Or to defensively deny age as a factor in their sexual performance. Some husbands attributed their reduction in sexual performance to the wife's loss of physical appeal. The wife may have put on weight, developed wrinkles, and in general let her appearance deteriorate. Physically, she no longer turned him on. We all know women, those we pass in the supermarket and elsewhere, who seemingly "care less" about the nonsexual image they project—at least toward their husbands. The same criticism can, of course, be leveled at their husbands.

Other husbands explained their drop in desired frequency by citing the myth of the natural promiscuity in men. "No man can stay turned on by the same woman year in and year out," argued one husband. "Variety puts the spice in life."

These husbands, as well as many of the husbands who blame their lack of ardor on their wife's loss of sexual appeal, have found what can only be described as a comfortable excuse—a copout. They have found a rationale which permits them to avoid a painful admission of sexual inadequacy. They are somehow convinced they *should* perform at a level (frequency) comparable to what they believe is the average for the super-virile male. And since they don't, they blame it on their wives.

Many husbands, reaching forty, face crises which include almost every area of their lives. Their occupational achievement may not be everything they hoped for. They may see the handwriting on the wall which tells them their dreams are fading. Their children are leaving the nest, rejecting parental values. And the middle-age man begins to read the obituary tables. He is no longer young. This can be a traumatic realization. It can mean a brutal confrontation between what is and what might have been, between dreams and reality. Sex can become as much a preoccupation in middle age as it ordinarily is in adolescence. It can become a substitute for the achievements dreamed of which never came true. The husband who planned the trip to Tahiti in a forty-foot sailboat when he was twenty-five, may transform his dreams into a love affair with a Tahitian maiden when he is forty-five. Aspirations of wealth may become fantasies of sexual conquest. There are frequently observed parallels between the painful frustrations of adolescence and those of middle age, yet while the transitions of adolescence are painful hurdles, youth can look forward to the rewards of adulthood; the man in his middle years can anticipate only a downhill road. And to most men, we have observed, this downhill road is a sexual one. If we were to select the single most evident dimension of one's life that is correlated with age, it would have to be sexual activity. Not because of a physiologic variable, a matter of aging tissues and glands, but because of what the individual tells himself (or herself) about the age at which he finds himself.

The husband in his forties or older who sees himself as "over the hill" in his career, financial achievement, or athletic ability, may withdraw into a shell of antisexuality. Or attempt, almost in desperation, to reclaim and invigorate his weakening manhood by chasing young women. The self-sentences, what Albert Ellis calls verbal mediations, seem to us to be the greatest determiners of middle-age behavior. The husband who sees himself as having reached the limits of his "masculine" goals (occupationally, financially, and sexually), may tell himself that any effort to turn the tide is useless. Either his marriage locks him in to a woman who no longer turns him on, or his job is a dead end, or he feels he cannot reach his teen-agers, or that his dream of a condominium in Acapulco is dead. The effect is the same. He feels impotent.

Fred McMorrow (*Midolescence: The Dangerous Years*, p. 12) has said "The way a man deals with aging, with sex, with career and with the thousand-and-one other elements that make up his life will depend on and reflect the way he has dealt with them all along. Beneath the outer self that seems to change in middle age lies a man basically consistent with himself. The anguish of middle age is in large measure the collision of that new man and the old one beneath the surface." We concur. The observation is supported by our interviews and by the data of others. What a man (or woman) is sexually at twenty-five is the best predicter of what he will be at forty-five. We found that couples who had been above average in frequency of sexual relations early in marriage and had maintained a high frequency, had very little reduction in middle age. Those who had a low frequency of sexual activity in the early years experienced a significant drop in middle age. This drop, however, was not, we feel, inevitable. Our interviews confirm what a number of investigators have noted: The more frequently one engages in sex, the more frequent will be the desire to do so. It may seem an absurd conclusion—the more you have sex, the more you'll want it. There is, however, strong evidence to support it. We know disappointingly little about the human sex drive and the variables affecting it. We know, of course, that it varies from individual to individual, apparently more than it does within an individual over time. The high-sex-drive man of forty-five may have a higher preferred frequency than the low- or even average-sex-drive twenty-year-old. Dr. Robert Chartham, British sexologist, has differentiated what he calls "voluntary" and "involuntary" sex drive. "Involuntary" sex drive is arousal which occurs without any appreciable external stimuli (e.g., visual, tactual). "Voluntary" sex drive is arousal which occurs in response to appropriate external stimuli. Although Chartham does not make it clear, it seems obvious that strength of drive is on a continuum; most times it is a combination of both. We may be in a state of mild "involuntary" drive and be brought to a high state of arousal through "voluntary"-drive stimuli. The "involuntary"-drive state can be expected to make us more attentive to external stimuli. If we are aroused, we will respond to external stimuli which might at another time be virtually ignored.

We may thus reduce the "involuntary-voluntary" continuum to a rule: The higher the "involuntary" drive, the lower the "voluntary" drive necessary to elicit full arousal; the lower the "involuntary" drive, the higher the "voluntary" drive necessary to elicit full arousal. This rule carries an important message for the man in his middle years. It may be that age itself brings with it a diminishment in sexual drive. It would be foolish to deny it. But the man and woman who desire high frequency and satisfaction in their sexual relations can, through utilizing available external stimuli, attain the sexual frequency of a couple with high sex drive. The wife can learn the skills most apt to turn him on. The husband can make love in ways that will arouse her, even if she is not initially turned on. They can both seek those stimuli which will have the highest potential as "voluntary" arousers. In doing so, they may, ironically, find more satisfaction than they did when they were first married.

Women suffer similar feelings as they age. A woman gazes in the mirror. She sees signs of aging and knows there is little she can do to turn back the clock. That's the way it is, she may feel, and there is little she can do about it. She looks at the firm, young bodies of the nude models and feels, "What's the use? I can do nothing about my sagging breasts, the stretch marks, the wrinkles. I can never compete with a twenty-year-old. Why try?"

Added to that may be a growing feeling of uselessness. Her children are grown, off on their own. Finances no longer exert the pressure that made her ability to budget so important in earlier years. She sees herself as no longer needed.

Both attitudes may be reinforced by other firmly ingrained attitudes. She may have accepted the notion that all men are, by nature, promiscuous, and that her husband, like all men, will succumb to the temptations of the "roving forties." Or she may believe what she fears, that a woman loses her sexual drive as well as attractiveness with menopause.

The individual's self-image is most important here. Each of these negative feelings are reflections of poor self-esteem, which is generally learned during childhood. These feelings can, however, be reversed. The wife can begin to see herself as attractive, capable, and worthwhile. But only if she assumes the roles which express those attributes. She can develop her talents, further her intellectual growth, and keep herself physically attractive. We all know women who are forty years old and look sixty, and others who are forty but are sexier than most twenty-five-years-olds. For the most part, these women reflect whatever is going on internally (emotionally). But there is also the matter of the effort applied toward physical enhancement: makeup, figure control, dress. How much is she concerned with keeping herself the woman who turned her husband on when they met? A wife may dismiss the matter with, "Men all have a thing for twenty-year-old girls with big boobs," but she defeats herself when she does. Appearance *is* important. It would be foolish to deny it. The woman who is motivated to present herself in the best, most sexually attractive, way may find helpful suggestions in many popular paperback books on makeup and hairstyle

and in *How To Be a Happily Married Mistress* by one of the authors
(Lois Bird).

Many wives of middle-aged men we spoke to expressed resentment
toward their husbands, whom they felt were interested only in young
girls (as represented in the pages of *Playboy*) or "perverse" sex. What
they resented, to put it in other words, was their husband's attraction to
external stimuli—when it wasn't provided by them (or when they refused to provide it). Such wives fail to see the advantage possible in
sexual arousal which is predominantly elicited by external stimuli. One
might even argue that arousal which is primarily elicited by external
rather than internal stimuli leads to more satisfying sexual relations,
since the efforts both lovers put into arousing the other not only greatly
increase the arousal state, but prolong the lovemaking—to the satisfaction of both. (Many young women have attested to the superiority
of the older lover.) Wives (and husbands) who value sexual relations,
whether at twenty or at fifty, will welcome any external stimuli that
will elicit arousal.

External stimuli should, in any case, be increasing as a part of
lovemaking with the passing years. If the couple's sexual love is growing as it should, their knowledge of one another's desires, and the innovations they have introduced, will broaden the spectrum of their external stimuli. Shared fantasies, erotic writings and films, exotic bedroom
décor, variety in settings, dress, and arousal techniques, will not only
keep their sex life alive, but make it even more fulfilling than when
they were young. Couple after couple confirmed the minimal importance of age as a factor in sexual frequency and performance for either
sex. The factors discussed—sexual-drive strength in early adulthood
and frequency of sexual relations during early years of marriage—had
predictive value in estimating what the couple might expect of their
sexual relationship in middle age and older. However, husband and
wife may effect this for better or worse by their actions. If sex has been
exploitive or used as a battleground, if one or both do little to keep
themselves physically attractive, if sex has become unimaginative, if
they have filled their lives with family, friends, work, and diversions
that allow them little time for relaxation with each other, or if they
have convinced themselves that sex dies with the onset of gray hair,
their initial sex drives and active lovemaking during the first years will
count for little.

More than all other factors seemingly related to age is the quality of
the overall relationship between husband and wife. Those couples who

were deeply, romantically, in love, who had worked to keep their honeymoon alive over the years, who thoroughly enjoy the other sex, and were turned on to each other emotionally, intellectually, and physically, seldom noted any significant decline in the quality or frequency of their lovemaking. They affirmed the truth that lovers never grow old, only richer in memories.

CHAPTER 15

Toward Psychosensual Loving

We didn't find any answers. But then,
maybe we didn't ask the right questions.
What are the right questions anyway?

An ex-husband

I remember I had several reasons for
marrying Helen. Now I can think of
only one: Helen. Does that mean something?

Karl, Helen's husband

Without love,
only the most courageous,
or the most foolish,
would prefer life
over death.

Joseph and Lois Bird
Love Is All

Sex is a physical drive. Love may accompany the satisfaction of the sex drive (or it may not), but only one who, tragically, has never experienced love would question whether sex can be fulfilling when love is absent. Physically satisfying perhaps, but never fulfilling. It can never reach the depths of what we are as human beings, and what we are capable of becoming. To climb the heights, sex education is not enough. We need to learn how to love. With an understanding of love, and an education in sexuality, we can then, as husband and wife, build a relationship which will make us one.

No one loves easily. In order to love, we must act against our nature. We are born egocentric. Everything within our nature cries out for us to act in selfish ways, to think first, and only, of ourselves. To think first of others, even those toward whom we are strongly attracted or toward whom we owe an obligation, is not "natural." Learning to love is virtually synonymous with maturing. The young child is seldom loving, and we don't expect it. The child learns to say, "I love you, Mommy," but he says it for the response he knows will be forthcoming from Mommy. It is immediate reward he seeks. As he matures, he learns to accept delay in his rewards. He learns to work for long-range goals. And it is long-range goals that provide the motivation for loving.

Love has been described as the "giving of self." Unfortunately, this does nothing to help us understand it. One's "self" cannot be given. And, we might add, if it could, who would want it? When we give to a loved one, it is with the hope that our gift will meet his or her needs or desires. The quality of the gift is, therefore, determined by the recipient. Does it fulfill the needs or desires of the recipient? Does this mean, however, that the lover *gives* to his loved one with no thought of any return? Must loving be totally selfless in order for it to be loving? If so, where is the motivation for loving to be found?

In sexual love, fulfillment is to be found only when we are able to get outside ourselves and find pleasure in pleasuring our partner. This is not a saccharine "It is better to give than to receive." There is a definite self-interest in the pleasuring given. This was confirmed again and again in our interviews. As we mentioned previously, we asked husbands and wives to rate the degree of arousal of a wide variety of sexual actions—strongly arousing, mildly arousing, neutral-nonarousing, anti-erotic (a turn-off). The eighty items were evenly divided between acts of pleasuring and those of being pleasured (*having your buttocks stroked/stroking his/her buttocks*). Predictably, those with the highest sex drive (as measured independently) checked the greatest number of items as "highly arousing" in both categories. Our interest, however, was primarily in the differences between the categories and the relationship, if any, the differences might have to the degree of satisfaction expressed in the individual's marital sex. The findings were the same for both sexes. Every individual in the group with the highest degree of sexual fulfillment checked as many or more items as highly arousing which were in the "giving pleasure" category as in the "receiving pleasure" category. Over half of them actually checked more such items! At the other end of the continuum, those who expressed the least satisfaction in the marital relations checked relatively few items involving giving pleasure as highly arousing. A husband in the fulfilled group, for example, said he could become most highly aroused while performing cunnilingus. A number of husbands in the least-fulfilled group, on the other hand, said they had difficulty maintaining an erection while pleasuring their wives unless the wife was simultaneously stimulating them, and many said they could be most aroused only when they didn't have to be "distracted" by making love to the wife.

Most wives who complained of a lack of sexual satisfaction with their husbands exhibited what we came to describe as the "Queen of the Nile" syndrome. They saw their role in sex as passive recipients of male attentions. Not just a role, a *right*. One wife insisted her husband act out her fantasy each time they had sex. "I like to lie back propped up on some pillows, shut my eyes, and just let him do wonderful things to me, to every inch of my body. I lie there imagining I have several men who are taking turns worshiping my body. They're all terribly excited." She said, "I know it's only fair to go along with what my husband wants once in a while, and I do, but to tell the truth, stimulating him, whether it's with my hands or mouth, does nothing for me." As we so often discovered, her husband held similar egocentric attitudes. "I can't get turned on acting like her sex slave," he told us. "I don't think any man get his kicks going through a long kissing and stroking routine."

There seems to be a question of cause and effect in this. Do such individuals avoid pleasuring their partners because they don't derive satisfaction in sex? Or do they fail to find satisfaction because they are reluctant to give pleasure? All the evidence points to the latter. We may be *born* egocentric, but we don't have to stay that way. We *can* climb out of the shells in which we see the world and other people only as they relate to (and have importance to) us, and become aware of the reality of persons—their needs, desires, idiosyncrasies, virtues, vices, achievements, failures, insights, and stupidities. And we can *choose* to meet the other's needs and desires, not out of any motive of self-sacrifice, but out of a clear recognition of the benefits to be found in doing so.

The benefits in loving are not immediately apparent, and most of us are probably far too aware of the benefits of being loved; not enough, those of loving. Love, as *giving*, is not an emotion. An emotion may accompany loving, but the emotion is not love. It is an emotion. The question is whether love leads to the emotion or the emotion leads to love. It could be either—or neither. We can love—giving to someone—feeling no emotion. There can be any number of motives. The only test of whether it is an act of love is whether it meets the needs and/or desires of the one loved. We all remember that first big crush. Emotion? It could be overwhelming. Feeling the emotions we felt, we were ready and willing to climb mountains and swim rivers for our loved one. The emotion was the motivator. And so long as emotion persists, it provides a strong motivation. But it doesn't always last. As an emotion, pure and simple, with no action on our part, it almost never does.

It is popular to view an emotion as something that just happens to us, totally out of our control. And it can take over in just that way, but only if we permit it to do so. Emotions, however, are too valuable to be handled in such a careless manner. The emotions that accompany love are the most sublime we can experience. If we could turn them on, rather than risk their occurring by chance, we all would. And we can. It depends upon the roles we select to play. A skilled actor throws himself into the role he is playing. He "becomes" the role. In doing so, he feels what the character he portrays would feel. The emotions follow the actions. We develop the emotions appropriate to the roles we choose to play.

In sex we can play many roles: child, parent, friend, boss, adventurer, master, slave, puritan, libertine—and lover. We may vary the roles from time to time, depending on our mood and the mood of our partner. Without the variations, sex can become tedious. It can die. Most of the time we are not aware of the role we are playing. We may deny playing a role at all. Many people with whom we discussed this subject said they felt that role-playing was phony or dishonest. Yet it is not a question of whether we choose to play a role. Anytime we interact with another person, we play a role. It is only a question of what role is appropriate to that interaction. And whether we play the role well.

Learning to be a lover (and it *is* learned; it doesn't come naturally) means learning to play the role of lover. There are, in order, three steps: (1) We learn to play the role of lover; (2) from playing the role, we develop fully the emotions which accompany the role; and (3) over time, the meaning of true sexual love emerges. How do we make deliberate what we have been taught should be free and spontaneous? And in sexual loving, how do we learn to act according to our reason when we have been taught to react according to our feelings?

"It all sounds so cold and calculating." "I could never do it; I'd feel hypocritical." "I don't think you should do anything in sex you don't feel like doing right then." "If you are consciously playing a role, what happens to the real you, to you as a person?" "I can't understand playing the role of lover; it makes it sound like it's all pretense; if I thought my husband was playing a role, I'd feel awful." These are typical, and understandable, reactions. They miss the point, however. When we suggest role-playing, we first suggest that the individual become aware of what he is presently doing, the role he is presently playing, and to assess his words and actions in terms of their effectiveness. We invite a guest to dinner. When he arrives, we greet him at the door, guide him to the living room, suggest he sit down in the most comfortable chair, and offer him a drink. We then make casual conversation until the meal is served. We play the role of host, a role appropriate to the interaction. The role differs in several respects from the one we play with a door-to-door salesperson. Or the role we play when our mother-in-law comes to dinner. Or the role we play toward one of our children's friends. If we interchange any of these roles, a social breakdown results. If we are to succeed in our interactions—on any and all levels—we cannot afford to be unaware of our roles, how appropriate they may be, and whether we are playing them well. During the course of a day, we may be called upon to play a dozen roles, more or less. The role of professional colleague vs. the role of therapist vs. the role of parent vs. the role of customer vs. the role of neighbor vs. the role of close friend, etc., and vs., most critically, the role of lover.

And how did we learn this diversity of roles? Through what sociologists call the "socialization process." We observe our parents and other adults as we are growing up. We see how they interact, and we follow their example. We learn how to relate to clerks, salesmen, the doctors, dentists, and repairmen, how to talk to strangers of both sexes, to parents and other authority figures. We learn which actions are rewarded and which punished. We learn the rules of courtesy and graciousness, which words will persuade and which words dissuade. And it is generally from our parents that we are given our first lessons in the role of lover. And there hangs the danger. We may have learned something no more appropriate than playing the piano with our nose. If Dad was the unromantic type who seldom gave Mom more than a passing peck on the cheek as he left for work, that was our model of the husband as lover. If Mom acted as if a pat on the fanny was a disgusting familiarity, she provided a model of the sexually loving woman. And in the sexually unliberated days of our youth, few of us ever saw examples of more graphic sexual love acted out. To our knowledge, there are no schools for lovers. This is unfortunate. Other than what they learn from motion pictures, television, and romantic novels, a young man or woman must rely on trial and error to learn the roles. And television and motion pictures have, in recent years, often presented models worse than the most antisexual parents. The roles can, however, be learned. By the time we marry, most of us have developed the appropriate role to some extent. The lingering kiss, the words of love, the romantic gift, the caresses, the sense of mystery. It is in living together, day by day, that we have the opportunity to develop this role to the fullest. All too often, however, we find that development stops with the wedding.

In lover role-playing, husband and wife must, therefore, take up where they left off: with the romance and excitement of the courtship and honeymoon. Generally, both partners very consciously played lover roles then. They didn't think of them as phony or "unnecessary." It was only when the emotional "high" wore off that these attitudes crept in.

The role of lovers did not stop, however, because the emotions turned off. The emotions diminished *because the lovers stopped playing the role.* By resuming the role, playing it deliberately, consciously, they can recapture all the exciting emotions they once felt (or intensify the feelings they still have).

Awareness is the key to the role of lover. The great lovers of history have seldom been noted for their physical beauty. They have all, however, possessed one skill to an above-average degree: the ability to perceive and interpret the desires of the loved one. They have the skill to then become the lover the loved one desires. They psych-out the appropriate role, and they play their role with the greatest expertise. And how do they develop this special skill? Through practice. A salesman develops it in dealing with prospective customers. The physician and psychotherapist develop it in dealing with their patients. The politician develops it in dealing with his constituents. It is simply a matter of observing, then making note of the actions, reactions, and verbalizations of others. The would-be lover concentrates all attention on the one who is the object of his/her efforts. To say, "I don't know what my husband/wife really wants," is an admission of a lack of observation and awareness. Every individual communicates his or her desires. It is simply a matter of "listening" to what is expressed. Language, as we have come to learn, is more than the written or spoken word. It is expressed in many ways. Body language is one. Our movements and postures reveal much about us. Facial expressions and voice inflections also say something.

Being aware of the other person calls for close observation of every cue. Loving that person means *acting* on these cues to give what he or she is seeking.

An actor studies his role. How would that character dress? Walk? Sit? Kiss? Make love? How would he speak to each of the other characters in the play? Is he emotional or unemotional? Serious or fun-loving? Strong or weak? Dominant or passive? Flexible or rigid? Self-sufficient or dependent? Would the character employ certain mannerisms to communicate feelings and attitudes? Studying the role becomes a matter of first understanding the character, then *becoming* the character. If the character is playing the role of lover, the actor must also know and understand this well or his characterization will be "out of character." The playwright doesn't characterize his male lead as a sophisticated lover in the first two acts only to have him talk with a toothpick in his mouth and pick his nose in Act Three. Not if he wishes him to stay in character.

What husband and wife do in becoming lovers is in no way different from the role-studying of skilled actors. Every detail is studied and practiced. Whenever they are to be together, the question, "How would a lover . . . ?" is asked. How would a lover greet him at the door? How would a lover kiss her when he leaves for work? How would a lover plan an evening out together? How would a lover act during an evening at home? How would a lover act when a crisis arises? How would a lover behave in the company of other couples? How would a lover dress for an at-home even for two? How would a lover undress for the loved one? How would a lover create an atmosphere of romance?

And just as a dedicated actor continually reassesses his performance and his interpretation of a role, the would-be lover assesses his actions in terms of the lover's role: "Is this how a lover would act?" "Is this what a lover would do?" "Is this the gift a lover would give?" "Is that what a lover would say?" "Is this how a lover would react?" "Are these the gestures of a lover?" The role may become easier and more comfortable with practice—certainly it becomes more rewarding—but it can never become "natural," "unconscious," "a habit," a role played without thought. Loving is a series of *conscious* choices, never a state of just "being yourself." Perhaps this is why there are so few lovers. It is popular to say, "I want to be accepted as I am." But why? Do we have a right to demand that our unacceptable behavior be accepted by others? In the relationship of marriage, many apparently think so. "I figure home is the one place where I can let it all hang out, where I don't have to put on a smiling front for anybody," was the way one husband put it. "Sure, I air my gripes to my husband," said a wife. "Nobody else would put up with them. After all, isn't that what marriage is for?" To which we answer, "Not any fulfilling marriage we have yet witnessed."

If there is any generalization we can make with certainty from what we have observed, it is that the sexual relationship of husband and wife is never better or more fulfilling than the relationship as a whole, and the relationship as a whole is never better or more fulfilling than the couple's sexual relationship. Everything they are to one another will be represented in their sexual relations. It is the arch paridigm of the marriage. It is the agent that brings into harmony what otherwise might be two antagonistic human beings. In fulfilling sexual love, husband and wife are able to blend their personalities, the whole becoming more than the sum of the parts. The reponsibility for fulfillment should not, however, be viewed by husband or wife as "joint." We are each, individually, responsible for our own happiness, success, and fulfillment. We each choose, through our actions and inactions, our own destinies.

This is perhaps the most difficult of all truths to accept. "I could have been a success if my wife had encouraged me." "I was programed by my parents to be nothing but a housewife." "It's my wife's constant nagging that makes my life so miserable." "I'm a nervous wreck because of my kids; they're deliberately driving me crazy." We have all made similar statements. They are the "If not for . . ." statements. "If not for my wife . . ." "If not for my background . . ." "If not for my lack of education . . ." "If not for having married so young . . ." "If not for the four kids we have . . ." "If not for my wife's attitudes toward sex . . ." I would be successful, happy, fulfilled, sexually satisfied, free, self-confident, everything I claim I would like to be. The "If not for . . ." statements permit us to avoid the bitter pill of reality: *What I am and where I am in my life at this moment is of my making.* If my wife is sexually unresponsive, isn't it true that either I chose to marry a woman who was unresponsive, or through my actions I have persuaded her to be unresponsive *to me?* If my husband seldom shows an interest in talking with me, isn't it true that I either married a man I knew was not the "talkative sort," or that during our marriage I have given him little reason for wanting to talk to me? *We attain the goals we set out to attain.* This truth has been repeatedly impressed upon us by the couples we have interviewed. Those with the most fulfilling relationships were those who relied on each other *least* for their individual happiness. And they were the ones who genuinely wanted the best possible relationship. At first, it would seem that this would include all couples. Would any man or woman marry, having as their goal an unhappy life with each other? All evidence indicates that for many wives and husbands the answer is, *Yes.* We live our lives with many self-fulfilling prophecies. The young rock-music fan goes to his first symphony concert. "I just know I'm going to hate it," he says, and, sure enough, he does. The husband-to-be accepts without question what he has heard: "You can never figure out a woman." Five years married, he complains he can't understand his wife. The rock fan makes no attempt to enjoy the symphony. The husband dismisses as futile any effort to "make sense" of what his wife is trying to communicate. They each reach the goal they set: the rock fan finds he does dislike classical music; the husband does succeed in misunderstanding women.

In no area of human activity is this more apparent than in sex. Those husbands who believed women were less interested in sexual enjoyment than men found themselves married to women who seemed, in fact, to have little interest in sex. Women who believed most men were boorish and unromantic in the bedroom tended to marry men who were boorish and unromantic in the bedroom. The self-fulfilling prophecy serves in part to explain the observed similarity of sex drive in most couples. The husband with a low sex drive does not strive to stimulate his wife to a higher level than his own. The wife with a high sex drive will not attempt to dampen her husband's ardor. We are attracted to, and marry, someone who has a similar sex-drive level. There are subtle cues which communicate this information despite the claim made by so many: "I didn't really know him/her before we married."

In each case where we observed significant change in the sexual relationship (and in other areas as well), either husband or wife (but seldom both initially) assumed the responsibility for the change, *independent of the other.* "I decided it was my life I wanted to change," a wife told us. "What he did or did not do about himself was up to him." A husband said, "I had been sitting around waiting for her to make the first move. It was stupid. Finally, I figured I would work on my own growth as a person, and when and if the day came that I could see myself as having it all together, I could take a look at where she was and decide then if I still wanted to stay with her. And you know what? Soon after I got off my backside and took responsibility for my own happiness, she began moving toward becoming a real woman. It became almost a race to see who could grow up fastest." The assumption of responsibility in the growth of sexual love means never evaluating the responsibilities assumed by one's partner. Two people are involved. That much is true. But it is not an interdependency. It is, rather, like two musicians playing a duet. The music they produce is a blend of their individual artistry. Each is individually responsible for the part he or she is playing. One cannot say, "I would not have played that sour note had it not been for my partner." Those husbands and wives with the least-fulfilling relationships most often attributed their unhappiness to the actions and inactions of their spouses. And they most often claimed they had done everything they could to "make it work." "I've been everything a man could ask for in a wife," is the plea of an unhappy woman. "But what can you do if your husband persists in making your life hell?" As expected, her husband had a different story. "She has never wanted sex. Right from the beginning, she said I was like an animal rutting in the field. She insisted her mother live with us, and her mother always sided with her against me. She's never let me feel like a man in my own home. And you know something? I've given her everything a man can give a woman. What more could she ask for?"

Speaking of loving or the failure to love, we have found, is perilous. We have seen the reaction from lecture platforms when we have spoken of the personal responsibility involved in loving (and the joy of loving). For those who have found the rewards in loving, the message has been positive. For others, the message has been "oversimplified." An angry member of an audience in Washington, D.C., said, "You make it sound as if any couple could be happy in their marriage if they just loved one another." A woman in Detroit accused us of "reducing everything down to loving." Another said, "All this emphasis on love and sex! I think there are other things more important in marriage." Eric Berne, the late author/transactional analyst, said he was frequently accused of "oversimplifying." His answer: "You're overcomplicating." By all means, love is a simple answer. But never an easy one. It calls for mustering every bit of our reserves of maturity and self-discipline. The total love relationship grows from our sexual love, like an inverted triangle expanding upward. And it is from this fact that meaning is found in the relationship of man and woman.

That meaning has been pursued by philosophers, theologians, psychologists, and poets over the centuries. When we asked couples to attempt to describe the meaning they found in their sexual relations, many of them drew upon these writings. Their words often appeared to be less their own than those of a writer who held an overall philosophical position to which they subscribed. Thus, those who were strongly religious tended to find a spiritual meaning in marital sex, employing phrases which paraphrased theologians and religious writers such as Paul Tillich and Teilhard de Chardin. Those with less religious orientation frequently employed the writings of humanist philosophers and psychologists (e.g., Erich Fromm, Carl Rogers, Abraham Maslow). And there were a number, mostly wives, who drew upon poetic metaphors.

We were interested in studying a possible relationship between the meaning husbands and wives found in their sexual relations and the degree of satisfaction and fulfillment they expressed. A number of writers have suggested that those who find the most profound meaning in sex will, as a result, derive the greatest fulfillment in the sexual act, or that those who find the greatest satisfaction will discover a deep meaning in it. We did not find support for these views in our interviews. Couples who reported the highest degree of satisfaction in sex were *least* able to verbalize any meaning found. One wife said, "I guess I don't understand the question. I've never thought about 'meaning' when we make love. It's just something which is great." A husband who is a professional musician said, "Trying to find 'meaning' in our sex life seems to me a little like what those guys do who write about jazz but who are not musicians. They're always writing about what they think the music is saying, always interpreting the hell out of it, but I wonder if any of them ever *feel* jazz on a gut level. Seems to me good sex is like good jazz: It just *is*." And a wife who described sex with her husband as "fantastic . . . just about the greatest thing in life," answered our question with, "If I don't find a 'meaning,' does that mean I find it 'meaningless'? Then I guess you'd have to say I find a sunset 'meaningless.' All I know is that it makes everything right in my world."

Several possibilities suggest themselves. Those husbands and wives who find the greatest fulfillment in their sexual relationship may feel that the experience is literally "indescribable," that any words they might use to describe any meaning found would be wholly inadequate. It may also be that those who have apparently given much thought to the meaning of sexual love have done so in an attempt to justify acts they feel would be otherwise unacceptable. Since the husbands and wives in the most-fulfilled group were those who were most free in accepting sexual pleasure, the need to rationalize would be less present.

There is even the further possibility that those who are highly fulfilled in their sexual relationship tend to be less philosophical and introspective than those who are less satisfied, that they tend to think less about meaning in all areas of life than do others. Although this would seem unlikely, there might be some truth to it. Those who trust themselves most fully seldom have time for introspection. They don't pause in their living to contemplate their psyches. And those who are most dedicated to living to the fullest are those who have the greatest probability of fulfillment in their marriages.

We asked a further question related to meaning: "Do you feel that your responses in sex and your sexual fulfillment are affected by your religious beliefs—or vice versa?" We explained that we were seeking answers to such questions as: "Is there a spiritual dimension to your sexual love?" "Marriage, for many couples, is a religious as well as civil commitment. Do you find a religious significance in lovemaking?" Many said that their early religious education had created problems for them in sex. A heavy emphasis on sin carried into marriage was a strong inhibiting force. Almost invariably, however, the negative influence operated only in conjunction with strong antisexual attitudes communicated by the parents. In exploring meaning, we were more interested in positive attitudes toward marital sex developed through a religious background.

Only a small percentage of those interviewed had not been exposed to some formal religious experience, although less than half were regular attendants at church and/or observed religious practices in their home. The answers to the questions we asked could, of course, come only from those who professed belief in a Supreme Being, whether or not the individual identified with any organized religion.

The answers were, in many respects, little different from those to the initial questions concerning meaning. Some husbands and wives (a minority) said they found religious significance in their sexual relations. "I feel it is what Our Lord intended when He blessed our marriage," a wife told us. "It is as if God is present when we make love," said another. "We always pray together before we go to bed. It makes our lovemaking something beautiful," a husband said. "If I couldn't find a spiritual meaning in it," a wife of almost twenty years told us, "it would seem filthy to me." A few, all women, said they frequently prayed or thought of things spiritual while engaged in sexual relations. "I think of the Blessed Virgin while my husband makes love to me. I read somewhere that even though a woman marries and gives up her physical virginity, by her thoughts and prayers she can still retain her spiritual virginity." (This wife claimed to have never experienced any feelings of sexual pleasure with her husband, had no other heterosexual or homosexual experience, and had never masturbated. She denied having any sexual problems.) Another said, "When my husband and I are joined in the marital embrace, I like to think of it as a religious ceremony, like I'm being deflowered in my bridal dress—all in white, with a choir singing: all holy and pure." Most husbands and wives who claimed they found *religious* significance in their sexual relations, however, did not report such feeling-level experiences. "It's more on a 'head' level than a 'gut' level," was the way one husband expressed it. His wife added, "My church teaches that marriage is a sacrament, instituted by God. It's holy. So, of course, sex between husband and wife must be holy, but I can't say I have any kind of spiritual feeling when we make love. It's much earthier than that."

As we found in response to the more general question regarding meaning, those who verbalized the most elaborated "theological meanings" were generally among the least sexually satisfied. Spiritual meaning, especially as expressed in religious pamphlets and books they had read, seemed to represent their attempt to live with what they had not been able to accept as moral and good. We were unable to find a relationship between devoutness (as measured by church attendance, individual and family prayer, religious reading, and statements of the importance of religion in the individual's life) and sexual fulfillment. Those who were very devout as well as sexually fulfilled did not, on the average, find more spiritual meaning in lovemaking than did those who were less devout and fulfilled.

Perhaps personal spiritual meaning ("on the gut level") emerges only with fulfillment in the couple's sexual love. The "spiritual meaning" *is* love. "What meaning do I find in sex? I learned what love is all about, if that's what you mean. I'm not religious in any formal sense. We go to church, but not regularly. It does seem to me, however, that *love* is very close to godliness—if that makes any sense," said a husband. A wife seemed to be expressing something similar when she said, "I learned how to love others through loving my husband. We make love, and the next morning I can smile at the whole world. Isn't that what is meant by having God within us?"

The meaning of love is *love*. The couples who consented to share their experiences confirmed our own experience. Everything we are as man and woman, husband and wife, is expressed in our sexual relationship. And everything that relationship is, and everything it is capable of becoming, will be a measure of the love we bring to it.

Seeking Professional Counseling

The individual or couple seeking help for sexual or other marital problems may have trouble knowing where to turn. Advice columnists are fond of suggesting the family doctor or clergyman. This may or may not prove a good starting point. Most physicians are not trained in counseling, and it has been only in recent years that medical schools have provided even minimal education in human sexuality as part of the four-year program toward the degree Doctor of Medicine. Some, but by no means all, seminaries and schools of theology offer course work, and in some cases practicum experience, in counseling. The extent and depth of these programs vary widely. Some clergymen take graduate work in counseling; most do not. Most doctors and ministers, however, are good referral sources.

Regardless of the source of the referral, however, the individual seeking help is entitled to ask certain questions of the therapist or counselor. Before undergoing surgery, we want to know that the surgeon who will be operating on us is a physician with appropriate training and experience in the surgical specialty. In general, a measure of protection is offered the patient through licensure requirements of the state Board of Medical Examiners, specialty boards (e.g., The American College of Surgeons), and the requirements for staff privileges in each hospital. Unfortunately, the professional qualifications of those who may choose to engage in counseling are not so clearly spelled out. Licensure requirements vary from state to state. In some jurisdictions there are *no* legal requirements for the profession of "marriage counselor." In recent years the situation has worsened with the spread of various esoteric group "therapies," self-proclaimed "sex therapists," and others who circumvent licensing regulations by assuming such titles as "Personal Problems Advisor" or "Personality Analyst."

In addition to professional qualifications, counselors differ in orientation, attitudes, values, and personal life experiences. One can argue that a surgeon need not be in perfect health in order to treat his patients skillfully. The parallel breaks down somewhat when it comes to counseling. Even with the best of intentions, it is not possible for the therapist or counselor to keep his own values and life experiences out of therapy. If he or she has had a series of bitter experiences with those of the opposite sex, it is bound to influence what is said in therapy. The thrice-married therapist who is involved in the "swinging" scene is hardly the one to counsel a couple committed to monogamous marriage. During the first appointment, it is certainly proper to ask pointed, highly personal questions of the counselor. And if the therapist is unwilling to provide frank answers, the patient or client would be well-advised to seek help elsewhere.

The following professional qualifications are based on the requirements of the more stringent jurisdictions. While requirements vary from state to state, it is felt that these requirements offer the best guidelines by which to judge qualifications of professionals who advertise themselves as psychotherapists or counselors.

CLINICAL PSYCHOLOGIST

The Clinical Psychologist and Psychiatrist are the only two counseling professionals licensed in some states by the state boards of medical examiners. This fact may be important where the patient carries a policy (group or individual) of health insurance.

To obtain a license to practice as a clinical psychologist an individual must: possess the doctorate degree (Ph.D.) from a university approved by the American Psychological Association; have submitted an original research thesis on a psychological topic; have completed an approved, supervised internship; and have passed a written and oral examination. The doctoral training is usually a program of about five and one-half years following graduation from college. Internship is one to two years and includes weekly face-to-face supervision.

PSYCHIATRIST

To qualify, an individual must: hold a medical degree (M.D.) from a recognized medical school; have completed one year of rotating internship; have completed three years of residency training in an approved hospital or institution devoted to the practice of psychiatry; and have passed the medical-board examinations of the state.

To qualify to be "boarded" by the American Board of Psychiatry, the individual must, in addition, complete two years of practice and pass an examination in neurology and psychiatry. Being "boarded," however, is not a requirement of practice.

SOCIAL WORKER

Social workers in private counseling practice generally have a graduate degree, Master of Social Work (M.S.W.), in psychiatric social work. This is a two-year post-college degree, including one year of supervised work experience. While a registered social worker must take an examination in social work, the examination does not include clinical questions related to marital problems. The prospective client is advised, therefore, to inquire about the social worker's qualifications and training.

MARRIAGE AND FAMILY COUNSELOR

In relatively recent years, some states have established requirements for licensure in marriage and family counseling for those who do not meet the qualifications in Psychology, Psychiatry, or Social Work.

To engage in the business of marriage, family, or child counseling, an individual must have: at least a Master's Degree in marriage counseling, social work, or one of the behavioral sciences; at least two years' supervised counseling experience, or at least two years' experience of a type which is equivalent to that obtained under the direction of a supervisor.

It should be noted, however, that exempted from these requirements are priests, rabbis, ministers of the gospel of any denomination; any person licensed to practice law or medicine; or the personnel of any organization which is nonprofit and charitable. In view of such exemptions, a prospective client of such licensees is doubly advised to inquire as to the counselor's qualifications.

Bibliography

In compiling the following bibliography, we enlisted the aid of the many husbands and wives we interviewed. We asked the husbands and wives to name the publications they had found helpful in the development of their sexuality and their relationship. To this list we then added a small number of authoritative works in the areas of psychology, psychiatry, reproductive biology, philosophy, and religion. We then had to face the question of whether we could recommend the entire bibliography (of course we could not), a selected number (which would represent nothing more than our tastes and values plus our judgments on the empirical validity of the material), or make no recommendations at all. We decided to take a middle course. We have indicated by asterisks those works most frequently mentioned as "helpful" by couples interviewed as well as those we feel are significant contributions to our knowledge of human sexuality and love. Quite frankly, we feel that some of the works frequently mentioned are superficial, inaccurate, or simply the works of hack sexploitationists. If an individual finds something of value in a work, and if it perhaps opens a door for him or her, we will not mount a professional platform to heap scorn on it. We have not included professional journal articles, and we have limited the number of technical books.

We encourage the reader to develop a knowledge of sexuality through reading as well as through personal experience. One cannot read too much about sex any more than one can read too much about art or music. Not only will reading lead to discrimination, it will contribute insights and innovations. And if the goal is sexual loving, it will aid in showing the way.

Abbott, E., *The Fifteen Joys of Marriage*. New York: The Orion Press, 1959.
*Allen, G., and Martin, C. G., *Intimacy*. New York: Pocket Books, 1972.
Ardrey, R., *The Territorial Imperative*. New York: Delta Books, 1966.
Armour, R., *A Short History of Sex*. New York: McGraw-Hill, 1970.
Arnold, F. X., *Woman and Man*. New York: Herder and Herder, 1963.
Augsburger, D. W., *Cherishable: Love and Marriage*. New York: Pyramid Books, 1971.
*Bach, G. R., and Wyden, P., *The Intimate Enemy*. New York: William Morrow, 1969.
*—— and Deutsch, R. M., *Pairing*. New York: Avon Books, 1970.
Bailey, D. S., *The Mystery of Love and Marriage: A Study in the Theology of Sexual Relations*. New York: Harper & Brothers, 1952.
—— *Sexual Relations in Christian Thought*. New York: Harper & Brothers, 1959.
Bartell, G. D., *Group Sex*. New York: Peter H. Wyden, 1971.
Baruch, D. W., and Miller, H., *Sex in Marriage*. New York: Hoeber-Harper, 1962.
Bassett, M., *A New Sex Ethics and Marriage Structure*. New York: Philosophical Library, 1961.
Beach, F. A., *Hormones and Behavior*. New York: Harper & Brothers, 1948.
Beach, F. A. (ed.), *Sex and Behavior*. New York: John Wiley, 1965.
*Belliveau, F., and Richter, L., *Understanding Human Sexual Inadequacy*. New York: Bantam Books, 1970.
Bernard, J., *The Sex Game*. Englewood Cliffs, N.J.: Prentice-Hall, 1968.
Berne, E., *Games People Play*. New York: Grove Press, 1964.
*—— *Sex in Human Loving*. New York: Pocket Books, 1971.
Bertocci, P. A., *Sex, Love and the Person*. New York: Sheed and Ward, 1967.
*Bird, L., *How To Be a Happily Married Mistress*. Garden City, N.Y.: Doubleday, 1970.

*—— *How To Make Your Wife Your Mistress.* Garden City, N.Y.: Doubleday, 1971.

*—— *How To Make Your Husband Your Lover.* Garden City, N.Y.: Doubleday, 1972.

*Bird, J., and Bird, L., *The Freedom of Sexual Love.* Garden City, N.Y.: Doubleday, 1967.

—— *Love Is All.* Garden City, N.Y.: Doubleday, 1968.

*—— *Marriage Is for Grownups.* Garden City, N.Y.: Doubleday, 1969.

—— *The Tennis Match* (tape recording). San Jose: Cognetics, Inc., 1971.

Blake, R., and Mouton, J., *The Marriage Grid.* New York: McGraw-Hill, 1971.

Blank, L.; Gottsegen, G.; and Gottsegen, M. (eds.), *Confrontation: Encounters in Self and Personal Awareness.* New York: Macmillan, 1971.

Blanton, S., *Love or Perish.* Greenwich: Fawcett, 1965.

Bossard, J., and Boll, E., *Why Marriages Go Wrong.* New York: Ronald Press, 1958.

Bowen, Elisa, *How Can I Show That I Love You.* Millbrae, Ca.: Celestial Arts, 1972.

Brecher, R., and Brecher, E. (eds.), *An Analysis of Human Sexual Response.* Boston: Little, Brown, 1966.

Calder, J., *Women's Sex Talk.* New York: Signet, 1974.

Cervantes, L. F., *And God Made Man and Woman.* Chicago: Henry Regnery, 1959.

Chapman, A. H., *Sexual Maneuvers and Stratagems.* New York: G. P. Putnam's Sons, 1969.

Chartham, R., *What Turns Women On.* New York: Ballantine Books, 1974.

Chesser, E., *Is Chastity Outmoded?* London: The Windmill Press, 1960.

Ciardi, J., *I Marry You.* New Brunswick, N.J.: Rutgers University Press, 1958.

Clark, L., *The Enjoyment of Love in Marriage.* New York: Crest Books, 1949.

—— *101 More Intimate Sexual Problems Answered.* New York: Signet Books, 1968.

Clinebell, H. J., and Clinebell, C. H., *The Intimate Marriage.* New York: Harper & Row, 1970.

Cole, W. G., *Sex in Christianity and Psychoanalysis.* New York: Oxford University Press, 1955.

Collein, J. L., *The Hypocritical American: An Essay on Sex Attitudes in America.* Indianapolis: Bobbs-Merrill, 1964.

Chapman, J. D., *The Feminine Mind and Body: The Psychosexual and Psychosomatic Reactions of Women.* New York: Philosophical Library, 1967.

Chesser, E., *Love and Married Woman.* New York: G. P. Putnam's Sons, 1969.

Comfort, A., *Sex in Society.* New York: Citadel Press, 1966.

*—— (ed.), *The Joy of Sex.* New York: Crown, 1972.

—— (ed.), *More Joy.* New York: Crown, 1974.

Daniels, A. K., *It's Never Too Late To Love.* New York: Pyramid Books, 1956.

Davis, M., *The Sexual Responsibility of Women.* New York: Dial Press, 1956.

—— *Sexual Responsibility in Marriage.* New York: Dial Press, 1963.

DeMartino, M. F. (ed.), *Sexual Behavior and Personality Characteristics.* New York: Grove Press, 1966.

Deutsch, H., *The Psychology of Women,* Vols. I, II. New York: Grune and Stratton, 1945.

—— "Frigidity in Women," in *Neurosis and Character Types.* New York: International Universities Press, 1965.

Deutsch, R. M., *The Key to Feminine Response in Marriage.* New York: Ballantine Books, 1969.

DeVinck, J., and Cotoir, J. T., *The Challenge of Love: Practical Advice on Freedom of Conscience and Happiness in Marriage.* New York: Hawthorn Books, 1969.

Diamond, M. (ed.), *Perspectives in Reproduction and Sexual Behavior.* Bloomington: Indiana University Press, 1968.

Downing, G., *The Massage Book.* New York: Random House, 1972.

*Downs, H., *Potential.* Garden City, N.Y.: Doubleday, 1973.

Duyckaerts, F., *The Sexual Bond* (John A. Kay, trans.). New York: Delta Books, 1971.

Eichenlaub, J. E., *New Approaches to Sex in Marriage.* New York: Dell, 1967.

Eisenstein, V. W. (ed.), *Neurotic Interaction in Marriage.* New York: Basic Books, 1956.

*Ellis, A., *The Art and Science of Love.* New York: Lyle Stuart, 1960.

―― *The American Sexual Tragedy.* New York: Lyle Stuart, 1962.

*―― *Sex Without Guilt.* New York: Lyle Stuart, 1966.

Ellis, A., and Abarbanel, A. (eds.), *The Encyclopedia of Sexual Behavior,* Vols. I, II. New York: Hawthorn Books, 1961.

Ellis, A., and Conway, R. O., *The Art of Erotic Seduction.* New York: Lyle Stuart, 1967.

―― and Harper, R., *A Guide to Rational Living.* Englewood Cliffs, N.J.: Prentice-Hall, 1961.

Ellis, H., *Studies in the Psychology of Sex,* Vols. I–VII. Philadelphia: F. A. Davis, 1928.

Fast, J., *What You Should Know About Human Sexual Response.* New York: Berkley, 1966.

―― *The Incompatibility of Men and Women.* New York: M. Evans, 1971.

Fielding, W. J., *Sex and the Love Life.* New York: Permabooks, 1961.

*Fisher, S., *The Female Orgasm.* New York: Basic Books, 1973.

Fliess, R., *Erogeneity and Libido.* New York: International Universities Press, 1956.

Ford, C. S., and Beach, F. A., *Patterns of Sexual Behavior.* New York: Harper & Brothers, 1951.

Francoeur, R. T., *Utopian Motherhood: New Trends in Human Reproduction.* Garden City, N.Y.: Doubleday, 1970.

Frank, L. K., *The Conduct of Sex.* New York: William Morrow, 1961.

*Friday, N., *My Secret Garden.* New York: Pocket Books, 1974.

―― *Forbidden Flowers.* New York: Pocket Books, 1975.

Fried, E., *The Ego in Love and Sexuality.* New York: Grune and Stratton, 1960.

*Freud, S., *Sexuality and the Psychology of Love.* New York: Collier Books, 1963.

*―― *Three Essays on the Theory of Sexuality* (J. Strachey, ed. and trans.). New York: Basic Books, 1963.

*Fromm, E., *The Art of Loving.* New York: Harper & Brothers, 1956.

Fromme, A., *Understanding the Sexual Response in Humans.* New York: Pocket Books, 1966.

―― *The Ability To Love.* New York: Pocket Books, 1971.

―― *Enjoy Being a Woman.* New York: Warner Paperback Library, 1972.

Geddes, D. R. (ed.), *An Analysis of the Kinsey Reports on Sexual Be-

havior in the Human Male and Female. New York: Deelton, 1954.

Geldard, F. A., *The Human Senses.* New York: John Wiley, 1953.

Gilbert, H., *The Meaning and Practice of Sexual Love in Christian Marriage* (A. Humbert, trans.). New York: Hawthorn Books, 1964.

*Glasser, W., *Reality Therapy: A New Approach to Psychiatry.* New York: Harper & Row, 1965.

Goldstein, M., and Haeberle, E. J., *The Sex Book.* New York: Herder and Herder, 1971.

Grant, V. W., *The Psychology of Sexual Emotion.* New York: Longmans, Green, 1957.

Greene, B. L. (ed.), *The Psychotherapies of Marital Disharmony.* New York: Free Press of Glencoe, 1965.

Grimm, R., *Love and Sexuality* (D. R. Mace, trans.). New York: Association Press, 1964.

Gunther, B., *What To Do Until the Messiah Comes.* New York: Macmillan, 1971.

—— *Sense Relaxation.* New York: Macmillan, 1971.

*Hamilton, E., *Sex Before Marriage.* New York: Bantam Books, 1970.

—— *Partners in Love.* New York: Bantam Books, 1970.

Harkel, R. L., *The Picture Book of Sexual Love.* New York: Cybertype Corp., 1969.

Hodge, M. B., *Your Fear of Love.* Garden City, N.Y.: Doubleday, 1967.

Hopson, B., and Hopson, C., *Intimate Feedback.* New York: Simon and Schuster, 1975.

Howard, J., *Please Touch.* New York: McGraw-Hill, 1970.

Hunt, M., *The Affair.* New York: Signet Books, 1969.

*"J," *The Sensuous Woman.* New York: Lyle Stuart, Inc., 1969.

Jackson, D., *Human Communication.* Palo Alto, Ca.: Science and Behavior Books, 1968.

Jeanniere, A., *The Anthropology of Sex.* New York: Harper & Row, 1967.

Johnson, E. W., *Love and Sex in Plain Language.* New York, Bantam Books, 1968.

Kaufman, J. J., and Borgeson, G., *Man and Sex.* Greenwich, Conn.: Fawcett, 1963.

Kelly, G. L., *Sexual Feeling in Married Men and Women.* New York: Permabooks, 1961.

Kennedy, E. C., *The New Sexuality, Myths, Fables and Hang-Ups*. Garden City, N.Y.: Doubleday, 1972.

*Kinsey, A. C.; Pomeroy, W. B.; and Martin, C. E., *Sexual Behavior in the Human Male*. Philadelphia: W. B. Saunders, 1948.

*Kinsey, A. C.; Pomeroy, W. B.; Martin, C. E.; and Gebhard, P. H., *Sexual Behavior in the Human Female*. Philadelphia: W. B. Saunders, 1953.

Klaf, F. S., and Hurwood, B. J., *A Psychiatrist Looks at Erotica*. New York: Ace Books, 1964.

Krich, A. M. (ed.), *Women*. New York: Dell, 1953.

Kronhausen, P., and Kronhausen, E., *Sex Histories of American College Men*. New York: Ballantine Books, 1960.

——— *The Sexually Responsive Woman*. New York: Ballantine Books, 1964.

——— *Erotic Fantasies*. New York: Grove Press, 1969.

Lang, Theo, *The Difference Between a Man and a Woman*. New York: Bantam Books, 1971.

*Lederer, W. J., and Jackson, D. D., *The Mirages of Marriage*. New York: W. W. Norton, 1968.

Lepp, Ignace, *The Psychology of Loving*. Baltimore: Helicon Press, 1963.

Lewin, S. A., and Gelmore, J., *Sex After Forty*. New York: Medical Research Press, 1952.

Lewis, H. R., and Streitfeld, H. S., *Growth Games*. New York: Bantam Books, 1972.

Lindner, Robert, *Must You Conform?* New York: Holt, Rinehart and Winston, Inc., 1956.

Liswood, R., *First Aid for the Happy Marriage*. New York: Pocket Books, 1971.

Lorenz, K., *On Aggression*. New York: Harcourt, Brace, and World, 1966.

*Lundberg, F., and Farnham, M. F., *Modern Woman, The Lost Sex*. New York: Harper & Brothers, 1947.

Malloy, M., *My Song for Him Who Never Sang for Me*. Los Angeles: Ward Ritchie Press, 1975.

Masters, W. H., "Sex Life of the Aging Female" in *Sex in Our Culture* (G. Graves and A. Stone, eds.). New York: Emerson Books, 1955.

——— and Johnson, V. E., *Determinants of Human Sexual Behavior* (G. Winokier, ed.). Springfield, Ill.: Charles C. Thomas, 1963.

—— *Human Reproductive and Sexual Behavior* (C. W. Lloyd, ed.). Philadelphia: Lea & Febiger, 1964.

*—— *Human Sexual Response*. Boston: Little, Brown, 1966.

*—— *Human Sexual Inadequacy*. Boston: Little, Brown, 1970.

*—— *The Pleasure Bond*. Boston and Toronto: Little, Brown, 1975.

McCorkle, L., *How To Make Love*. New York: Grove Press, 1969.

Mead, M., *Male and Female*. New York: William Morrow, 1949.

Menninger, K., *Love Against Hate*. New York: Harcourt, Brace, 1959.

Money, J., *Sex and Internal Secretions* (W. C. Young, ed.). Baltimore: Williams & Wilkins, 1961.

Morris, D., *Intimate Behaviour*. New York: Random House, 1972.

Newhorn, P., *Primal Sensuality*. Greenwich, Conn.: Fawcett Publications, 1974.

Nolte, C., and Nolte, D., *Wake Up in Bed Together!* New York: Stein and Day, 1975.

*O'Neill, N., and O'Neill, G., *Open Marriage*. Philadelphia: Lippincott, 1971.

Otto, H. A., *More Joy in Your Marriage*. New York: Hawthorn Books, 1969.

*—— *Total Sex*. New York: Peter H. Wyden, 1972.

Packard, V., *The Sexual Wilderness: The Contemporary Upheaval in Male-Female Relationships*. New York: David McKay, 1968.

Pillay, A. P., and Ellis, A. (eds.). *Sex, Society, and the Individual*. London: Methuen, 1960.

Rainer, J., and Rainer, J., *Sexual Pleasure in Marriage*. New York: Messner, 1959.

Reik, T., *Psychology of Sex Relations*. New York: Farrar, 1945.

Rhymes, D. A., *No New Morality: Christian Personal Values and Sexual Morality*. Indianapolis: Bobbs-Merrill, 1964.

*Robinson, M. N., *The Power of Sexual Surrender*. Garden City, N.Y.: Doubleday, 1959.

*Rogers, C. R., *Becoming Partners: Marriage and Its Alternatives*. New York: Delacorte Press, 1972.

Rubin, I., *Sexual Life After Sixty*. New York: Basic Books, 1965.

Russell, B., *Marriage and Morals*. New York: Bantam Books, 1959.

*Schutz, W., *Joy*. New York: Grove Press, 1967.

Schwarz, O., *Psychology of Sex*. London: Penguin, 1967.

Shostrom, E., *Man, the Manipulator*. New York and Nashville: Abington Press, 1967.

——— and Kavanaugh, J., *Between Man and Woman: The Dynamics of Intersexual Relationships*. Los Angeles: Nash, 1971.

*Smith, G. W., *Me and You and US*. New York: Peter H. Wyden, 1971.

*Stein, M. L., *Lovers, Friends, Slaves*. New York: Berkley, 1975.

Stevens, J. O., *Awareness*. Menlo Park, Ca.: Peninsula Lithograph Co., 1971.

Stokes, W. R., *Married Love in Today's World*. New York: Citadel Press, 1962.

Street, R., *Modern Sex Techniques*. New York: Lancer Books, 1963.

Tenenbaum, S. A., *A Psychologist Looks at Marriage*. New York: A. S. Barnes, 1968.

Thielicke, H., *The Ethics of Sex* (J. W. Doberstein, trans.). New York: Harper & Row, 1964.

Thorp, R., and Blake, R., *Wives: An Investigation*. Philadelphia: Lippincott, 1971.

Tinbergen, N., *The Study of Instinct*. Oxford: Clarendon Press, 1951.

*Van De Velde, T. H., *Ideal Marriage: Its Physiology and Technique* (S. Browne, trans.). New York: Random House, 1965.

*Vatsyayana, *Kama Sutra* (R. Burton and F. F. Arbuthnot, trans.). London: Luxor Press, 1967.

von Urban, R., *Sex Perfection*. London: Arrow Books, 1952.

Wahl, C. W. (ed.). *Sexual Problems: Diagnosis and Treatment in Medical Practice*. New York: Free Press of Glencoe, 1967.

*Watts, A. W., *Nature, Man and Woman*. New York: Mentor Books, 1960.

Weber, L. M., *On Marriage, Sex and Virginity* (R. Brennan, trans.). New York: Herder and Herder, 1966.

Wells, J. W., *Comparative Sex Techniques*. New York: Lancer Books, 1968.

*Wolpe, J., *Psychotherapy by Reciprocal Inhibition*. Stanford: Stanford University Press, 1958.

*——— and Lazarus, A. A., *Behavior Therapy Techniques*. New York: Pergamon Press, 1966.